160 2103 1 5

D0586348

WITHDRAWN

Upstream/Downstream

Issues in Environmental Ethics

Upstream/Downstream

Issues in Environmental Ethics

Edited by Donald Scherer

 Temple University Press
Philadelphia

18 FEB 1993

GF
80
·U7

Temple University Press, Philadelphia 19122
Copyright © 1990 by Temple University. All rights reserved
Published 1990
Printed in the United States of America

The paper used in this publication meets the minimum
requirements of American National Standard for Information
Sciences—Permanence of Paper for Printed Library Materials,
ANSI Z39.48-1984 ∞

Library of Congress Cataloging-in-Publication Data

Upstream/downstream : issues in environmental ethics / edited by
  Donald Scherer.
      p.   cm.
    Includes index.
    ISBN 0-87722-747-0 (alk. paper)
    1. Human ecology—Moral and ethical aspects.   2. Environmental
policy.   I. Scherer, Donald.
  GF80.U67   1990
  179'.1—dc20

                                        90-11106
                                        CIP

Contents

Acknowledgments

This book would not have been possible without the generous support and encouragement of the George Gund Foundation of Cleveland, Ohio. The Foundation's belief in the importance of studying the complex relationships between human beings and the natural environment was very encouraging to me when I began talking to the scholars whose work is reflected in these essays. I wish to thank the Foundation for their support of the Fall 1988 conference where preliminary versions of most of these papers were read and discussed with an audience of scholars, environmentalists, and government officials. May the longstanding concern of the Foundation with such thoughtful endeavors itself prove a powerful upstream current for the downstream of our ecological future.

I also thank the authors whose papers are represented within. The care they have taken with their essays and their concern for the issues they discuss are heartening. And, as in so many other projects, my office staff of Pat Bressler, Diane Petteys, and Margy DeLuca have been invaluable.

Upstream/Downstream

Issues in Environmental Ethics

Introduction

Environmental ethics was born in the early 1970s. Clean air and water legislation had recently been passed, and the Environmental Protection Agency (EPA) had been formed. But in the minds of many, portents of disaster loomed. Energy use was growing exponentially and, many feared, unsustainably. Topsoil was eroding precipitously. Many animal and plant species were becoming extinct. New technologies were affecting the natural environment in unknown ways, and locally rising incidences of cancer, mutation, and birth defects were seen as the unhappy fruits of environmental destruction.

Many social critics urged society to view our newly discovered environmental problems as problems about the biases of our society. Our values, they urged, were unsustainable because they were capitalist. Fundamental changes in the distribution of power, they urged, were the solution to our environmental woes. But the history of this discussion does not substantiate an easy indictment of capitalism because it quickly became apparent that centrally planned economies create approximately as much pollution as market economies. And it is plausible that the freer the flow of information within a society, the less the dangers of new technologies.

Indeed, markets and technologies, despite the lag times they involve, have made countless adjustments to various unsustainable practices of earlier times. Topsoil erosion is decreased by low till technologies. Superefficient furnaces conserve nonrenewable fuels. There is a brisk market in recycled aluminum, and communities are beginning to recycle plastics as well as paper, cardboard, and glass. The environmentalist predictions in the early 1970s of "unsustainability" have themselves contributed to the development of new resources and new technologies designed to modify but sustain our lifestyles.

The concept of unsustainability, then, has not become the focus of environmental ethics. In contrast, the idea that the anthropocentrism of our thought and the anthropomorphism of our lives had led us to ignore important values became central. Many environmentally concerned persons saw Aldo Leopold as a prophet boldly speaking of a new age of heightened environmental sensitivity.[1] He envisioned an age of values attuned to the world in which we live, its values not anthropocentric but geocentric, its models not anthropomorphic but ecosystemic. Human beings would be seen not as conquerors and sub-duers of nature but as children of a world they are destined to protect. They would view themselves not as protected from nature's harm but as cautiously adjusting their actions to the broader rhythms of life.

And in the intervening years, philosophers have responded, deve-loping environmental conceptions of value less individualistic (Cal-licott), much more inclusive (Taylor), and much more systemic (Rolston) than the work of other ethical theorists.[2] Important as it has been, their work has also shown its own shortcoming, for they have made painfully clear the difficulty of inferring from *the value of the ecosystem* to *how human beings ought to act*. The very breadth of the conception seems to imply that all actions involve conflicts of value. Consequently, the mere appreciation of some value is compatible with the decision that the value must be sacrificed in view of its conflict with some other value. While few environmental ethicists would want to use such conflicts as a license to revert to simple anthropocentric policies, the hard fact, in the light of these recent books, is that envi-ronmental ethicists have at most produced a *theory of value*. They have not produced a *theory of action* inferable from the former.

A related issue for environmental ethicists is the likelihood of being able to develop and apply a general theory of action to real environ-mental problems. Many environmental concerns, from the destruction of tropical forests to the falling of acid rain, from the runoff from the farmer's field to the long-term storage of long-term radioactive wastes, have become significantly more urgent, even while philosophi-cally significant work in value theory has yielded few practical results.

Moreover, researches—philosophic, scientific, and legal—into var-ious environmental problems have suggested that the values in conflict do not seem constant across environmental problems. The conditions under which farm animals are raised and various uses of animals in testing and experimentation raise problems apparently based on the sentient, emotional, and cognitive capacities of those animals. But the plight of individuals seems much less central for those who compare the merits of preservationist and conservationist approaches to populations, communities, and ecosystems. Because different environmental issues appear to involve different values, the utility of trying to develop an encompassing theory of action has become suspect for many environmental philosophers.

Thus, different combinations of values seem to be at stake in different environmental problems, and the research agenda for many environmental philosophers reflects the hypothesis that fruitful conclusions about appropriate courses of action may best emerge, not from an all-encompassing ethical theory, but from a careful consideration of recurrent situations in which particular constellations of values yield typical conflicts.

One set of environmental problems attracting considerable philosophical attention we may call upstream/downstream problems. These problems differ from the issues mentioned above because of the human involvements in them. When the wastes in one community's water affect the water supply of a community downstream or the emissions of some factory become parts of the air persons breathe downwind, a significant portion of the ethical problem is a very particular sort of human mistreatment of humans. When the wastes are technological hybrids without a history of environmental effects, a significant portion of the ethical problem is the ability of technologically driven action to outstrip human powers of foresight, thereby challenging standards of responsibility. And when new forms of social organization and new technologies combine with the natural facts of upstream/downstream relations, challenges arise both to the standards of conduct codified in law and to the entire system of norms of which our morality is a significant part.

The first hypothesis, then, that the chapters in this volume address, is that the study of upstream/downstream issues will reveal a particular constellation of values that yields a typical set of conflicts. The second hypothesis, following on the first, is that the study of these conflicts will suggest conclusions about what courses of action may best work to alleviate them.

We may then ask what sorts of facts tend to make upstream/downstream issues distinctive. Here we may begin from the observation that upstream/downstream issues are sensitive to population density. On the American frontier during the nineteenth century, for instance, settlers followed the rule of thumb that water purifies itself in six miles. The rule was important because nobody treated sewage. Consequently, new settlers needed guidance about how far downstream they should stake claims in order to ensure the quality of their drinking water.

Beyond intimating the importance of population density for upstream/downstream issues, this simple bit of frontier history can be used to indicate the importance and difficulty of understanding upstream/downstream relations. First, because of the initial low population density, newcomers had *choices* among alternative tracts more than six miles downstream from any other settlers. Second, the usefulness of water is *plural*: Water is used for waste removal and for cleaning, as well as for drinking. Third, the rule of thumb about water's self-purification, while generally true, was true relative to the *uses* to which humans put the water, upstream and downstream. There were no toxic chemical dumps upstream, nor did any downstream industrial processes require any special purity. And, finally, the rule of thumb was available because people had a decent working *knowledge* of what dangers were implicit in polluted water. The knowledge rested rather securely on a knowledge of the few naturally dangerous pollutants typically found in waters.

How do these things help us understand upstream/downstream relations today? Even as humans pursue frontiers in outer space, on the ocean floor, and in the Amazon, many spatial frontiers have closed. The human population has quintupled to over 5 billion persons within the past 150 years, and the industrialization that began in North America and Europe is swiftly encompassing the globe. In the 1860s, more than 90 percent of the earth's billion-plus human beings lived in rural areas; today over 70 percent of a Third World country like Mexico is urban. Accordingly, population density has made atypical the naturally purified downstream niche. The norm of metropolitan sewage treatment plants has replaced the norm of settling at least six miles downstream. In other words, where the independent *choices* of individual frontier families sufficed for maintaining a safe and adequate water supply, communal systems reflecting complex technologies and regional planning have become our norm. The interdependence of persons on complex social and technological organizations grows out of the sensitivity of upstream/downstream issues to population density.

Population density also feeds the growth of *multiple uses* of resources. Water, long used to carry human bodily wastes, now carries human industrial wastes. And when the exhaustion of some resource leads humans to make resources out of other ecosystemic elements, the wastes of that resource creation process, as well as the wastes in the use of that new resource, are still removed in long-familiar ways. Water carries the residues of chemical fertilizers, and wind, the carbon dioxide and sulfur dioxide.

But as these intensifications occur, they of course include interactions. Causation within ecosystems is hardly linear, and human understanding of causation in ecosystems is sketchy at best. Thus, thresholds of risk are crossed from benign to harmful uses. And synergisms of uses occur. Rules of thumb about the self-purification of water and air become false and useless. *Stable patterns* of resource usage we clearly lack.

And with changes in the resources human use, the pollutants carried downstream and downwind also change. And as they change, the purification rate for one pollutant carries no implication for the purification for another. In many environments, *nobody knows* the pollutants involved, much less their virtually countless synergisms.

Accordingly, it becomes problematic to sustain the assumption that the natural environment can be treated with impunity simply as the arena for human activity and the storehouse of our potential resources. In frontier times, human society was more easily arranged (low technology, at six-mile intervals) so that the assumption was not falsified. Even if the assumption is confused all along, it tends not to show itself as false in frontier societies. But when geodemographers map the incidence of human cancer along the Great Lakes basin, finding its nadir on the upstream tributaries and its peak at the mouth of the basin, the reality of environmentally related disease becomes vivid. We do not affect the natural environment with impunity.

The rise of cities teaches further lessons. Rural environments make human habitats significantly different from urban environments. It is not merely the difference that comes with replacing wells with municipal waterworks. Nor is it simply the easier urban access to schools, doctors, and other social services. The personal anonymity of urban environments promotes rootlessness, and the juxtaposition of ethnic traditions creates tensions. At the same historical moment when population density exponentially increases human interdependence, the alienation of individuals from traditional social settings means the decay of amenities that have facilitated social intercourse.

Cities, which are often literally downstream, give "downstream" a new meaning when resources such as timber and ore flow from upstream to downstream environments, there to be transformed into products. Resources are bought, transformed, and sold. Markets develop, and power comes to surround centers of exchange located in downstream centers. And we need to remind ourselves of the ethical quandaries to which these developments can lead. Let us recall that in the 1590s, when London was becoming an international center of exchange, William Shakespeare wrote *The Merchant of Venice* about the comparable experiences of Venice more than 200 years earlier.

In those days, however, markets were small; subsistence farming was the common human way of life. Few people were then employed; in so advanced a city as London, the factory is the creature of the eighteenth century. But as factories were created, jobs, employment, and wages, the social realities of the "modern age," began to emerge. People started working outside the home. Since their labor was specialized, they needed their wages to buy what they did not supply themselves. Markets began to expand, fed by the still-increasing involvement of persons in "the labor force."

But a lesson of the nineteenth and twentieth centuries is that markets bring with them the vicissitudes of change. If demand increases, the factory increases its pollution, straining to keep pace with demand. If demand declines, the lack of funds to pay workers vibrates through a regional, state, or world economy. If demand increases, more workers are drawn to the city, and the demand for social services increases, with the provision of those services lagging in a classic pattern. If the demand declines, the economy flags, discouragement and crime increase, and human drug use—from alcohol to cocaine—rises. If demand increases, the well-off seek the upstream retreat, the mountain hike or vacation home, that removes them from the stress and squalor of downstream life. If demand decreases, potential vacationers rethink, and the economy of economically downstream but geographically upstream vacation areas suffers. Aldo Leopold remarked on these obvious upstream/downstream patterns of modern life almost half a century ago.

And such patterns in turn generate social responses. Social services arise—Head Start programs and state fisheries to prevent a declining quality of experiences, and drug rehabilitation and river-dredging programs to overcome problems of especially degenerate environments.

But nobody wants the proposed new regional jail to be built locally. Everybody petitions against the opening of a new landfill, since by now most people have at least a vague knowledge of the dangers of leaching, even when the landfill accepts only the five pounds of wastes we Americans individually generate daily. Why should that new outpatient program for the mentally disturbed be built in our neighborhood? Can't we have a town of light industries, schools, parks, and appropriate places of worship?

These, then, are the environments and sentiments in which have evolved the NIMBY ("Not in my backyard") chorus to what beleaguered residents now universally call LULUs ("locally unwanted land uses"). As desirable and necessary as a shelter for battered wives and children may be, we do not want potentially violent men drawn to our neighborhood. As inevitable as pollution may be, we do not want to live with unusually high downwind mortality rates. Downwind is vulnerable, and the weakness of the weak is reinforced after they have been unable to resist the establishment of physical or social pollution upstream of themselves. Resentments arise where the ability to resist has fallen short, and that resentment, if widespread and deep, can form the social environment for declining expectations, community apathy, and rising rates of drug use and crime.

The cry of NIMBY bespeaks distress and suspicion that "they" are trying to impose the unwanted pollution on "us." But beneath the distress, even deeper, is a fear of the unknown. What are the pollutant by-products of this manufacturing process? How do we know that these mentally ill persons are really safe? Don't we have a duty to protect our children from the drug dealing that may follow a drug rehabilitation program into town?

It is no accident that NIMBY and LULU are among the novel acronyms of our time because they arise from the newly technological and urbanized environment of human life. The technological base of developed economies and the mass of people and diversity of contemporary culture represent great novelty. Granted, technology has been important to human life for about 100,000 years and cities for at least 10,000. Even so, 90 percent of all chemical compounds on the earth today have been invented in the past forty years, mass urban culture is the child of the twentieth century, and the highway system and airports of postwar American life are without precedent. Human beings thus have no significant tradition on which to build the norms they need to maintain themselves, much less to thrive, in a dense and highly interactive upstream/downstream world.

Living in an Upstream/ Downstream World

How, then, can we develop an ecologically sensitive understanding of our upstream/downstream world? The key is to note fundamental features of organisms and successful ecosystems. Thus, while all living creates waste products, the evolution of an ecosystem presupposes that the system develops means through which the wastes have no more than a marginal impact on the system and thus on the species within it. On the one hand, many long-established wastes serve as resources elsewhere in the system. On the other hand, successful organisms learn to identify and avoid potentially harmful wastes by relying on the wastes to degenerate naturally in areas avoidable by the organisms at least while the danger remains.

Clearly, then, upstream/downstream relationships take on significance arising from the closing of frontiers. The increased quantity, as well as the new kinds, of wastes floods the ecosystemic abilities to absorb them. The avoidable areas become scarcer as closed frontiers put a premium on space. Technological development makes exponentially less certain what wastes are harmful. And human beings, ever seeking new ways to better their situations, even in the face of great population increases, learn to make their actions more "efficient" by externalizing the costs associated with containing or treating wastes. If the fertilizers a farmer uses run off the field into surrounding streams, the costs of phosphorous-stimulated algae growth are borne not by the farmer but by fish and by water recreation interests downstream. If the food service manager uses plastics to offer a more competitive price to the sponsor of some event, then the costs of filling the landfill with nonbiodegradable materials is borne neither by the food service manager nor by the event sponsor, but by our grandchildren. Beyond the geographical and cultural upstream/downstream flows, chemically induced birth defects and a 100-year provision for wastes dangerous for 100,000 years portend the ultimate "downstream" vulnerability of future generations. More vulnerable than the poor, they cannot even protest, "Not in my backyard." Such is the upstream/downstream world in which we live.

Our upstream/downstream world is also characterized by changed social norms. The earliest human beings clearly lived in small bands. Bilateral relationships among persons long known to one another are normative for such bands. Small-group interactions remained similarly normative in the agricultural society that had until recently characterized human life for thousands of years.

To grasp the ethical significance of this fact, consider the characteristics of small-group interactions in agricultural communities. In such environments, many relationships are bilateral: Your action primarily affects me, and vice versa. The bonds of responsibility are strengthened by the clear consequences of our treatment of each other. Many relationships are reciprocal and are known to be so. In such social environments, person A and person B know that they will someday exchange roles, so the question "How would you like it if somebody did that to you?" has a clear portent. Similarly, the thought that my action will be of insignificant consequence is falsified. After all, when there are few agents, the action of each plays a significant part, and the action of each will be widely known by others. For, indeed, others know us. There is no norm of anonymity. The social tracking system is in the perception and storytelling of others, not in the record of computer-stored bureaucratic forms.

Even when roles are not fully reversed, even when our ancestors knew that they would never really be in the others' shoes, they often saw that their continual interactions within their small communities provided many incentives to cooperation. The continued interaction of persons well known to one another enhances the basic quid pro quo of social existence: "I could do this for you if you would do that for me."

These were among the powerful norms of past societies, but they have endured great recent stress. Upstream/downstream environments have undermined several conditions that supported these norms. As persons move from country to town, from town to city, and from city to suburb, the pressure arises for norms that tolerate anonymity. Traveling and shopping nationally, for instance, creates an impetus toward credit cards. As relationships become less bilateral, reciprocity decreases, and enlightened self-interest is less obviously adequate to ensure that others will be treated as one would also wish to be treated. The very concrete implication of the population explosion is the existence of mass markets, which in turn imply the probable insignificance of the individual's action for the outcome of the operation of the market. The increased pool of any individual's acquaintances and the quickened evolution of the social environment make searching for advantageous quid pro quos not only more necessary but also more difficult.

One can see much of this writ large in the philosophy of John Locke (1632–1702) and his most important implementor, Thomas Jefferson. Locke's political philosophy has as one of its important underpinnings a labor theory of value. People's labor, Locke held, is the source of almost all the value pieces of land ever come to have. Thus, Locke urged, a person is entitled to own the land whose value has derived from his or her labor. And this, Locke suggested, is fair because the person's having title to the land would both benefit others insofar as the owner's labor created salable value and deprive no one else on the assumption that places like America, with its open frontier, exist to leave others with "as much and as good" as the owner appropriates.

Now Thomas Jefferson was a careful reader and great admirer of John Locke. Much more than his federalist contemporaries, Jefferson saw the "honest, yeoman farmer," through the eyes of Locke's labor theory of value, as the fundamental source of America's greatness. All such citizens required to secure that greatness, Jefferson believed, was unused land they could cultivate and therefore lay claim to. And as President Jefferson, he purchased the Louisiana Territory so that the

country's industrious and rational "yeoman farmers" and their de-
scendents could work and claim new lands, leaving as much and as
good for others for, Jefferson estimated, 500 years.[3] It was the one act
that that strict constitutionalist feared was unconstitutional, the purchase of territory without any constitutional provision explicitly
granting the president that power, the one act he did on the basis of
his fervent belief in the power of human beings motivated to make a
better life for their children and grandchildren. And from Jefferson
through Jackson, through Reconstruction and almost to the end of the
nineteenth century, one homestead act followed another, each legis-
lating that those who staked a claim and labored to improve a parcel
would thereby become its owner. Although Jefferson had estimated
that the Louisiana Territory would take 500 years to settle, the frontier was closed before the century was out, as frontiers from Hawaii to
Alaska were also pursued.

Now we have come full circle. We began with grasping the closing
of land frontiers as one of the primary disturbers of traditional social
norms. Now we see that the political philosophy and the legislation on
which American frontiers were developed assumed an agricultural
economy, assumed easily accessible and profitable quid pro quos, relied on the social context to reinforce persons in taking responsibility
for individually significant actions, saw no need to make provision for
controlling pollutant by-products, and never entertained the new-
fangled possibility that the toughest battles humans might have with
"nature" would be with the pollutants humans would introduce to
the natural environment.

Today, then, we live in an upstream/downstream world. Environmental philosophers tend to view that world as constituted by how
new facts about the human condition redefine both the social and the
natural environment in which we live. The question addressed in this
volume is not so much "How should we humans treat the natural
environment?" as "What should we humans do, what norms should
we adopt, to promote human responsibility for the well-being of both
other human beings and the natural environment?" For the study of
ecosystems presses on us an understanding of human life, human
communities, and human norms as respondent to and creator of environments. The history of the past century is a history of vastly up-

heaved natural and social environments arising mostly in closed frontiers, using enormous energy and vast technologies to sustain unprecedented human residents of the novel environments we call metropolitan areas.

Our social world is thus characterized by decreased reciprocity, less apparent quid pro quos, more anonymity, more multilateral relationships, and less individual significance. Accordingly, the problems of environmental ethics arise not only from the human transformation of nature but in fair measure from the human transformation of human society.

The eight chapters that follow provide eight perspectives on aspects of this contemporary predicament. In the first, Donald Scherer works from the preceding characterization of upstream/downstream issues, asking how new norms might emerge to respond to the problems endemic to upstream/downstream environments. But in order to do that, Scherer puts the entire problem in a larger perspective: Human beings are social animals who have developed language, technology, norms, and conventional practices. All these things prove useful for facilitating the creation and maintenance of environments, physical and social, within which social coordination proves generally beneficial. What sorts of developments are appropriate, then, in the light of the peculiarities of upstream/downstream environments?

Ernest Partridge provides an overview of our relationship to future generations. As many people are concerned only about themselves, their children, and their grandchildren, many philosophers have argued on one basis and another that people living today can have no obligations to persons of future times. Certainly our relationships to such persons are nonreciprocal, and by hypothesis such persons are unable to enter into quid pro quos. Although they are only metaphorically "down the river of time," the metaphor of a river of time does capture the characteristics attributed above to upstream/downstream relationships. Interestingly, then, Partridge finds each of the five prominent arguments offered to sustain the "no obligations" thesis deficient. More important, he suggests what bases such upstream/downstream obligations have.

Partridge's essay sets the stage for that of Dale Jamieson, who focuses on the human understanding of the Greenhouse Effect. He urges that, by operating on inadequate philosophies, society is abrogating its obligations to future generations. Positivist models of science and society, on which much of American society has been built, make several important assumptions, among them that there is a radical separation between facts and values and that scientists, applying appropriate methods, can ascertain the facts. Many others have added the technocratic assumption that these facts can be ascertained quickly enough to devise a technological resolution to any problem. But the rigidity of fact–value distinction is hardly clear from ecological considerations: Observers must be able to distinguish real data from noise, and technological solutions are not always so feasible when social interactions are central to the nonlinear causal chains defining the problem. These are among the considerations that, Jamieson suggests, must shape a more responsible response to the Greenhouse Effect.

Kristin Shrader-Frechette challenges the use of hydrogeological models along similar lines. While it has been almost axiomatic in scientific research that one ought to use the best models available, Shrader-Frechette urges that the best models may not be adequate to answer certain practical questions of applied science. Suppose the hydrogeological complexity of an area lends plausibility to the claim that no extant hydrogeological model is sufficiently sophisticated to yield reliable predictions about what contamination might result from the siting of a waste depository in a given area. What use should we then make of the "best available model"? Shrader-Frechette questions the ways in which such models have been used to decide the siting of hazardous wastes.

The next two chapters focus on the role of law, especially as it responds to the social character of upstream/downstream issues. As we have noted, upstream/downstream issues are characterized by anonymous and multilateral human relationships in which individuals have little significance. Even in the empires of the ancient world, it began to become apparent how law could become a normative structure for handling the complex interactions of large masses of people. Among Western societies, the law is prominent in the establishment and enforcement of social norms. In the United States, the immense changes outlined above have been accompanied by the development of the most litigious society on earth. Yet to many people it seems that at its widest the power of law is intranational. Canadians and Americans are certainly sensitive to the limited impact of the law in responding to the acid rain that has fallen into Canadian lakes. Thus, to many people, the law can successfully respond to upstream/ downstream issues only in the presence of traditions common to a nation and the substantial enforcement powers typically missing from international affairs.

Accordingly, Daniel Magraw, a professor of law, and James Nickel, a professor of philosophy, focus on this apparent limit to the usefulness of law. They bid us notice the many substantial ways in which international law is followed even with legal enforcement powers missing. Using the contrasting frameworks provided by Thomas Hobbes and John Locke, they argue that however hostile or congenial humans may naturally be, international law, even in its present form, can be and is a substantial normative force reshaping the vulnerabilities of downstream environments.

Mark Sagoff focuses on a particular use of the law of property rights. The Fifth Amendment to the Constitution of the United States guarantees that individuals shall not be deprived of their property by the government without just compensation. But regardless of the importance of this "takings" clause of the Fifth Amendment, it has never been used to argue against the police power to prevent a man from using "his" club to assault his neighbor. What upstream/downstream issues bring into focus is the possibility that the property owner's action may have or substantially contribute to ecological breakdowns. A famous case concerns Ronald Just, who owned some swampland that was useless to him unless he filled in the swamp. But filling in the only remaining swampland in that area of northeast Wisconsin would render the swamp unable to serve its vital ecological functions. In many indirect ways, many individuals would suffer if, for example, the water passing through the swamp no longer was cleansed and several species of fish lost their breeding grounds. What legal norm is appropriate, given the right of a property owner to use property for private gain without governmental interference and given the right of others to be protected from what the law calls noxious uses of one's property?

In legal theory, much of this discussion centers on the political philosophy of John Locke, especially his labor theory of property rights. Working from such a labor theory of property rights, Ellen Paul has argued that such a philosophy justifies a strong interpretation of the "takings" clause of the Fifth Amendment to the Constitution of the United States. Since, as Paul points out, the government is forbidden from taking the property of an individual for the public good without providing compensation to the property owner, the property rights of the owner, she concludes, require the government to compensate the owner if the government should prohibit such profitable uses of the property as destroy some resources to the public detriment. It is this argument of Paul's that Sagoff attacks.

Another dimension of upstream/downstream issues is that many downstream problems result not from the acts of any individual but from some combination of the acts of many. Often, no one upstream individual alone is causing significant harm. Bart Gruzalski wrestles with finding an adequate basis for attributing responsibility for pollution when each polluter adds so little pollution as to do no damage alone. This is especially problematic when the rest of the polluters add so much pollution as to be quite damaging without any contribution from the one. What, he asks, is an appropriate standard of responsibility in the face of individual insignificance?

Standards of responsibility are fundamental to the norms of any society. And certainly the prevalence of multilateral relationships suggests why cost–benefit analyses, developed first in the New Deal and now widely applied by businesses as well as governments, have become one of our standard tools for ascertaining responsibility. But what value do traditional cost–benefit analyses capture, and are there significant values they have ignored? Alan Gewirth offers a twofold argument. Traditional cost–benefit analyses, he holds, are inadequate for assessing the losses of substantial goods and liberty that result from pollution, particularly pollution in the workplace. Only by directly assessing the value of a life and the value of liberty, he argues, could cost–benefit analyses accomplish their purported end. And, as he urges, this argument carries significant implications for how traditional cost–benefit analyses would need to be reshaped in order to provide an adequate assessment of losses involved in and consequent to a loss of health.

The common theme of these essays is that the environments in which we live, environments so much of our own making, have outstripped older conceptions of responsible human living within the environment. The global consequences of our actions and the uncertainty of our actions belie the inadequacies of our scientific models and force us to question the meaning of responsibility in the face of uncertainty. Our legal standards are challenged by interjurisdictional disputes; our best theories of property do not clearly yield the results their conservative champions seek. Our standards of responsibility are challenged by individual insignificance, and new standards, based on the analysis of costs and benefits, seem inadequate to handle the most basic of human goods.

The characteristics of upstream/downstream relations, as the authors in this volume argue, drive us toward revised standards of responsibility. Where a reliance on a technical conception of rationality narrows the focus of what being human means, this volume attempts a few initial steps toward new understandings of human responsibility in an upstream/downstream world.

Notes

1. For a basic introduction to the work of Aldo Leopold, see his *A Sand County Almanac: With Other Essays on Conservation from Round River* (New York: Oxford University Press, 1949).

2. J. Baird Callicott, *In Defense of the Land Ethic* (Albany: State University of New York Press, 1987); Paul W. Taylor, *Respect for Nature: A Theory of Environmental Ethics* (Princeton: Princeton University Press, 1986); Holmes Rolston III, *Environmental Ethics: Duties to and Values in the Natural World* (Philadelphia: Temple University Press, 1988).

3. From a European viewpoint, the Louisiana Purchase had an entirely different upstream/downstream significance. Jefferson borrowed the money for his purchase from British bankers so that he could pay Napoleon, who sold the territory to obtain the funding to support his war against, among others, the British. This is one model of an actual upstream/downstream relationship.

Donald Scherer

Chapter 1

The Molding of Norms and Environments

An upstream/downstream relationship is one in which an action taken "upstream," that is, at a given point in time and space, has a significant effect "downstream," that is, at a rather inconspicuously later time or in a significantly distant space. In this chapter, I suggest that such relationships tend to result in problems for natural and social environments because of the significant normative problems the relationships pose. In order to make this argument, I first characterize upstream/downstream relations. Then I sketch an account of the development of morality within evolutionary theory. The account I present rests in part on evolutionary theory proper, but also on archaeological theories about human development. To these I add some philosophic understandings of the functioning of language.

Once I have provided this account, it should be clear that morality is an integrated and functional part of a system of norms that probably has had survival value. Yet that survival value developed for independent human populations living in small bands. The corollary of this view is that a normative system functional for largely independent human populations may not prove functional for highly interdependent populations in upstream/downstream relationships. Accordingly, in the final section of the essay, I suggest some appropriate adjustments for a normative system in the face of upstream/downstream interactions.

The Anomalies of Upstream/
Downstream Environments

I begin by characterizing upstream/downstream environments because I believe that the difference between human relationships within
these environments and human relationships within environments
that human norms more successfully govern explains why traditional
human norms often fail in upstream/downstream environments.

1. A central characteristic of upstream/downstream environments
is that within them causation works, or is perceived as working, in
only one direction. What happens upstream is perceived to cause effects downstream, but not vice versa. Consequently, those who live
upstream do not fear harms caused to them from downstream. In
contrast, a fundamental reinforcer of human norms is "Someday you
may be in my position, and how would you like it if I . . ." Thus, when
one human community is upstream and another down, the two communities will typically not perceive *reciprocity* as constraining their
relationship.

2. Even without the strong reciprocity that obtains when two parties regularly and literally exchange places, many human relationships
are unproblematic because the interrelationship involves a *quid pro
quo.* But upstream/downstream relationships, being (perceived as)
unidirectional, do not strike persons as providing a basis for a quid
pro quo. In a particular case, the fortuitous fact may be that A is
upstream of B with respect to water flow, while B is upstream of A
with respect to prevailing winds, but upstream/downstream relations
often lack this symmetry.

3. Indeed, the *specialization of roles* characteristic of urbanized human interactions is a central factor in minimizing (apparent) quid pro
quos. For the specialization of roles implies that communities are related by several interrelationships most of which reflect the initiatives
of different groups of people.[1] And multilateral relationships are not
easily perceived as providing quid pro quos.

4. A further effect of the population explosion is the increased importance of *thresholds.* It can easily happen that many agents upstream will cause effects none of them would have individually
caused. The chemical effluents industries emit, the runoffs of farmers'

fields, and the Ohio State University stadium full of trash the people of Ohio throw away every week are equally good examples of threshold problems. Here we see at work the historical limits of our assignments of responsibility. Responsibilities are obviously harder to assign and coordinate when the number of assignees is large and unfixed, and the identities of involved parties are not clearly known.

5. The problem of thresholds exhibits but does not exhaust another anomaly of contemporary upstream/downstream environments. Upstream/downstream environments often foster *consequent social environments that constrain* the actions of persons, corporations, and governments. Many upstream/downstream problems that would be solvable under conditions of perfect coordination plague us today, and some of the most significant norms of contemporary life reinforce the difficulties of coordination. First, to the extent that the actions of individuals are anonymous, monitoring the acceptability of those actions is difficult. But anonymity is often the outgrowth of privacy and of traditionally broad conceptions of liberty allied with narrow definitions of harm, definitions inherited from the frontier traditions of northern Europe and nineteenth-century United States.[2] Second, the moral constraint of producers to meet consumers' needs is reinforced by norms of competition within free markets. An instrumental value placed on secrecy used to promote a competitive advantage reinforces producers as they strive for efficiency. Third, in the modern world, jurisdictions of government are used to protect the intrajurisdictional economy. Whether we are talking about acid rain in eastern Canada, the exportation of products that do not meet U.S. safety standards, or thousands of examples that have nothing to do with the United States, governmental coercion frequently prioritizes the protection of a local constituency over the long-term health of persons and ecosystems. But, given the plurality of jurisdictions and interactions, superior coordinations are difficult to achieve and maintain. Numerous situations occur that are like Prisoners' Dilemma situations. Thus, even nations with considerable power can be coerced from actions that their jurisdictional authority might otherwise coordinate.

6. Upstream/downstream environments are also characterized by *ignorance* of several varieties. In part, upstream/downstream environments are simply markets in which perfect information is not to be

expected; especially, how the actions of third parties will affect contemplated actions is often unknown. And our detailed knowledge of ecosystems is quite sketchy. While it is apparent that ecosystems tend to be resilient, many limits of a given ecosystem's resilience are usually unpredictable except within a rather broad range. Finally, the evolutionary impact of fertilizers and pesticides continually introduces significant novelty (and thus unpredictability) into environments, affecting human health and liberty. These forms of ignorance work to excuse even more harmful consequences than they cause.

7. It may be obvious that an effect has occurred downstream when it is not at all obvious who, upstream, is responsible for that effect. This *anonymity* occurs for several reasons: At the outset, it may be unclear that the downstream effect has an upstream cause. Or the occurrence of the effect may be due in part to midstream ecosystemic transformations that nobody understands. Or many upstream agents may have contributed to the cause. And norms concerning the protection of trade secrets may promote public ignorance of how an effect occurs. And even the upstream agents may be unaware of how the effects of their actions interacted.

Moreover, upstream/downstream environments are problematic because of the interaction of all these factors. For example, consider the common maxim I discussed in connection with reciprocity: "How would you like it if you were in my position and I . . ." In addition to reciprocity, the use of this maxim presupposes that we can identify a party whose causal role ties responsibility clearly to that party. Accordingly, the threshold effects and the problems of ignorance typical of many macroenvironmental problems also limit the usefulness of the maxim in the world today.

Morality within the Structure of Evolutionary Theory

I now turn to an account of the development of norms. My goal in developing this account is to highlight why upstream/downstream relations turn out to be anomalous.

Norms in the Nonhuman Environment

Human beings are social animals. From an evolutionary viewpoint, a social species pursues the hypothesis that the ability to survive will be enhanced if individuals coordinate their behaviors, even in ways that include the vulnerabilities of interdependence. In other words, social species pursue the evolutionary hypothesis that the gains of forming the interdependencies of a society outweigh the costs.

For social primates, opportunities for learning are among the important gains. To the extent that the survival of a species depends on either the variety or the fineness of individuals' awarenesses or response discriminations, a capacity for learning improves survivability. It is not surprising, then, that the young of a species with prolonged immaturity use their immaturity to learn to correlate various awarenesses of the environment with adaptive response behaviors.

Unlike most fish, amphibians, and reptiles, then, social primates cannot tolerate the juvenile deaths of most individuals of their species. To be successful, the environment of their young must not regularly undermine their existence. Human beings, like other social primates, use interorganism cooperation to soften the environment for their juveniles. Indeed, the evolutionary strategy of social primates regularly includes interorganism cooperation in mother–infant interactions, male–female sexual interactions, safety-providing interactions, hostility-minimizing strategies, and food-procurement interactions.[3]

To understand morality, I find it very important to note the extra-moral social environment in which human moral norms arise. For example, the perceived cuteness of infants is among the motivators of adult caregivers, particularly mothers, to tend to the interests of infants. The regular sexual attractiveness and receptivity of sexual partners is among the motivators of cooperative relations between sexual partners. The increased intelligence and, later, the increased technological capacities of a band make the band more successful in protecting weaker organisms from harm as they also make food procurement more successful.[4]

But an increasingly social environment for animals also magnifies potential social threats of harm: As infants grow, they become not only less cute but also more inclined to pursue their own goals. Sexual attractiveness and receptivity promote promiscuity, jealousy, rivalry, and animosity. Adolescent males and organized neighbors magnify the potential sources of harm. And when success in food procurement promotes toleration of population growth, the need for food resources increases.

Still developing the complexity of the social context within which moral norms arise, we may note that both the affection of parents for children and the domination of parents over children control pre-adolescent children's growing independence. Moreover, children tend to love even those parents who neglect or mistreat them. Independently, the interactions of parents and child can come to promote affection and concern for one another. Selective sexual attractiveness moderates the conflicts to which generalized sexual attractiveness and receptivity give rise. And when the members of small bands depend on one another, at least for facilitating the meeting of basic needs, the need for ongoing cooperation deters the overt expression of sexual desire. Similarly, dominant mature males check the aggressiveness of adolescent males until the adolescent males grow older, less antisocial, and more cooperative in their behavior.[5]

The evolutionary strategy of social primates thus gives rise to social environments in which goals are best achieved through a division of labor. Indeed, even without language, chimpanzee mothers train their offspring to achieve successes that require each to do his or her part. And again, without language, one chimpanzee can express approbation or disapprobation when another has or has not done something crucial to the success of an interdependent undertaking. I think of this behavioral syndrome as a prototype for what it certainly is not yet, namely, an assignment of responsiblity.

But all of the above probably existed before language came to be.[6] We can therefore provide a *genetic definition* of a norm of behavior applicable to all social primates, including prelinguistic human beings.[7] "Norms of behavior" can mean "usual patterns of behavior, the maintenance (and hence the reinforcement) of which promotes the successful continuation of primary, life-sustaining behaviors." The implicit teleological explanation of such norms is their promotion of life-sustaining behaviors.[8]

Language and the Development of Human Norms

Given this background, let us recall the broadest outlines of early human history. Between 2.5 million years ago and 100,000 years ago, the size of our ancestors' brain grew from approximately 600 cc to 1500 cc.[9] Then, between 100,000 and 90,000 years ago, an unparalleled technological revolution occurred. In that revolution, hunting implements evolved more quickly than in the preceding million years. Pottery was invented. And vast changes in human life resulted: Only through superior hunting implements did the larger, fiercer mammals become regular prey; only with a liquid diet, made possible by pottery, could human individuals survive the loss of their teeth; only with pottery could alcoholic beverages be brewed.[10]

From this vast technological revolution, in conjunction with the fact that human brain size then reached a zenith from which it has since declined by about 10 percent, I accept the inference of some anthropologists that language evolved at about that time.[11] For language gives new speakers increased ability to mark finer distinctions and to mark them in a more standard public way. If social animals are going to coordinate with one another noninstinctively, they must interpret the sensory stimuli they receive from their environments and from one another as indicating the appropriateness of a particular interactive pattern. The development of language, then, allows social animals to make various features of circumstances salient by naming them, thereby facilitating the learning of norms and improving the quality of coordination. For, through language, one organism directs the attention of another to particular characteristics of their environment. Soon enough, the development of vocabulary will make it true that language users, while focusing their eyes in the same direction, can coordinatively look first at one aspect of their environment and then at another. Thus language allows organisms to observe environments more distinctly and to know more certainly that each has made the same observation.

Besides the beginning evolution of descriptive capacities, proto-language, whenever it evolved, probably involved directive capacities. Certainly commands and prohibitions were early directives. But the domination of children by parents and the hierarchical organization of primate bands suggest that commands and prohibitions were soon supplemented by permissions.[12]

And since our ancestors were social long before they were linguistic, language must very early have caused coordinative planning to evolve. If uses of language can refine organisms' environmental awareness through selective attention, then uses of language can also enhance organisms' coordinative capacities. For language, with its power to make obvious the need for creating a salience not present in an environment, can be used to present the ideas that what an animal *will* do will allow two animals to achieve a desired outcome.[13] Is it not plausible that language about the future should have arisen in part out of situations in which one social animal wanted to direct another linguistically skilled animal to act in such a way that a delayed gratification would occur?

Linguistic abilities may then be used to facilitate voluntary exchanges since many exchanges will occur only if they are voluntary, and voluntary exchanges rest on the mutual preference of what the other has to what one has. In many circumstances where coercion is a self-defeating or impossible motivator, the first may seek to induce the second through some prospect of a currently nonexistent benefit. Here we discover the creation of projects as social realities—that is, two parties each understand that they have a common understanding of what they are trying to achieve. And projects, which nudge the future into the linguistic realm, thus appear as an ancestor of the concept of contract.

From the outset of the use of language, some sentences occasionally proved unacceptable to their hearers.[14] Descriptive sentences hearers are sometimes disinclined to believe; directive sentences they are sometimes disinclined to follow. But bands of social animals in ongoing relationships sense that frustrated uses of language are bound to be *reciprocal.* Thus their sense of ongoing interrelationships motivates disinclined hearers not simply to ignore the disagreeable sentence.

Accordingly, counterclaim is a likely alternative. But claim and counterclaim are not by themselves a coordinating device; they merely mark the perceived lack of a basis for coordination. And because of the advantages of noncoercive interaction, some basis for achieving voluntary coordination will evolve. Such a basis is the invention of procedures for determining "who is right"; that is, which claim—counterclaim is to be accepted. Here a new use of language arises: Procedures of verification and justification evolve as outgrowths of the failure of claim—counterclaim to produce a resolution of differences.[15]

Language-speaking social organisms, however, even if they have built verification and justification procedures into their linguistic interactions, do not always act to bring about the greatest common good. The self-interest of the individual may not coincide with the self-interest of the group. And individuals sometimes act on desires contrary to their own self-interest. Of course, a child's desire to please parents and a weaker individual's fear of a stronger group member will promote many coordinated outcomes even when individuals are not otherwise so disposed. But, often enough, those natural motivations will be missing or overridden.

We now step closer to what we might call responsibilities. If the social environment includes a division of labor,[16] and language includes directives, sentences can evolve to assign roles coordinated for achieving a desired result. With the language of justification and a language of the future, it becomes possible to articulate that if each of the feasible assignments of responsibility is carried out, a mutually desired goal will be met. Praise and blame, as essentially linguistic acts, can then supplement and sometimes even supplant nonlinguistic expressions of approbation and disapprobation.[17]

Now, consider what had to happen to language with the coming of the agricultural revolution. Any agricultural process involves an investment of labor that bears fruit only at some later time. Thus, in the intervening moments, those who have not invested the labor may arrange to benefit from it. Obviously, if such interventions are regular, the interventions will discourage agricultural development unless preventing the interventions is arrangeable. Such arrangements included practices of boundary demarcation and security watches even before the advent of written language. The protection of cultivated lands led headmen to create the specialized social role of protector, the precursor of both the police and the military.[18]

The idea of real property, already complex, gains in complexity with the introduction of written language, for a title or a deed to a piece of real property is a certification by some authority in a publicly accessible and publicly retrievable way that henceforth some individual shall have an authority over that land not shared by others.

To see more clearly the role of records in the regulation of behavior, let us consider how written language originated.[19] When goods are placed on ships, ship captains frequently have nothing of comparable worth to exchange for those goods. Clearly, exchange will be facilitated—theoretically, even in a barter society—if ship captains can use goods they later receive in distant ports to compensate those who earlier put goods on their ships. But when the ship captain returns to port, nothing may remain in the environment of the port to show what goods were placed on the ship months earlier. Or, if anything remains, it may be only the memories of persons present both earlier and later. When expressions of memory conflict, however, a conflict about proper compensation will arise. The temporal absence of what is to be exchanged creates the problem of precision in defining what it is that is not present but is to be exchanged. Social order and the advantages of continuing commerce will then push toward creating a practice of record making.

The practical problem of consigning goods to ships does not consist simply in the problem of the unreliability of memory about which goods were placed on which ships. Consignment, like more primitive exchange practices, rests on an understanding of an appropriate quid pro quo. Indeed, notice how the elements of what we still take contracts to be respond to the problems created by consignments of goods to ships. Because contracts are records of agreements, they create a salience in the later environment that encourages compliance. Because contracts have witnesses, the reliability of the record itself is vouchsafed, and the salience is harder to deny. Because contracts have sanctions, there is also a response to the inevitability of risk associated with the future, independent of human best efforts.[20] Because sanctions fall upon particular parties, incentives are created for minimizing the risks.[21] Because the mutual satisfaction goes unattained unless by some specifiable future time the party of the second part gains the satisfactions due, contracts have terms. The material roots of the concept of contract, then, are totally contained within the advantages and risks of exchanges of something now for something later.

Another common use of language among primitive people is to recount stories, for storytelling can build intragroup cohesion. Whether they are historical, legendary, or mythic, the stories are repeated, and from Greece to Israel, from India to China, one finds the development of oral traditions. In each of these traditions, the stories are eventually written, and at least the more privileged males in these successful cultures have the leisure to read the texts, reflect on them, and memorize much of them.

This process of reflection creates an inward focal point for action. We may infer this creation from noting that the most ancient written codes are entirely behavioral in content. For instance, the original form of the Ten Commandments has, rather than the commandment "Thou shalt not steal," the commandment "Thou shalt not steal a man." That is, the original commandment prohibited not theft but the kidnapping of free men. Correspondingly, the original meaning of *covet* was "steal"; the commandment prohibited stealing one's neighbor's house, his wife, his manservant, his maidservant, his ox, his ass, or anything else he might own. The form of the commandments that comes down to us in Exodus generalizes the prohibition against stealing to cover both kidnapping and property, thereby freeing the commandment about "coveting" to be reinterpreted more inwardly.

The art of storytelling stimulates and the process of reflecting on texts develops the concept of vicarious experience. What would I have done in his position? What must it have felt like to have to make such a choice? And in the light of such questions, a different breed of thoughts arises: What kind of inner strength must he have had to have acted so well?[22] What ideal of manliness (that is, what virtue) allowed him to act so well in those circumstances?[23] What traits of character distinguish the man we rightly idealize from other men? Would that through my meditation on these treasured stories I could become such a man myself![24]

This new breed of thoughts grows through classic literatures into a cultivated inwardness. Spokesmen begin to articulate norms idealizing those who identify themselves with the cultivation of a set of virtues.

Thus the common theme of Confucius, the Upanishads, Israelite prophets, and Greek playwrights is that the worth of a human life is measured by the kind of integrity it develops and maintains. This discovery of the soul mightily expands a normative discourse by requiring that the justification of norms should include not only the effects of external behaviors but also the effects of the taking of the action on the self-consciousness of the agent. The concepts of dignity, self-respect, and autonomy, which seem so central to the modern moral consciousness, take their original shape out of sustained reflection on the stories of the people.

It is tempting to think that we have reached the subject matter of ethics only with our discussions of responsibility and contract, and with the concept of conscience implicit in the discussion of self-consciousness. But I propose that it is a mistake, in thinking about upstream/downstream environments, to confine our discussions to such explicitly moral norms. Certainly many sociologists would be ready to emphasize that the attractiveness of moral norms is greatest within the middle classes. And we know that the reciprocity of community building means most to the parents of the young. If we believe that upstream/downstream relations create disturbing harms, then, we can scarcely afford to confine our search for solutions to strictly moral norms. As powerful as moral norms are, they are a very specialized glue of social cohesiveness, not necessrarily well adapted to every social environment.

Restructuring the Human Normative Environment for Upstream/ Downstream Environments

I take the problem of upstream/downstream relations to be one of recalling the contrast between upstream/downstream relations to interactions more definitive of the norms I have been explicating and then of suggesting how the restructuring of upstream/downstream relations can bring such relations within the power of an effective normative structure.[25] The point of the history I have sketched is that moral norms have developed and have always operated within a broader natural and human environment, including many nonmoral norms. Thus, the solution of upstream/downstream problems may well require more than an adjustment of moral norms.

If I have previously respectably characterized upstream/downstream environments, I propose now to turn to the question of the restructuring of the human normative environment to respond to the anomalies of upstream/downstream environments. The concern we must address is that moral norms have their efficacy within a framework of reciprocities and quid pro quos that upstream/downstream environments apparently undermine.

1. To the extent that social norms are strengthened by *reciprocity*, it is important for people to structure environments so that any real reciprocity has a perceived salience. For we commonly fail to recognize reciprocities to which we are subject. Perhaps we are unacquainted with the other party to whom we are related. Perhaps the reversal of roles is based in differences of place or time. Perhaps the causation we perceive as linear is really systemic. But certainly the normative structure is buttressed to the extent that persons are led to realize that, to some significant extent, everybody lives downstream. When middle-class persons escape to vacation retreats and find a remote, almost pristine lake environment, fed in part by an industrially polluted stream, they can begin to sense the need for a higher level of personal responsibility. A mountaintop retreat offers no escape from recycling when the mountain county, which must haul trash over fifty miles to the only remaining landfull, triples the price of trash pickup. Such experiences tell people they cannot act with immunity, even when no one-to-one reciprocity constrains them.

2. In many ways, however, the wealthy of a community and the wealthy of the world insulate their downstream environments and buy themselves upstream environments so that upstream/downstream relations will not be reciprocal. The people of advanced nations do not begin to know how well they have managed to make their own environments atypical. Consequently, the resolution of upstream/downstream problems must rely not only on a limited existing reciprocity but on *quid pro quos* as well.

Now, prototypically, upstream environments are characterized by resource abundance, resource manipulation, perceived purity, and opportunities for self-renewal. In contrast, downstream environments are characterized by product availability, consumption, pollution, and concentration of power. In other words, the relations between proto-typical upstream and downstream communities are asymmetrical.

Yet this asymmetricality is itself the basis for many quid pro quos. Materials collected upstream are transformed downstream, but pollution produced upwind is carried downwind. Developed products are marketed to consumers. And only in a frazzled urban downstream environment do many develop the power through which they buy their own mountain retreat. Even though in a mass society non-reciprocal relationships tend to predominate, nevertheless, especially in a society where markets freely develop, quid pro quos arise, strengthening individuals' interdependence.

3. The efficiency of much of the *specialization of roles* we practice arises from the externalization of costs. But an important aspect of the problem of pollutants carried downwind and downstream is that the cost of the pollution is externalized by being exported. And yet, in a society of specialized labor, we far too easily accept role designations as defining acceptable delegations of responsibility, thereby exacer-bating the problematic tendencies of upstream/downstream relations.

Consider the amazingly ubiquitous role of consumer in conjunction with the fact that as a society we generate five pounds of solid waste per person per day, even though we never seem to reach that average number of pounds of trash outside our homes on garbage pickup days. When, as consumers, we eat our fast food, we let McDonald's handle the litter we put in its place for them. When patients enter a hospital, they accept the use of disposables that create over eighteen pounds of waste per patient per day. When we buy our supermarket food, we accept the externalities of high-tech agriculture that has pro-duced the food. When 16,000 students come to Bowling Green State University, they let the maintenance department put their trash in 320,000 giant plastic bags per year. Even when we go to parties, we accept our host's decision to use paper plates and plastic eating uten-sils. All these role specializations create externalities. And an exter-nality simply is a cost for which no beneficiary accepts responsibility.

In contrast, municipalities across the nation are finding that nobody wants their trash. More and more communities cannot buy anybody else's landfill space. This scarcity is, of course, forcing the internalization of costs. It has led Michigan and several other states to decree a time by which every community must accept responsibility for its own wastes.

Role specialization, then, is a two-edged sword. It creates real efficiencies through the economies skill and talent bring into play, but it creates pseudoefficiencies by the externalization of costs. The normative structures we need to evolve, then, require not only that we eschew externalization to which upstream/downstream relations naturally tend but also that we learn how to recognize when our delegations of responsibility externalize costs.[26]

Notice that responsibility is often delegated to parties who have incentives or obligations to minimize costs. Many hospitals try to make a profit, and Bowling Green State University is mandated to accept low bids. But these incentives and obligations move both the hospitals and the university to reduce costs by externalizing them. The immorality of passing significant costs along to nonbeneficiaries thus argues for revising structures that promote or mandate externalizations.

4. At a popular level, the traditional moral response to the problem of *thresholds* has been "What would happen if everybody did that?" This question, of course, has been used to promote absolute prohibitions. But the model of emergency vehicles on city streets tells us that the fact that disastrous results would follow if everyone did something does not necessarily justify an absolute prohibition. The only reason for adopting an absolute prohibition will be the infeasibility of creating an effective rationing system for distinguishing acceptable below-threshold uses. Thus the siren on an emergency vehicle is a symbol of the possibility of making feasible the selective violation of generally desirable norms.

5. *Individual insignificance* has for centuries been recognized as detrimental to socially responsible behavior. And a traditional social response to individual insignificance has been to make the individual's response matter socially so that the weight of that social response interaction makes up for the physical insignificance of the individual's response. Conservative social theorists have long noted the value of integrating individuals into selective societies. Within those societies, a

weight quite significant to an individual may attach to actions that, on a larger scale or on other measures, are insignificant. Communities of all sizes therefore need to work very hard at making individuals aware of themselves as members of the community so that identification with the community and its well-being can become a weight in the individual's decision making. Moreover, communities can be strongly reinforced for such identity-creating activities because when such community-minded identities are widespread, what were individually insignificant actions become community successes.

6. Only life in an extraordinarily stable environment avoids the problem of a receding horizon of knowledge, and *ignorance* is accordingly a problem to which there is no one solution. Here I confine myself to two general methodological suggestions for minimizing the havoc that ignorance portends in a mass technological society. While there is much merit to the argument for a more thorough testing of products, I want to urge, independently, the introduction of different products in different environments. Such a generalized procedure has two advantages: We better account for differences in the environments into which the products are introduced, and, even more important, the different environments effectively become test environments for different products, so knowledge of safer efficiencies can be gleaned while the scope of dangers is minimized.

Notice also that if testers of new products are publicly known as having responsibility for conducting the tests, and especially if the dangers of the product are not externalized, then community pressure will develop to minimize danger in the conduct of the test. And, similarly, if the tester does not disproportionately benefit from one outcome of the test over another, then the tester will not be tempted to tamper with test results. Or if the tester is known to have an interest in the outcome of the test, then a test publicly known to include dangers to the local citizenry will create pressure for the independent review of the process and outcome of the test.

Let me then recollect some of what I have been saying about role specialization, thresholds, insignificance, and ignorance. Responsible responses are promoted when the individual is downstream of her or his own action. So the desirable products, commodities, and so on, are those that do not spew their pollution downstream; any residues remain in the neighborhood of the polluter to affect the polluter and be known by the polluter's neighbors as the polluter's.

7. In small-town economies, the reputation of a business was often used to generate business. Reputability, after all, has a value in many transactions. Some years ago, the Cooper Tire Company recaptured some of that value by a mass advertising campaign in which Cooper tires were touted as the tire with two names inside, the name of the company and the name of the individual tire maker. The company wanted to use increased worker pride to improve product quality while using the image of old-fashioned craftsmanship to attract more customers. But its action suggests what could become a powerful general strategy of erasing anonymity. To the extent that customers can know producers, the producers are encouraged to take pride in their work and the customers are provided a social environment within which a basis for personal trust reemerges. Advertising campaigns, telephone sales, and computerized mailing lists are all high-tech means available for overcoming *anonymity*. Block Watch programs, working with police officers on a local beat, are a very-low-tech means to the same end. And thus, to the extent that anonymity promotes attitudes of nonresponsiblity and irresponsibility, new means, both high tech and low, should be developed for re-creating and strengthening ties of responsiblity.

I hope that I have constructed a suggestive list of means through which it becomes possible to respond to the problems that upstream/downstream environments typically create. Upstream/downstream problems can become more resolvable by rechaining the sequences of events, by promoting new saliences, by allowing individuals to act in concert, by creating resources and thus new abundances, and by creating models and practices of foresight. Through such structures, norms of responsibility will flourish. For it is often possible to create and to highlight reciprocities, quid pro quos, and a less anonymous and broader sense of responsibility to others. Nevertheless, we do well to remember this: Upstream/downstream problems arise out of the variety of ways in which upstream/downstream environments disrupt the normative structures of human life. Accordingly, the best corrections of these problems are unlikely to be confined strictly to moral norms.

A natural environment that is literally upstream or upwind of another tends to create a social environment that magnifies downstream or downwind problems. But we human beings mold our environments. We think of our technologies as the molding forces, but I hope I have shown the prominent social dimensions of upstream/downstream problems. Human beings are also molders of their social environment. Money, traffic signals, and the insertion into a network television script of sympathetic characters concerned about a closed landfill all show us that our molding of the social environment has vast power to modify the impacts of naturally upstream and upwind environments on their downstream and downwind counterparts. Upstream/downstream problems need to be resolved by molding the human environment to minimize its wastes and internalize their costs.

Notes

1. This specialization of roles is reinforced in its effect by the population explosion, which magnifies the possibilities of interdependence without quid pro quos.

2. On this point, see Eugene Hargrove, "Anglo-American Land Use Attitudes," *Environmental Ethics*, Summer 1980.

3. Here I follow Donald Symons, *The Evolution of Human Sexuality* (New York: Oxford University Press, 1979).

4. Ibid.

5. Here I follow Donald Johanson and Maitland Edey, *Lucy* (New York: Simon and Schuster, 1981), chap. 16.

6. Obviously some definition of language is implicit here. Following Wittgenstein, *Tractatus Logico-Philosophicus* (London: Oxford University Press, 1922), and *Philosophical Investigations* (New York: Macmillan, 1953), I am thinking of language as including units that can be separated and recombined into new comprehensible structures.

7. By a *genetic definition* of norms, I mean a definition of what norms would have been in an original state, however different they may have evolved to be.

8. I cannot pause here to explicate my assumption that social animals will like approbation and dislike disapprobation because such likes and dislikes have survival value inasmuch as they strengthen the social bonds that support the species' social survival strategy. Thus the survival value that is at the root of such other affectations as any animal's desire for sweets or for

sexual gratification also underlies a social animal's response to approbation and disapprobation. For a much fuller and plausible discussion of these and related issues, see Robert Frank, *Passions within Reason: The Strategic Role of the Emotions* (New York: Norton, 1988).

9. C. Loring Brace, "Biological Parameters and Pleistocene Hominid Life-Ways," in *Primate Ecology and Human Origins*, ed. I. S. Bernstein and E.O.L. Smith (New York: Garland Press, 1979).

10. C. Loring Brace, lecture, Bowling Green State University, 1986.

11. Ibid. While I am inclined to believe that language probably evolved about 100,000 years ago, my position here requires no more than the minimal evolutionary implication that human language is a product of evolution.

12. A related point arises from a practice that anthropologists cannot date but that is probably almost as old as language: the use of something approximating definitions. For if there is a language, there is the possibility that a hearer will not understand a particular communication. And with the possibility of misunderstanding, the need arises to secure some proposed coordination. Obviously, this need will sometimes be met by a speaker who physically moves a hearer's body in appropriate ways, but just as obviously a misunderstood animal will often repeat itself. And sometimes when the animal repeats itself, it will repeat itself "in other words." The indifference of the speaking animal to alternative locutions will then become an operational understanding of synonymy, and the beginning of a practice of defining will have emerged. If the use of other words in the face of misunderstandings proves efficacious, then the general power of language to call attention to features of the "environment" will be invoked to call attention to a particular linguistic aspect of the human environment: the use of other words to overcome misunderstandings. The use of words in this way will then evolve toward the practice of seeking alternative linguistic expressions. When this practice becomes well known, it may be made even more salient by being named *definition*.

13. Similarly, what one animal will have will be a satisfactory exchange for what the other party already has or will have. Here I build on the work of N. Bischof, "On the Phylogeny of Human Morality," in *Morality as Biological Phenomenon*, ed. Gunther Stent (Los Angeles and Berkeley: University of California Press, 1978).

14. I do not know that primitive language is spoken, so talk of "speakers" and "hearers" is literally appropriate. I note, however, that the term "hearers" above is merely a convenient way of saying "organism to whom a sentence is addressed."

15. I do not assume that the question of "who is right" can be answered only through the language of justification. Of course not. For example, a stronger animal may urge that an utterance is right because he made it. My point is that the natural fact of disagreement among speakers creates the social environment in which disagreement-resolving procedures, including justification, come to have a point. The goal here is to sketch the interaction between justifiable norms and the natural and social environment in which they exist.

16. And a division of labor, not only along sexual lines but also hierarchical, is observable in higher primates.

17. Whereas previously individuals might be harmed or stroked because of what they had done, language can be extended to allow punishment and reward to develop. That is, organisms can say, "I am hitting you because" or "I am giving you these things because."

18. I have not the space here to tell the more complex story, which includes the evolution from dominance relationships among prelinguistic primates through the concept of an authority at a specialized labor, to the person who begins to issue statements of coordinative arrangements, which eventually come to include delegations of authority a coordinator has come to be perceived as rightfully exercising. For a fuller discussion of that issue, see Ronald Cohen and Elman R. Service, eds., *Origins of the State* (Philadelphia: Institute for the Study of Human Issues, 1978).

19. At least in the eastern hemisphere, where the earliest extant written records are Phoenician shipping consignment lists.

20. And here is a significant root of the concept of compensation.

21. And here is another root of a concept of responsibility, a concept now clearly extended beyond the bounds of kinship and affection.

22. The word *fortis*, from which we derive not only *fort* but also *fortitude*, means "strength" as I use the term here.

23. The word *virtue* etymologically means "manliness."

24. Here I loosely paraphrase Psalm 1.

25. Here I work from the presumption that a goal of human coordination is to avoid having to choose between the meeting of human needs and the maintenance of those social practices that have enhanced human identity and the richness of human society and human life. Ideal forms of action, then, maintain or expand supplies to meet demand (production incentives), control demanders to balance supplies (population control, rationing and wage and credit controls), substitute materials and procedures that do not endanger the quality of human life (pollution control, where some pollutants are material,

some social), and redistribute opportunities and materials so that failures in any of the above do not prevent persons from having life's recognized basic goods.

26. Here the discussion drifts toward the topic of ignorance, to which I return below.

Ernest Partridge

Chapter 2

On the Rights of Future Generations

"Time," wrote Thoreau, "is but the stream I go a-fishing in."
And so do we all. As we look upstream and downstream along the
river of time, beyond the scope of adjacent generations and concurrent
lives, numerous ethical paradoxes, puzzles, and perplexities emerge.
And while most would agree that it would be morally reprehensible
for our generation to "trash the future" in a spree of resource depletion and environmental destruction, thus devastating the lives of
successors we will never know, we are hard pressed to explicate the
ethical concepts or articulate the ethical theory that might best express
and condemn such moral dereliction. Fundamental to this puzzle is
the apparent nonreciprocity across generations, typified by the cynical
taunt "What has posterity ever done for me?" Strictly speaking, nothing.[1] Conversely, posterity is in no position to demand compensation
from us. The "downstream" course of the river of time is swift, invari-
ant, and unidirectional.

One prominent candidate for the portentous task of articulating the
moral bonds between the generations is the notion that our effects on
the remote future are ethically constrained by the "rights claims" of
posterity on us, and consequently by the burdens of moral duty en-
tailed by these rights. The numerous objections to this approach have
led many philosophers to seek other justifications for such constraints,
such as unreciprocated (i.e., "imperfect") duties to the future, utility
calculations, and so forth. Some have even claimed that future persons

have no claims whatever on our resources. These objections to the "rights approach" have been based on a few allegedly "essential" differences between actual persons and future (or "potential") persons— most prominently, their *temporal remoteness, incapacity, nonactuality*, and *indeterminacy*. Despite all these objections, I argue that members of future generations have rights claims on us, *now*—although some of the rights claims that obtain among contemporaries do not apply across nonconcurrent generations.

Although fewer rights might obtain across generations than within them, I further argue that the rights that remain may nonetheless be stringent. The duties we have to our successors may be more than merely praiseworthy "duties of beneficence." Instead, some of these duties are, in Kantian terms, "perfect duties," morally required *now*, because of the rights of future persons.

"Rights": An Analysis

Recently, several environmental writers have put the word rights to some imaginative uses and contexts, thus placing this essential moral concept under considerable strain and complicating the task of circumspect moral philosophers. For example, while most of us would agree that we are not free to do what we please with regard to insentient nature, describing these constraints as "rights of nature" (or, in particular, of rocks and trees) extends the concept far beyond its paradigm application to persons and sentient beings, thus diluting the concept of much of its moral significance.[2]

In this chapter, I steadfastly resist the temptation to extend the concept of rights beyond its paradigm application. Following Joel Feinberg's splendid analyses, I instead locate the conceptual ground of moral rights in *interests* and *valid claims*. Accordingly, only beings that can be benefited or harmed, *in and for themselves*, as philosophers say, can properly be said to have rights.[3] Thus a line may be drawn to include sentient animals but to exclude inanimate nature. Beings "within" may thus be said to have rights by virtue of their *interests* in (perhaps) being benefited or (more fundamentally) in not being harmed. Interests, so defined, entail valid claims on those in a position to affect the rights bearers (a point to be elaborated shortly).

My exclusive focus of concern, however, is with human persons, by which term philosophers mean beings for whom *sentience* is the simplest prerequisite of moral significance. "Human rights" (more correctly, "personal rights") are grounded in the remarkable cluster of capacities, and consequent interests, that designate *personhood*—that is, use of an articulate language, self-concept and self-consciousness, time perspective, hypothetical (practical) thinking, abstract reflection, responsiveness to moral principles, and so forth—in short, what philosophers have come to mean by "moral agency."

Accordingly, by "moral rights" I mean valid claims made either directly or by proxy against particular persons, groups, and institutions, or indefinite individuals, or even "the world in general." These claims announce to others that obligations and duties to the rights holders are to be honored and that their liberties and opportunities are not to be curtailed. Furthermore, I endorse H. L. A. Hart's principle that "to have a [moral] right entails having a moral justification for limiting the freedom of another person and for determining how he should act."[4] Parenthetically, this limitation of the freedom of the other constitutes his *duty* to the rights bearer. *Rights*, in short, entail *duties* on the part of others.[5]

With a couple of additional clarifications and qualifications, our analysis of *rights* might bear the burden of argument that follows. First, the duties and rights referred to herein are, unless otherwise indicated, to be interpreted as prima facie, and thus subject to being overridden by competing and compelling rights and duties. Second, duties and rights apply to circumstances situated between the extremes of inevitability and impossibility, and thus are subject to the agency of responsible, free, and rational persons. To quote and elaborate on an old maxim, "*Ought* implies *can* (possibility), and yet *might not* (non-inevitability)." Finally, if A has a rights claim upon B, and B is thus correspondingly duty bound to A, the moral burden is on B, and thus applies to such time as B can act on his duty.[6]

Note that according to this account, the class of individuals deliberately affected by dutiful acts need not be restricted to contemporaries. If duties are presumed to be derived from the rights of others, however, some interesting controversies emerge. To explore this further, let us borrow from Kant the terms "perfect duties" and "imperfect duties." "Imperfect duties" (e.g., of kindness, beneficence, and charity) do *not* entail corresponding rights (e.g., rights to kindness, to beneficence, to charity). "Perfect duties" follow from the claims of rights holders (e.g., the duty to pay one's debts or not to interfere with another's freedom to speak). That we have imperfect duties to posterity (say, duties of beneficence) is, I believe, granted by most of the critics that I deal with in this essay. My point of contention with these critics is the stronger and more interesting claim that duties to the future include the ("perfect") duties of actual persons to respect the rights of their successors. I claim that there *are* such rights. My adversaries contend that there are not.

But if some critics accept "imperfect" uncorrelated duties to the future and reject the "perfect" duties based on the alleged rights of future persons, why not settle for the imperfect duties and be done with it? Why need we insist that future persons have rights? What difference does it make?

It might make an enormous moral difference. A duty to respect another's rights generally carries greater weight and has priority over an "imperfect" duty to be charitable. For example, we assume that we can write a check to the March of Dimes only if we have cash on balance after paying our bills and installment debts. Our creditors have a *right* to our money; the charitable agencies do not. Need is irrelevant; the situation is unaltered by the fact that our creditor might be Exxon and that the potential beneficiaries of our charity include the wretched of the earth. In short, rights have a stringency and urgency that benefactions do not.

But there is more. Beings with rights deserve *respect*—especially so, if these "beings" are persons. Rights, as Joel Feinberg insists, command our attention and demand our response.

> Their characteristic use and that for which they are distinctively well-suited, is to be claimed, demanded, affirmed, insisted upon. They are especially sturdy objects to "stand upon," a most useful sort of moral furniture. . . . Having rights enables us to "stand up like men," to look others in the eye, and to feel in some fundamental way the equal of anyone. To think of oneself as the holder of rights is not to be unduly but properly

proud, to have that minimal self-respect that is necessary to be worthy of the love and esteem of others. . . . To respect a person then, or to think of him as possessed of human dignity, simply *is* to think of him as a potential maker of claims.[7]

Thus, if future generations have rights claims against us, they will have no cause to be grateful to us for preserving a viable ecosystem, for they will have received their due. In contrast, if we violate this ("perfect") duty, our duty implies that moral indignation, not simply regret, is their appropriate response. Moral duties born of rights weigh more heavily on the duty bearers. Thus, to the degree that our policymakers and legislators respond to valid moral arguments, the interests of future generations will be far better served if we can succeed in defending the notion that succeeding generations have rights claims against the living, who in turn have the moral duty to respect and respond to these rights. In other words, this stronger claim transforms the moral case—a point of no small significance for those whose job it is to propose and defend environmental policies with long-term significance.

Why might future persons *not* have rights claims against us? I have found five persistent arguments against these claims, to which I now turn.

The Repopulation Paradox[8]

The first objection must be treated briefly, though not because it can be easily and quickly disposed of. On the contrary, this is a deeply perplexing problem that we must merely mention and step around, lest we enter a thicket from which we cannot emerge in the allotted space. Otherwise, the larger part of the topic will not be addressed.

In a troubling and provocative paper, Thomas Schwartz argues that any effective attempts to "improve" the living conditions of the remote future will so alter "genetic shuffle" of future meetings, matings, and births that such policies will, in fact, "repopulate" that future with *different* individuals. Accordingly, since none of the individuals in future A will exist in ("improved") future B, no *individual* will be benefited ("made better off") as a result of this policy. It follows that since any attempts to "improve the future" will, strictly speaking, benefit no one, *there are no obligations to future generations.*[9] And if there are no duties to the future, it follows that future generations have no rights.

Schwartz's challenge has provoked carefully crafted responses by such noteworthy philosophers as Gregory Kavka and Derek Parfit, neither of whom is convinced that this argument has severed all moral commerce across generations.[10] Elsewhere, I have, like Kavka and Parfit, also (1) accepted Schwartz's argument that long-term policies effectively "repopulate" the future, and (2) rejected his inference therefrom that we have no obligations to the future. Briefly, my reply is that while "radical genetic contingencies" absolve us of obligations to act "in behalf of" future persons as *individuals*, this moral absolution does not entail a permission to disregard the remote consequences of our policies. Since relevant moral principles bind us to persons *in general*, and not to particular individuals, we remain obligated to improve the life prospects of (variable) future persons. Schwartz's error, therefore, is a failure to treat this moral problem from the "moral point of view." Instead, he assumes the perspective of hypothetical, though radically indeterminate, future persons.[11]

This is, of course, a summary, not an argument. The argument itself takes us into the thicket and, in effect, into another essay. Thus we must instead walk around this obstacle, using our assumption that this puzzle can be solved as our "ticket" to the next section of this essay. Those familiar with, and unalterably convinced by, Schwartz's argument need read no further, since all that follows assumes that future persons have claims on us to affect favorably the conditions of their "eventual" lives.

The Time-Span Argument

The time-span argument against the rights claims of posterity objects that duties and rights cannot meaningfully be said to hold over long periods of time and between persons with nonconcurrent lives, who are thus denied reciprocal communication and interaction. But with this argument, time itself is the foremost reason for this moral disconnection.

Do long durations of time erode moral responsibilities? For the moment, consider causal and epistemic connections through time, rather than moral connections. According to informed scientific opinion, some technological innovations and social policies enacted during the last few decades, and others now being contemplated, may result in both short-term advantages for some of our contemporaries and devastating long-range effects for our successors. Such long-term effects, which are tied to their remote causes by quiet, continuing, and accumulating processes, are called, by ecologists, time-lag effects. Consider that the manufacture of thousands of nuclear weapons, and the decision to invest heavily in nuclear fission energy, has resulted in the production of highly toxic, long-lasting, radioactive by-products. Some of these substances (i.e., the actinides) must then be isolated from the biosphere for hundreds of thousands of years.[12] If, in the intervening time, a geological event should cause the release of these materials into the biosphere, the results could be catastrophic. The time lag between the disposal of these substances and their possible reappearance is unknown and unknowable.

Another case concerns the accumulation of chlorofluorocarbons (CFCs) in the atmosphere. In the past four decades, several million tons of these "inert" compounds have been released into the atmosphere. There is significant evidence that CFCs, now irrevocably in the atmosphere, are drifting up into the stratosphere where they will deplete the ozone shield that protects the biosphere from harmful ultraviolet radiation. Because of these warnings, the release of CFCs into thje atmosphere has been sharply curtailed by law. Nonetheless, it appears that the worst effects of ozone depletion might become evident well into the twenty-first century, which means that because of time-lag effects, the deadly results might not affect the generation that introduced these substances into the atmosphere.[13] Of course, a similar reflection might be made regarding the Greenhouse Effect in the atmosphere or the slow but inexorable spread of chemical toxins in the aquifers.

The point of this recitation should be clear: Events enacted or contemplated within the lifetime of the present generation may, through time-lag effects, produce benefits for this generation and perhaps the next, at the eventual cost of bringing devastation on those who will be born a century or more hence. Moreover, informed persons now alive recognize these possibilities, and scientific techniques now available might provide even more exact assessments of the long-term impact of our technology.

The moral implications are apparent: If, indeed, because of their long-term time-lag effects, our activities and policies reach across generations to cause significant changes in the life conditions of posterity, and if, furthermore, we know this and can choose alternative policies, can we continue to pretend that we have no *duties* to this posterity? If it is within our knowledge and power to cause or prevent grave harm to future generations, can we still maintain that future generations have no *rights* to be spared such injury? Can we, in short, acknowledge our foresight, capacity, and choices significantly to affect the life conditions of future generations and at the same time disclaim moral responsibility across the same time span? I think not. Instead, I suggest that our power to affect the lives of posterity, and our scientific foresight of the results thereof, requires us to extend our moral responsibility to the limits of this anticipation, capacity, and choice.

Perhaps one reason why the notions of "duty to" and "rights of" posterity might seem strange is that we have not become accustomed to the moral implications of recent scientific and technological developments. Consider again the technological impacts cited above. Scarcely sixty years ago, atomic energy was merely being contemplated in a few physics laboratories, and artificial disruption of the chemistry and physics of the earth's atmosphere seemed preposterous. Today, though environmental scientists know better, the logic of ordinary discourse has yet to reflect this profound change in the human biotic and moral condition. Only a generation or so ago, within the memory of many of us, we could innocently believe that the effect of our generation on its successors was totally beyond human predictability and agency and thus not within its moral competency. No longer. With the contemporary extension of foresight and power has come a corresponding extension of moral responsibility.

Time span, of itself, cannot be construed as an argument against duties and rights. Quite the contrary, these moral relationships are inextricably bound to durations of time. Contractual obligations, and their correlative rights, endure from the time of the agreement to the time of its consummation. The duty to forebear from injuring others and the rights that correspond thereto last as long as the agent is capable of deliberately causing or permitting preventable injury, which is to say, usually throughout one's lifetime. And, if someone is duty bound not to cause deliberate harm during his or her lifetime, is that person any less duty bound to prevent such injuries that may occur after his or her death because of neglect *during* the person's lifetime? If one is both aware of the harm that might be caused and capable of preventing it, does it matter if the calamity takes place five years after one's death? Five hundred years? Five hundred *thousand* years? I suggest that foresight, capacity, and choice, not time (however long) are the morally relevant factors here.

To summarize this point: If we have a general duty not to cause avoidable pain, this means the pain at *any time* of *any being* who, at the least, is a member of the ongoing entity called humankind. Time does not diminish the prima facie force of duty, although it may be conjoined with a diminished certainty or efficacy of one's attempts to fulfill that duty.[14] In such cases the factors of *probability, efficacy*, and deliberative *choice*, as such, not time, are morally relevant. And with recent advances in scientific knowledge and technological power, we are losing our ability to hide behind the excuses of ignorance and impotence.

The "No-Claims" Argument

Another common objection to the claim that future generations have rights is that posterity, being "merely potential," is incapable of claiming these alleged rights. And without *claims*, it is argued, there can be no *rights*.

Bertram Bandman expresses the "no-claims" position directly (though he nonetheless affirms *some* rights of posterity).[15]

> To have a usable right means that one is in a position to make an effective claim for one's right. Legal philosophers from John Austin on distinguished between primary and secondary rights, the first being a right to an action itself, and the second being a back-up or remedial right, one that provides a remedy if the

first is blocked. Consequently, rights also imply back-up rights or the right to claim one's rights. Future generations can only correctly be said to have the rights to breathe clean air if there is provision for them to claim that right. And there are various conditions that may undercut such a right, such as the end of life on earth, acute scarcity, absence of clean air, low priority placed on clean air in relation to other more urgent human goals.[16]

A common and forceful response to the no-claims argument is that individuals incapable of claiming their rights may have these rights defended by others acting in their behalf. (While Bandman makes an implicit acknowledgment of the possibility of representing others' rights, he has little more to say about it.) Thus the rights of animals can be legally represented by private agencies such as the American Society for the Prevention of Cruelty to Animals (ASPCA), and the rights of infants can be claimed and defended by appointed counsel or public agencies. Of particular interest to us is the explicit legal protection of the rights of future persons. For instance, a person can stipulate in his or her will that certain funds be held in trust for the education of yet-unborn grandchildren, who can properly be said to have a legal *right* to these funds, even though the children do not, as yet, exist. Still more to the point, the National Park Act of 1916 specifies that the National Park Service shall protect and keep the land in its charge "unimpaired for the enjoyment of future generations." The Park Service, in other words, is the legally appointed guardian of posterity's *rights*, a point that must be constantly reiterated by the Sierra Club, among others.

The critic might reply that these are examples of rights *protected by law*; that is to say, the claims made by, or in behalf of, the rights holders are legally recognized. Most of posterity's alleged rights, however, although they might be argued on moral grounds, lack legal standing. These rights can not be legally claimed by, or in behalf of, posterity, and thus there are no "back-up rights" (i.e., no institutional sanctions against, or remedies for, violations of these rights).

Moral philosophers routinely distinguish between *moral* and *legal* rights. But surely this distinction, however significant, is not sufficient to sustain the suggestion that without legal protection and recourse, future generations cannot be said to have rights at all. For one thing, this notion runs counter to our normal mode of speaking, and our ordinary "considered moral judgments" (to borrow Rawls's phrase). We are well aware of legally sanctioned violations of moral rights: the Nazi race laws, slavery in the pre–Civil War United States, Soviet suppression of dissent by means of "anti-slander" laws, and so on.

It is noteworthy that such conflicts between legal and moral rights *preclude* the possibility of the offended individual claiming his or her (illegal) moral rights. Before the Emancipation Proclamation of 1863, slaves who exercised their moral right to be free could find no legal "remedy," as the fugitive slave Dred Scott was to be told by the Supreme Court in 1857. In contrast, persons enslaved after 1863 could call on the power of the state to acknowledge their claim and sustain their right to be free. The Proclamation did not alter the moral force of the prima facie right to be free, but it totally reversed, in the southern United States, the ability to *claim* that right. Indeed, the growing moral consciousness of the injustice of slavery was a significant factor in bringing about this reversal.

Accordingly, legal means are not the *only* means to "claim" a right. In the words of Joel Feinberg, a person can be said to have a moral right "when he has a claim, the recognition of which is called for— not (necessarily) by legal rule—but by moral principles, or the principles of an enlightened conscience."[17]

It is commonly said that "you cannot legislate morality." The Prohibition amendment and laws against such private vices as prostitution and gambling are cited as examples. However well the rule might fit these examples, it is, as a generalization, patently absurd. Morality *can* be legislated, and *is* properly legislated time and again. Prohibition taught us a much more qualified rule: "You cannot impose by legislation the private morality of a determined but unrepresentative minority." Universal moral rights to life, liberty, and property are, in free societies, guaranteed by the rule of law. A universal abhorrence to murder gives rise, in all civilized societies, to legal sanctions against it. Furthermore, as the public moral consciousness (following perhaps the teachings and example of moral educators and exemplars) extends to new realms of moral awareness, the legislators respond, and still more rights claims are recognized and protected by law. Thus, at the time of the founding of this republic, there was no legal recognition (and little cultural acknowledgment) of the "right" to a free public education. The right was legally recognized only after a long and sustained struggle by such men as Franklin, Jefferson, Mann, and Parker. The right of future generations to enjoy designated areas of unspoiled natural beauty and the duty of the living to protect these areas were proclaimed by such men as Thoreau and Muir before this right and this duty were enacted by the National Park Act of 1916. To be sure, laws often determine whether or not a right can effectively be *claimed*. But it is equally the case that laws are often enacted in response to the public consciousness of a preexisting right—a right the claim to which morally *should* be sustained and protected by the force of law. In other words, defenders of the "positive law tradition" who insist that the possession of rights entails effective legal claims and remedies beg the essential moral issue. For only if the *moral* case has merit *should* legal means be enacted to ensure the protection of the alleged rights.

This all may be well and good, but the essential problem remains: If, as must be granted, posterity is itself incapable now of claiming or appointing a surrogate to claim its rights, who, then, is authorized to represent posterity? The answer, quite directly, is anyone who is able and willing to defend posterity's rights on the grounds of rational and general moral principles. In such debate, it is the *principles*, and the validity thereof, that count, not who the advocates might be. The pre-abolition slaves could not legally claim their rights, nor could they appoint surrogates. But fugitive slaves, and their defenders, could and did argue for abolition on the basis of moral principles. Similarly, animals and infants cannot claim their right not to be cruelly treated, nor can they appoint defenders. They are, instead, defended by the courts or by public agencies, which, in a well-ordered community, are the surrogates of everyone. So should it be with the rights of future generations. Ideally, their rights will be protected by the laws and by the legitimately appointed and elected representatives of the community. In the less-than-ideal actual world, the advocates of the interests of posterity (many of them self-appointed) must often present the case for posterity's legally unrecognized rights in the arena of moral debate, in the hope and expectation that the public conscience will come to demand that the laws of the living be extended to protect the rights and interests of posterity.

The Nonactuality Argument

Among the most common objections against the rights of future generations is the contention that since posterity does not exist *now*, it makes no sense to speak of posterity having rights *now*. Thus Ruth Macklin states:

> The ascription of rights is property to be made to actual persons—not possible persons. Since future generations can only be viewed as consisting of possible persons, from any vantage point at which the description "future generations" is applicable, it would follow . . . that rights cannot properly be ascribed to future generations."[18]

The nonactuality argument might be subdivided into two interpretations: (1) the charge that posterity is "merely imaginary"; and (2) the contention that posterity's rights apply only in posterity's own time. Let us examine these points in order.

1. *There are no duties owed to imaginary persons.* In an unpublished paper, Stuart Rosenbaum argues this point with great confidence:

> I take it as obvious that the general principle that obligations cannot be owed to merely potential individuals needs no defense. (Consider my potential harems—there are an indefinite number of them. Am I obligated to plan for all of their financial securities, or for the care of all of their potential children? And if not all, but only some, then which?) If there is something unique about future generations which exempts them from this general principle, I am unable to discover what it is. Consequently, I take this objection to the claim that future generations have rights to be conclusive against it.[19]

A careful reading of Rosenbaum's paper reveals that he is as good as his word. The principle that "no obligations are owed to protential persons" is reiterated, but it is given "no defense." The closest he comes to an argument for his "general principle that obligations cannot be owed to potential individuals" is his parenthetical comment about his potential harems: "There are an indefinite number of them. Am I obligated to plan for all of their financial securities, or for the care of all of their potential children?" In reply, I must agree that a philosophy professor today need care little about his "potential harems." But the case would be quite different if one were an Arabian prince or a Mormon elder a century ago. In that case, one *would* have a duty to plan for the security and well-being of potential wives and children. Indeed, the example is by no means farfetched, for it *is* the duty of every young person contemplating marriage and parenthood to make provision for one's potential spouse and children.

Thus there is, indeed, "something unique about future generations" that distinguishes them from Rosenbaum's imaginary harems. Very simply, the harems are imaginary and highly improbable; future generations, though also imaginary, are, barring catastrophe, virtually certain. And since the most likely catastrophe, nuclear annihilation, is a matter of our own choice, the uncertainty of human survival scarcely provides an absolution of responsibility toward the future. Surely these differences give us ample reason to reject this analogy and with it this argument.

2. "*Future generations . . . should correctly be said to have a right only to what is available when they come into existence, and hence when their possible future rights become actual and present.*" This objection is raised by Richard DeGeorge, who continues:

> Prehistoric cave men had no right to electric lights or artificial lungs since they were not available in their times, and we have no right to enjoy the sight of extinct animals. To claim a right to what is not available and cannot be made available is to speak vacuously. Some future people, therefore, will have no right to the use of gas, or oil, or coal, if, when they come into existence, such goods no longer exist. If the goods in question

are not available, *they* could not be produced with a right to them.[20]

But surely the distinction between our "right to enjoy the sight" of *some* extinct animals (say, dinosaurs), and posterity's right to clean air is, from a moral point of view, quite essential! We have no right to "enjoy" dinosaurs because it was, *at all times*, impossible for us to "have" them. (Recall that we have rights only to things that are possible but less than inevitable, and within the agency of rational and capable beings.) No rational, morally responsible beings deprived us of the dinosaurs; they vanished millions of years before any creature evolved to a state of moral accountability ("The Flintstones" and "Alley Oop" to the contrary, notwithstanding). The same cannot be said concerning the availability to us of passenger pigeons or, much more to the point, the availability to future generations of clean air and energy sources (be they fossil fuels or some yet to be developed alternatives). It is, to some degree, within the knowledge and power, and thus the moral purview, of contemporary persons to determine whether future generations shall have clean air and energy sources.

But surely it seems paradoxical to claim that persons *in the future* can have rights *in the present*. I grant that it *seems* so, but I insist that the claim is intelligible. So that we might unravel this subtle point, I suggest that we shift our time perspective to the past and consider the case of the cedars of Lebanon. In ancient times, the Phoenicians cut the fabled trees from the mountains and thus brought devastating floods and silt down to the valleys below. Can we not say that the Phoenicians, by this policy, defaulted in their duties to the present inhabitants of Lebanon? Furthermore, were not these contemporary persons correspondingly deprived, *in the past*, of their rights to an abundant and beautiful environment? It would seem that the duty to protect the right of the present Lebanese to have the cedars applied to those who were in a position to protect this right: the ancient Phoenicians. This follows from the rule that rights and duties apply to *possible* circumstances, that is, to circumstances that fall between the limits of impossibility and inevitability. The savages who lived in the region before the dawn of history, and who were presumably incapable of causing lasting damage to the forests, had no duty to forebear from what was, for them, the impossible. The Romans and Saracens who followed the Phoenicians found barren hills and thus had no duty to protect the nonexistent trees. All this bears some strange implications for the perspective of time present. For example, the present-day Lebanese *had* (!) no rights claims on the savages or on the Romans and Saracens. Neither do the Lebanese *have* rights today to trees that cannot be had. (For the sake of argument, I am assuming that the damage was irreversible and thus that the cedar forests, once destroyed, could not have been restored at any subsequent time.) The "rights" of the present generation to the cedars of Lebanon belong to the past tense. These rights could entail duties only applicable, first, to the predecessors of the Phoenicians, who were capable of destroying the trees, but who fulfilled their duties by protecting the cedars; and, second, to those who violated these duties by destroying the cedars. Thereafter, there were no more rights or duties, for the trees were (I assume) forever gone.

But does it not seem strange to speak of rights, long past, of present persons? I grant that it does, and suggest that this strangeness may be sufficient reason to prefer "duty talk" to "rights talk" in such cases.[21] But the very application of duties and rights across generations constitutes an unusual use of these concepts, which are usually applied among contemporaries. The strangeness of this use of "rights" is compounded by the fact that "rights" are not commonly referred from the contingent present back to the immutable past. We are not encouraged to cry over spilled milk, or accustomed to lament long-lost forests. Such issues are no longer "live." Indeed, we may be little aware of what we have lost. Nevertheless, the same situation seems far less odd when viewed from the perspective of the predecessor generation; when, for example, we speak of the rights claims of future generations falling on the present generation. Accordingly, while it may seem odd to speak of the right of the present Lebanese to the lost cedars, we would have little difficulty making sense of a recorded complaint, by some ancient Phoenician environmentalist, that the cedars should be carefully managed in deference to the rights of future generations.

The Indeterminacy Argument

The final objection to the notion of the rights of posterity might be called the *indeterminancy argument*. Ruth Macklin presents it quite forthrightly:

> While it is appropriate to ascribe rights to a class of persons, in general, such ascription is inappropriate when the class in question has no identifiable members. Now the class describable as "future generations" does not have any identifiable members—no existing person or persons on whose behalf the specific right can be claimed to exist.[22]

Of all the objections so far, I find this one to be the most curious in that while it appears time and again, it seems to be among the easiest to answer. Indeed, we need not look to posterity to find examples of duties to, or rights of, "unidentifiable persons." Such individuals exist among our contemporaries. For example, Joel Feinberg offers the example of "the duty of care that every citizen is said to owe to any and every person in a position to be injured by his negligence. I have this duty to some degree even to the uninvited trespasser on my land."[23] Notice that the duty of the landowner is owed not to identifiable persons, or even to probable persons, but only to (indefinite) possible persons in the (undetermined) future, whosoever they might be. And what of duties *of* "the indefinite"? Here, too, examples are easy to imagine. For instance, my right not to be physically assaulted entails the duty of *any* (indefinite) persons who might, at *any time* in the (undetermined) future, have occasion or opportunity to do so. I have a right not to be assaulted by anyone who will be conceived tomorrow and might assault me twenty years later. Does Macklin wish to deny that these are rights and duties properly so called? And if they are, and surely common usage so indicates, then in what sense are "future generations" less "definite" than the person, now alive, who might be injured eight years hence by say, my failure, *now*, to cover an abandoned mineshaft on my mountain property? Does such a person have any more right not to be injured than his now-unborn (thus "indeterminate") child, who will be six years old on that date?

It might be countered that if, as a result of my negligence, someone will in the future be injured, the victim's identity at that time will be made quite "definite" to me (presumably by his lawyer), which is not the case with injuries to posterity. But the objection misses the point. My duty not to be negligent is a duty to *anyone* who might be injured, and if my duty is fulfilled there will, *ipso facto*, be *no* "definite" victim, and, moreover, the rights of unidentified multitudes will thereby be respected.

Now all this may appear to be well and good when applied to our contemporaries. But will duties to, and rights of, the indefinite still be morally valid if the "indefinite" are not yet alive; if they are *possible* future persons?[24] I believe that these moral requirements might be meaningfully applied to such cases. To illustrate this point, consider Galen Pletcher's very apt "paradigm of the campsite":

> If I have been camping at a site for several days, it is common to say that I have an obligation to clean up the site—to leave it at least as clean as I found it—for the next person who camps there. We assume, of course, that the person who will use it next does exist somewhere; but it is not necessary to assume this, just as it is not necessary to know who he or she is, or when he or she will use the site. We have an obligation which might be called an "obligation-function," because it is to some as yet unspecified person or persons. There is a preliminary "right function" in this case, which can be stated: "for any x, if x is a person who wants to camp at this site, then x has a right to a clean campsite."[25]

Significantly, the morally operative consideration here is not the time of the next use, or the *identity* of the next camper. It is that the area *might* be used by an unknown and indeterminate individual with an interest in having a clean campsite.

But does this example have bearing on the posterity question? Clearly it does. Pletcher continues:

> If, happily, I have discovered a campsite so removed from the beaten track that the next person to discover it is someone who wasn't even alive when I last camped there, it still is true of that lucky person that he has a right to a clean campsite, and

I had an obligation to secure to him that state of affairs. My conclusion can thus be stated: If any moral obligations or rights can properly be stated in terms of "obligation—or right-functions," then these apply also to future generations.[26]

The next camper has a "right" to a clean campsite, not because of *who* he is (as an identifiable person), or *when* he is, but for *what* he is—a sentient, rational person (thus of our moral community) who might have an interest in enjoying the use thereof. That he may, at this moment, be *nonexistent* is, morally speaking, *nonrelevant*. The argument is all the more urgent when we speak not of a campsite where a camper might possibly visit but of a planet on which another generation, and then another, must *dwell*.

The Upshot—Some General Principles

The nonactuality and indeterminacy arguments share a common error that I believe we are now prepared to identify. Both arguments commit the fallacy of *false criterion* or (viewed differently) of *hasty generalization*. Criteria that correctly apply to certain kinds of rights are, I believe, falsely assumed to apply to rights in general. I have argued these points informally by citing counterexamples to the claims (of Rosenbaum, DeGeorge, and Macklin) that future generations do not have rights due, respectively, to their "mere imaginability," their "nonactuality," and their "indeterminacy." It is time to offer an analysis of the concepts that underlie my refutation of these arguments.

We begin with a simple, and I believe uncontroversial, acknowledgment that not *all* species of rights that obtain among contemporaries are the sorts of rights that can be held by future persons against their predecessors that are now actual. Thus, if future generations have rights *now*, then these are special kinds of rights (though they may be stringent, nonetheless). My analysis follows on a partial adoption, and an extension, of Joel Feinberg's analysis of rights—particularly of the contrasting pairs of "active/passive rights" and "*in rem/in personam* rights."[27]

Feinberg defines the first pair as follows: "*Active* rights are rights to act or not to act as one chooses; *passive* rights are rights not to be done by others in certain ways." He provides the following examples:

> Among one's active rights may be such as the rights to go where one will and say whatever one pleases, often referred to concisely as "the right to liberty." Among one's passive rights may be such as the rights to be let alone, to enjoy one's property, to keep one's affairs secret, or one's reputation un-damaged, or one's body unharmed. These are often charac-terized collectively as "the right to security."[28]

The *in rem*/*in personam* distinction is as follows:

> The distinguishing characteristic of *in personam* rights is that they are correlated with specific duties of determinate individ-uals, . . . [for example], the rights of landlords to collect rent from their tenants, and the right of the wrongfully injured to damages from their injurers. *In rem* rights, on the other hand, are those said to hold not against some specific namable per-son or persons, but against "the world at large." Examples in-clude a homeowner's right to peaceful occupancy of his own house, and anyone's rights to the use or possession of the money in his own purse or pocket. Corresponding to these rights are the legally enforced duties of non-interference im-posed on everyone. *Everyone* has a duty to keep off my land without my permission.[29]

Feinberg has a third distinction, between *negative* and *positive* rights:

> A *positive* right is a right to other persons' positive actions; a negative right is a right to other persons' omissions or fore-bearances. For every positive right I have, someone else has a duty to *refrain* from doing something.[30]

This third pair (negative/positive) does not have an important role in this analysis, since the rights of future persons can be either *positive* (e.g., the right to have certain resources available) or *negative* (e.g., the right not to be poisoned by radioactive wastes).

Similarly, the *in personam/in rem* distinction also has no direct application to the posterity issue, since, once again, *both* kinds of rights apply to future generations. Thus the putative rights of future generations might be directed, *in personam*, against a specific person (e.g., a Congressman about to vote on a nuclear energy bill) or *in rem*, against "the world at large" (e.g., against any and all citizens in a position to influence that same legislator's vote).[31]

But while the *in personam/in rem* distinction does not, in itself, advance our conception of rights that are, and are not, applicable to posterity, this distinction is important for what it suggests, namely, still another distinction, *not* explicated by Feinberg, yet relevant to the issue of the moral status of future persons. This pair, which I call *denotative rights* and *designative rights*, might be thought of as correlates to *in personam* and *in rem duties* (*not* rights). Thus by a *in personam* duty we may mean a duty responsive to the rights claim of ("denotatively") identifiable *individuals*, and by an "*in rem* duty" we mean a duty correlated to the rights of a class of persons identifiable by description (by "designation"). As Macklin has clearly indicated, denotative rights are clearly *not* applicable to future generations because of the "indeterminacy" of future generations. But Pletcher's "campsite paradigm" demonstrates, with equal clarity, the applicability of *designative* rights to future generations.

If these distinctions all hold—if, that is, valid cases of "rights" can be found to fill these special categories—then the nonactuality argument (of DeGeorge and Rosenbaum) and the indeterminacy argument (of Macklin) both commit the fallacy of false criterion. In both cases, the criterion for *one* type of a right is falsely taken to be the criterion for *all* rights. In the first case, Richard DeGeorge claims that the fact that future persons cannot act or exercise their personal rights *now* entails that they *have* no rights *now*. His argument is sound with regard to *active* rights, but *not* with regard to *passive* rights. Ruth Macklin states that "it is [in]appropriate to ascribe rights to a class of persons . . . [with no] identifiable members." As noted, she is correct with regard to denotative rights, but not with regard to designative rights. In the two previous sections, I have presented a number of exemplifications of such rights of future persons that demand action or forebearance in the present. All these cases indicate how persons now alive can *now* deliberately set in motion events and circumstances that will affect the quality of life of future persons, regardless of the analytic truth that they are nonactive, even nonactual, now (see the examples of nuclear waste and ozone depletion above). Furthermore, these options now before us affect future persons *generally* (i.e., "by description" or *designatively*—see "the campsite paradigm" above).

Conclusions

If my analyses have been correct, then neither *temporal remoteness, lack of direct claims, nonactuality, indeterminacy,* nor *nonreciprocity* disqualifies future persons from our moral community.[32] These five features present, I believe, the most serious challenges to the claim that future persons have rights, and thus that the living have strong "perfect" moral duties toward them. Perhaps I have overlooked a convincing and fatal objection. Unless and until such a refutation is offered, however, I believe that we can be assured that the moral categories of rights and corresponding duties, which morally bind us to our contemporaries, can meaningfully be said to bind us to our successors as well.

The primary burden of this essay has been to demonstrate the plausibility of acknowledging that future generations have *rights*. The question of the *content* of those rights lies beyond its intended scope. But when such issues arise, they may bring forth still more objections to the alleged rights claims of posterity. Some of these objections are not significantly different, in kind, from objections to the rights claims of contemporaries (such as the impoverished people of the Third World).

Consider, for example, the following observation of Richard De-George:

> Speaking of the rights of future generations as if their rights were present rights . . . leads to impossible demands on us. . . . Consider oil. . . . It is a nonrenewable resource and is limited in quantity. How many generations in the future are we to allow

to have present claim to it? Obviously if we push the generation into the unlimited future and divide the oil deposits by the
number of people, we each end up with the right to a gallon or
a quart or a teaspoon or a thimble full.[33]

This objection is, I believe, effectively answered by Douglas MacLean,
who writes: "Moral requirements apply not to the distribution of resources themselves [among generations], but to the distribution of
whatever it is that makes resources valuable."[34] Thus, he correctly
points out, the claims of future generations might not be to particular
material or energy resources, but to the availability, *somehow*, of the
benefits that these resources produce. Accordingly, our duties to the
future might be met by utilizing our necessarily brief and transitory age
of abundant fossil fuels to develop technologies that might produce
and utilize such "next generation" fuels as biomass, photovoltaic cells,
fusion reactors, or whatever unanticipated sources may yet turn up.
Therein might be an intelligible, and even practicable, interpretation
of the "Lockean proviso" that we leave "as much and as good" for
our successors.

The question of the *content* of the rights of future generations is the
subject for another essay—still better, a book or a career. In closing,
the following sketch must suffice: Posterity's claims on us are less for
gifts than for forebearances and options. *Positively*, we should bequeath the assimilated records and skills of our civilization, in li-
braries, archives, and universities. Beyond that, our duties are primarily of a *negative* sort. While we may share few of the aesthetic tastes,
or even the cultural mores, of our remote successors, we can still sur-
mise much regarding their fundamental needs. They will require just
institutions, basic energy and material resources, a functioning atmosphere and flourishing ecosystem, and an unpolluted and unpoisoned
environment. A just provision of many of the items on this list might
be achieved by little more than prudent stewardship of our own inher-
itance.

At length, perhaps our own brief moment alongside the river of
time will be justified and fulfilled if we can gaze "upstream" with
gratitude at what we have received, then "downstream" with pride
and satisfaction at what we will bequeath.

Notes

Acknowledgments: This chapter has its origins in the third chapter of my doctoral dissertation, "Rawls and the Duty to Posterity," University of Utah, 1976. An earlier and briefer version of the paper was read at the annual meeting of the Philosophy of Education Society, Vancouver, British Columbia, April 1976, and appears in the proceedings of that conference. It has undergone extensive revision and expansion since then. I gratefully acknowledge support from the Rockefeller Foundation and the National Science Foundation during the development of these ideas and this chapter.

1. And yet, in a figurative sense, we may "owe" a great deal to posterity. I so argue in "Why Care about the Future?" in *Responsibilities to Future Generations*, ed. Ernest Partridge (Buffalo: Prometheus Books, 1981), 203–18.

2. My dissatisfaction with this "extension" of the concept of rights is spelled out in "Environmental Ethics without Philosophy," in *Human Ecology: A Gathering of Perspectives*, ed. Richard Borden (College Park: Society for Human Ecology, 1986), 7, 140–45.

3. Though Feinberg has defended this analysis in numerous books and publications, perhaps the best-known source is "The Rights of Animals and Unborn Generations," in *Philosophy and Environmental Crisis*, ed. William Blackstone (Athens: University of Georgia Press, 1974). I accept Feinberg's analysis of *rights* virtually intact. My profound intellectual debt to this outstanding philosopher will become obvious to readers as they proceed with this essay. Less apparent, though no less significant, is my personal debt to Professor Feinberg.

4. H. L. A. Hart, "Are There Any Natural Rights?" *Philosophical Review* 64 (1955): 183.

5. The reverse is not the case: There may be duties without rights—for example, some duties of *beneficence*. This qualification is not important to my argument, however.

6. "Act" is interpreted broadly here and thus includes forebearances. (See my discussion of "negative rights" below.)

7. Joel Feinberg, "The Nature and Value of Rights," *Journal of Value Inquiry* 4 (Winter 1970): 252.

8. This is my term for the problem. Other names are "the non-identity problem" (Derek Parfit), "the paradox of future individuals" (Gregory Kavka), and "the case of the disappearing beneficiaries" (Thomas Schwartz). Citations follow.

9. Thomas Schwartz, "Obligations to Posterity," in *Obligation to Fu-*

ture Generations, ed. Brian Barry and R. I. Sikora (Philadelphia: Temple University Press, 1978), 3–13.

10. Gregory Kavka, "The Paradox of Future Individuals," *Philosophy and Public Affairs* 11, no. 2 (Spring 1982): 92–112. Derek Parfit, *Reasons and Persons* (New York: Oxford University Press, 1984), 351–441.

11. Thomas Schwartz, "Should We Seek a Better Future?" Paper read at the annual meeting of the American Philosophical Association, Pacific Division, Sacramento, Calif., March 1982. Since that presentation, the paper has more than doubled in size. My reply here to "the repopulation paradox" is complementary to my final argument for the rights of future generations.

12. William H. Millert and Albert J. Fritsch, *Nuclear Energy: The Morality of Our National Policy*, CSPI Energy Series 4 (Washington, D.C.: Center for Science in the Public Interest, October 1974), 41–47. See also Harvey Wasserman and Norman Solomon, *Killing Our Own* (New York: Delta, 1982), 193–302. For an acknowledgment of this problem by a proponent of nuclear power, see Alvin Weinberg, "Social Institutions and Nuclear Energy," *Science* 177 (July 7, 1972).

13. Ralph J. Cicerone, "Changes in Stratospheric Ozone," *Science* 237 (July 3, 1987): 35–42. James Gleick, "Even with Action Today, Ozone Loss Will Increase," *New York Times*, March 20, 1988. Richard A. Kerr, "Stratospheric Ozone Is Decreasing," *Science* 239 (March 25, 1988): 1489–91. See also Dale Jamieson's contribution to this anthology.

14. For a splendid statement of this point, see Parfit's criticism of "The Social Discount Rate," *Reasons and Persons*, Appendix F. In actual fact, the efficacy of an action and the certainty of its results generally diminish with time; but this is a contingent, not a logically necessary, fact. There are conceivable, and probably actual, exceptions. Indeed, I have just cited two of them. The damages caused by nuclear wastes and ozone depletion are *more likely* to occur in the remote than in the immediate future. Furthermore, in the ozone case, though the manufacture of all chlorofluorocarbons may soon be banned, the severity of the consequences of their past use will increase with time.

15. Bertram Bandman, "Do Future Generations Have the Right to Breathe Clean Air?" *Political Theory* 10, no. 1 (February 1982): 95–102. While this paper is useful for its clear expression of the no-claims argument, and while it appears to arrive at a conclusion similar to my own, Bandman's argument strikes me as incoherent. Furthermore, though this argument has a superficial resemblance to my section "The Indeterminacy Argument," below (which I developed independently of Bandman), close scrutiny will reveal significant differences.

16. Ibid., 96.

17. Joel Feinberg, *Social Philosophy* (Englewood Cliffs, N.J.: Prentice-Hall, 1973), 67.

18. Ruth Macklin, "Can Future Generations Correctly Be Said to Have Rights?" in Partridge, *Responsibilities to Future Generations*, 151–52.

19. Stuart E. Rosenbaum, "Do Future Generations Have Rights?" Paper read at the annual meeting of the American Philosophical Association, Eastern Division, Atlanta, Georgia, December 28, 1973. The topic of the symposium was "Can Future Generations Correctly Be Said to Have Rights; e.g., the Right to Clean Air?" Papers by Galen Pletcher, Richard DeGeorge, Ruth Macklin, and Annette Baier, presented at that symposium, were later revised and included in my anthology *Responsibilities to Future Generations*. I am grateful to Dr. William P. Alston of Rutgers University for sending me copies of the papers read at that meeting.

20. Richard T. DeGeorge, "The Environment, Rights, and Future Generations," in Partridge, *Responsibilities to Future Generations*, 161.

21. Nevertheless, this is talk of "perfect duties" (with correlative rights).

22. Macklin, "Can Future Generations Have Rights?" 152.

23. Joel Feinberg, "Duties, Rights and Claims," *American Philosophical Quarterly* 3, no. 2 (April 1966): 139–40.

24. It may be important to keep in mind a distinction here between those who are "indefinite" due to our limited knowledge ("epistemologically indefinite," including persons at all times) and those who are "indefinite" in the sense that their eventual existence is contingent (call them "ontologically indefinite"—a class comprised of future persons). Cf., in this regard, the final lines of the paragraph before the preceding ("Does Macklin wish to deny").

25. Galen Pletcher, "The Rights of Future Generations," in Partridge, *Responsibilities to Future Generations*, 168.

26. Ibid.

27. Cf. Feinberg, "The Nature and Value of Rights"; and Feinberg, *Social Philosophy*, chap. 4.

28. Feinberg, *Social Philosophy*, 60.

29. Ibid., 59.

30. Ibid.

31. Bandman, "Do Future Generations Have the Right?" 99, errs in overlooking the fact that the *in rem/in personam* distinction refers to *duty bearers*, not to *rights holders*. Thus he incorrectly concludes that future generations do not have *in personam* rights.

32. Again, I will not claim to have demonstrated here that "repopulation" due to effective policy choices fails to absolve us of our duties to posterity. I attempted that task elsewhere.

33. DeGeorge, "Environment, Rights, and Future Generations," 161. I would not wish to associate DeGeorge with the naiveté of this fragmented quotation. He subjects this rather gross observation to a subtle and sophisticated analysis. Furthermore, he is quite aware of, and to some degree endorses, the response I present below.

34. Douglas MacLean, "Introduction," *Energy and the Future* (Totowa, N.J.: Rowman and Littlefield, 1983), 5. Many of the contributors to this valuable anthology offer elaborations on this seminal theme.

Dale Jamieson

Chapter 3

*Managing the Future: Public
Policy, Scientific Uncertainty,
and Global Warming*

In every society, people have speculated about the future and
modulated their behavior in the light of their speculations. Today,
however, we are in a novel position. We are in the process of radically
altering the fundamental planetary systems that produced life on
earth. As a result, the world we bequeath to our children and grandchildren will be very different from the one in which we live. Since the
changes we are instituting are global in scope, it will not be possible
for our descendants to move on to greener pastures across the seas or
mountains. Escape cannot be to another continent or hemisphere,
only to another planet or solar system.

The atmosphere is one area that is undergoing dramatic changes as
a result of human activity. Because of our injection of carbon dioxide
and various other gases into the atmosphere, the world of the twenty-
first century may well have a climate regime that is outside the parameters of what humans have experienced in the entire course of their
evolution. According to a report issued by the National Aeronautics
and Space Administration, the Commission of the European Community, and the World Meteorological Organization, "we are conducting
one giant experiment on a global scale by increasing the concentration
of trace gases in the atmosphere without knowing the environmental
consequences."[1]

Some of the consequences of this experiment are clear. The earth's
mean temperature will increase, sea levels will rise, and extreme clima-

tic events will become more frequent. Much remains unclear, however. The more we focus our inquiry on details, the less we really seem to know. In the light of such scientific uncertainty, it is difficult to know what policy prescriptions make sense. We can speculate about the future, but, in this case at least, it is difficult to know how to modulate our behavior in the light of our speculations.

This chapter consists mainly of ruminations on these themes. I begin with a brief description of the environmental problem to which I have referred: global warming brought about by the injection of greenhouse gases (i.e., carbon dioxide, methane, nitrous oxides, and chlorofluorocarbons) into the atmosphere. I then sketch one plausible picture of how we might think about managing this problem. On this view, information flows like a wild river, and the relations between science and policy are linear and well kept. I show that however beautiful this picture may be, it is more like a surrealist painting than a photographic snapshot. I go on to identify some important issues that I believe are involved in global warming, and sketch some guidelines for policymaking.

In what follows there are few, if any, deductive arguments. Instead, I try to conceptualize an important issue in a way that is illuminating, highlighting some important features and drawing some significant morals. A lot of analytic work remains undone.

The Greenhouse Effect

Carbon dioxide was first identified as a constituent of the atmosphere by Joseph Black in 1754.[2] Early in the nineteenth century, the French mathematician François Fourier speculated that certain atmospheric gases might inhibit heat from escaping, thereby warming the earth's surface. In 1861, John Tyndall measured the absorption of infrared radiation by carbon dioxide and water vapor, and showed that slight changes in atmospheric composition would significantly raise the earth's surface temperature. By 1870, scientists were able to make measurements of atmospheric carbon dioxide comparable in precision to those made today. In 1899, T. C. Chamberlin theorized that changes in the earth's climate could be explained by changing carbon dioxide concentrations.

In 1896, the Swedish Nobel Prize-winning physicist Svante Arrhenius speculated about the possibility of anthropogenic atmospheric change. He thought that the release of fossil fuels might increase atmospheric carbon dioxide, thereby affecting both climate and terrestrial biological processes. He estimated that a doubling of atmospheric carbon dioxide would increase the earth's mean surface temperature by about 4 to 6 degrees centigrade. Arrhenius's ideas were rejected when it was discovered that water vapor also absorbs long-wave (infrared) radiation. Since it absorbs so strongly in the same general spectral regions as carbon dioxide, it was thought that carbon dioxide could have little influence on infrared radiation.

Arrhenius's ideas were revived in 1938 by the British engineer G. S. Callendar, who suggested that a high proportion of the carbon dioxide released by industrial activity remained in the atmosphere and that there might already be observational evidence of global warming. Callendar thought that such a warming should be welcomed. He wrote:

> In conclusion it may be said that the combustion of fossil fuel, whether it be peat from the surface or oil from 10,000 feet below, is likely to prove beneficial to mankind in several ways, besides the provision of heat and power. For instance the above mentioned small increases of mean temperature would be important at the northern margin of cultivation, and the growth of favorably situated plants is directly proportional to the carbon dioxide pressure. . . . In any case the return of the deadly glaciers should be delayed indefinitely.[3]

Callendar's views were rejected because observations did not seem to bear out his predictions, and because there was skepticism about whether increases in atmospheric carbon dioxide really would result in increasing the earth's surface temperature.

During the mid-1950s, the work of Gilbert Plass, and of Roger Revelle and Hans Suess, brought the speculations of Arrhenius and Callendar into the scientific mainstream. Revelle and Suess pointed out that an experiment was in progress that "could not have happened in the past nor be reproduced in the future."[4] They proposed that measurements relating to changes in atmospheric carbon dioxide and its effects on climate be made a priority during the International

Geophysical Year of 1957. In 1958, Charles Keeling, a colleague of Revelle and Suess at Scripps Institute of Oceanography, began measuring atmospheric carbon dioxide in Hawaii and Antarctica. By 1963, the evidence for increasing atmospheric concentrations of carbon dioxide was strong enough for the Conservation Foundation to convene a meeting to discuss its implications. This meeting came to the conclusion that a doubling of atmospheric carbon dioxide would result in a temperature rise of about 3.8 degrees centigrade. In 1965, the President's Science Advisory Committee published a report warning of this possibility. This document was the first public acknowledgment by a government body of the possibility of anthropogenic climate change. The issue was now on the table.

Although there are some dissenters, widespread agreement exists in the scientific community that atmospheric concentrations of carbon dioxide and other greenhouse gases are increasing, and that as a result we are already committed to an increase in the mean temperature of the earth's surface of 1.5 to 4 degrees centigrade.[5]

The evidence for the increase in atmospheric carbon dioxide rests mainly on Keeling's observations. They show a 9.5 percent increase in atmospheric carbon dioxide since 1958 (see Figure 3.1). This increase correlates with increases in fossil fuel consumption. Although it is more difficult to determine earlier concentrations of atmospheric carbon dioxide, there is evidence of a 19 percent increase over the past century.[6]

In addition to carbon dioxide, greenhouse gases include methane, nitrous oxides, ozone, and chlorofluorocarbons (CFCs). Although the behavior of these gases is not as well understood as that of carbon dioxide, their concentrations are increasing much more rapidly, and on a molecule-for-molecule basis they absorb infrared radiation much more strongly than carbon dioxide. It is widely believed that in the next century they will be as significant for climate change as carbon dioxide.[7]

While the overall results of an increase in the earth's mean surface temperature of 1.5 to 4 degrees are not well understood, there is a great deal of agreement that the expected warming will have a dramatic effect on rainfall patterns and climate variability. There will also

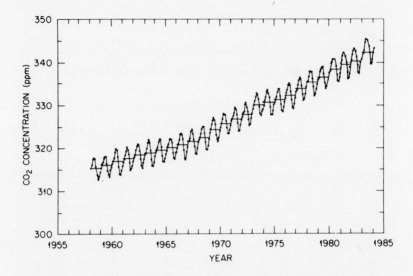

Figure 3.1. Atmospheric CO_2 in parts per million by volume (ppmv) concentrations at Mauna Loa Observatory, Hawaii. Measured amounts show seasonal fluctuations, primarily of biological origin, superimposed on an exponential growth. Source: C. Keeling, "Atmospheric CO_2 Concentration—Mauna Loa Observatory, Hawaii, 1958–1985," *U.S. Department of Energy Report No. NDP-0011R1* (Oak Ridge, Tenn.: Carbon Dioxide Information Center, 1986).

be significant effects on sea levels and on biological and ecological systems. These changes could greatly affect human societies. For example, it has been estimated that 12 to 15 percent of Egypt's arable land could be flooded by a "greenhouse-induced" sea-level rise. This area is home to about 48 million people and contributes 15 percent of Egypt's gross national product (GNP).[8]

The injection of greenhouse gases into the atmosphere appears to be a problem. For this reason, this behavior and our responses to its effects seem to be good candidates for management. The next section discusses one approach to management and exhibits a picture of how some think science and policy are related.

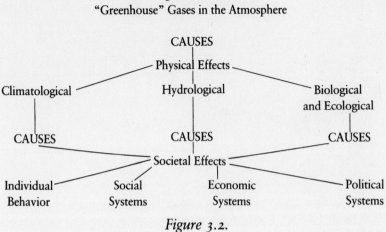

The Problem:
Increasing Concentrations of
"Greenhouse" Gases in the Atmosphere

CAUSES

Physical Effects

Climatological   Hydrological   Biological
and Ecological

CAUSES   CAUSES   CAUSES

Societal Effects

Individual   Social   Economic   Political
Behavior   Systems   Systems   Systems

Figure 3.2.

One Picture of the Relation between Science and Policy

Consider the following picture: We begin with a problem (see Figure 3.2), in this case, the problem of increasing concentrations of greenhouse gases in the atmosphere. These increasing concentrations cause various physical effects, which in turn cause various societal effects. Many of these effects are regarded as undesirable. The goal of management is to prevent, mitigate, or adapt to these undesirable effects.

In order to manage successfully we need information (see Figure 3.3). The role of physical science is to produce information regarding the physical effects of increasing concentrations of greenhouse gases. Physical effects include climatological effects, hydrological effects, and biological and ecological effects. With respect to global warming, such effects are likely to include increasing global mean temperature and precipitation, rising sea levels, drier soils, species extinctions, and shifting patterns of biological activity. Once information about physical effects is developed, it is transferred to social scientists, who evaluate the effects of these physical changes on individual and social behavior and economic and political systems. These effects may involve

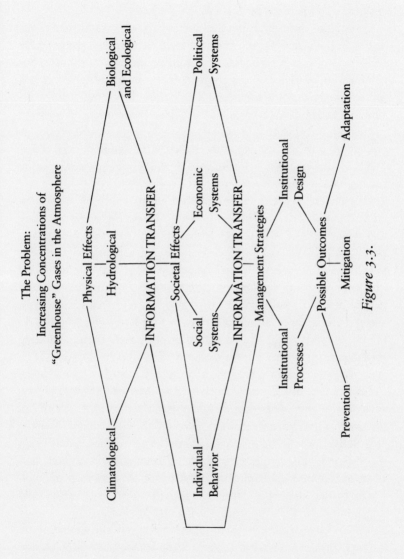

Figure 3.3.

impacts on individual lifestyles, the availability and price of food, migration patterns, economic development, the stability of national governments, and patterns of international relations.

Information from both physical and social scientists is then transferred to policymakers and their advisers (philosopher–kings). One response would be to welcome or ignore the anticipated changes. But if the effects of such changes are regarded as undesirable (and this is presupposed by calling something a problem), then some policy interventions would seem to be called for. These interventions may aim at preventing or mitigating the predicted physical or societal effects, or individual or collective adaptation. Policy interventions may be implemented by designing new institutions or institutional processes, or by redirecting existing ones.

This picture of the relation between science and policy consorts with what may be regarded as a (broadly) "positivist" view of science and value. This view is deeply entrenched in American science and public life. According to this view, there is a radical distinction between facts and values. Determining the physical and societal effects of increasing concentrations of greenhouse gases is, on this view, a factual matter to be resolved empirically by value-free science. This stage of the inquiry is purely descriptive; normative considerations do not enter into it at all. The next stage involves assessing and selecting management strategies. This is the normative, value-laden stage. Here such notions as equity, fairness, and efficiency come into play. The difference between the two stages is this: Management and policymaking are matters of decision, while scientific inquiry is a matter of discovery. Since scientific inquiry involves the determination of the way things are, it is the proper domain of experts. Since management involves resolving conflicts of values, interests, and preferences, it is the proper domain of democratic participation. Management and policy are matters of politics rather than expertise. Preferences are created equal, but judgments about what is the case are not.

This picture (or some of its variations) underpins the way we think about many important public issues. The Environmental Protection Agency (EPA) has instituted a version of this approach in its regulatory procedures.

During Ronald Reagan's presidency, the federal government turned away from prohibitive regulatory policies and toward policies that permitted some environmental degradation as a consequence of economically worthwhile activities. Instead of the absolute standards envisioned in the legislation of the early 1970s, notions of "acceptable risk" and "optimal pollution" gained currency.

When William Ruckelshaus began his second tenure as EPA Administrator, he instituted an analytic approach to the development of new regulations. On this approach, when potential risks are being investigated, the inquiry is to be divided into two stages. The first stage is the risk-assessment stage. This involves the identification of a hazard, the establishment of a dose–response curve, the construction of an exposure model, and finally the characterization of the risk. These activities are regarded as purely scientific; values are not supposed to enter at this stage. The second stage is the risk-management stage. On the basis of the results of the risk assessment, policies are established and regulations are written. Since risk-management decisions involve matters of value, public participation is appropriate. These decisions need not be left to the experts. Many factors affect people's tolerance for a particular risk: whether it involves communities or scattered individuals, whether it is familiar or unfamiliar, whether individual intervention is efficacious or not, and so on. Knowledge of these attitudes and opinions are important when making management decisions.

In the philosophical community there is growing dissatisfaction with models of decision making rooted in positivist conceptions.[9] Recent work in the philosophy of science has convincingly demonstrated that facts and values are tightly interwoven in actual scientific practice. Skepticism about science as an objective, value-free inquiry has been so great that it has become difficult to keep the public out of what once were regarded as strictly scientific matters. We see this in controversies over scientific uses of animals and embryos, over recombinant DNA research, over the determination of carcinogenic substances, and over the appropriate level of AIDS funding. Activists for various causes increasingly see scientific rhetoric as a mask for substantive value commitments. They seek to expose value dimensions and make policy debates more open and participatory. On the other side, many scientists are frustrated by what they regard as incompetent management decisions. They decry what they see as the scientific illiteracy of policymakers and the general public. While some members of the public and various organized interest groups want the domain of values to swallow that of facts, many scientists seem to want the converse. They seem to think that if we knew the facts, then the correct policy responses would fall out, without detouring through messy discussions of values and interests.

Despite growing dissatisfaction with the positivist picture, it remains influential. Whatever we may think about its ultimate tenability in other spheres, it is useful to see why the picture I have painted of the relation between science and policy is not a good model for us to adopt in our attempts to manage global warming.

Some Flaws in the Artwork

There is, as I have said, an emerging consensus that we are already committed to a warming of the earth's mean surface temperature of 1.5 to 4 degrees centigrade. In looking for support for this view, there are two main sources to which one may turn: actual climate observations, and model-based projections. Both sources face difficulties and have limitations. Let us consider the first source first.

The summer of 1988 was noteworthy for how quickly the problem of global warning moved from being a matter of professional attention to a major public concern. During that summer, the Greenhouse Effect made the cover of *Newsweek* magazine, the front page of the *New York Times*, and even the Democratic party platform. In addition, Senator Tim Wirth of Colorado introduced a multibillion-dollar spending bill to combat the Greenhouse Effect. Wirth's bill had fifteen cosponsors from both political parties.

It is clear what brought the Greenhouse Effect to center stage. Much of the United States spent the summer in the grip of extreme heat and serious drought. As a result, agricultural production declined dramatically.[10] In addition, water levels in the Mississippi River system continued their decline, resulting in channel closings and ship groundings.[11] On the Eastern Seaboard, demand for electricity to run fans and airconditioners hit an all-time high. Airconditioners were even in short supply.

Many people have felt for some time that our climate is changing. Their suspicion seemed confirmed by a headline in the *New York Times* on Friday, June 24, 1988: *Global Warming Has Begun, Expert Tells Senate*. This headline was misleading, however. The heat and dryness of the summer of 1988 was consistent with the hypothesis of global warming, but by no means established it as a fact, nor even provided very strong evidence for it. There are well-known problems with inferring climate change from observations of present climatic conditions.[12]

One problem is that annual mean temperatures can vary greatly within a stable climate regime. Climate change that involves a 2-degree centigrade change in mean temperature is very small by comparison. For this reason, it is difficult to distinguish the "signal" from the "noise."

The second difficulty is the "multiplicity" problem (also called "data snooping").[13] In order to identify a statistically significant shift in temperature it is necessary to examine each year in the light of preceding and succeeding years. But this means that each examination will fail to be independent of previous ones. Subjecting overlapping sets of observations to statistical analyses makes it difficut to be sure that an apparently significant change is really statistically significant. If we make one set of observations, the probability of not reaching statistical significance at 5 percent is 95 percent. With two sets of observations taken together, the probability of not reaching statistical significance is 95 percent squared, or 90.3 percent. With three sets of observations taken together, the probability is 95 percent cubed, or 85.7 percent, and so on. By taking different looks at the same data, we increase the chances of finding an apparently significant deviation that is really just due to chance.[14] In the case of climate change, we have no choice but to look at overlapping data sets. For this reason, it will always be problematical to determine on the basis of observation whether a climatically deviant year marks a climate change or is due to chance.

The evidence for global warming that many in the scientific community find convincing does not come from observation but from projections based on general circulation models (GCMs). These models are enormously complex. Each model run requires solving about 200,000 equations, and solving each equation requires many calculations. The projections of a warming of 1.5 to 4 degrees centigrade come from calculating the consequences of a doubling of atmospheric carbon dioxide. More than a hundred independent studies have indicated that such a doubling will increase global mean temperature within this range.[15] Despite their complexity and sophistication, there are problems with and limitations on these models.

First, there are enormously complicated feedback relations in the global system. Some of these have been taken into account, but it is not clear whether they have been adequately represented. Consider the case of clouds. If the earth's surface warms as predicted, then more clouds will be formed. Additional cloud cover will contribute to warming by trapping more heat, but it will also contribute to cooling by reflecting more of the sun's energy. A warmer surface would also mean less snow and ice cover, which would mean less reflectivity (albedo) from the earth's surface. This would contribute to a warmer surface, which would contribute to more cloud formation, and so on back through the cycle. Although the effect of cloud cover has been modeled, no one can be sure that it has been modeled correctly.

There are also problems in assessing the roles of the oceans and biomass. Although it is clear that the oceans are a sink for both heat and carbon dioxide, it is not clear how much of a sink they are or how they might behave as the atmosphere changes. Similarly, it is clear that biomass, especially huge forests such as those of Amazonia, is an important carbon sink. But it is unclear exactly how important, and how biomass productivity might be affected by global warming. In theory, at least, biological productivity should be greater in a carbon-dioxide-rich world.

In general, the overall carbon budget is not well understood. Of the carbon dioxide released by human activity over the past century, probably less than half is in the atmosphere. It is not entirely clear where the rest is, or what the principles are that govern its storage. It is sobering to remember that none of the atmospheric models predicted the Antarctic ozone hole. There could be other surprises in store for us.

A second problem area for the models concerns their lack of resolution. Modeling efforts divide the earth's surface into thousands of grid points and treat the areas between grid points as undifferentiated. They assume, for example, that climate, clouds, and topographical features are uniform throughout areas of about 500 square kilometers. This lack of resolution is problematical because many of the forces that profoundly influence climate are much smaller in scale.[16]

Thus far we have discussed the uncertainties involved in our knowledge of the physical effects of increasing atmospheric concentrations of greenhouse gases. It is now time to turn our attention to the difficulties involved in assessing the societal effects.

On the picture of the relation between science and policy that we are considering, information about physical effects is transferred to social scientists so that this information can be used in assessing societal effects. As a result of this transfer of information, uncertainties about the physical effects ramify. Any doubt that attaches to the reliability of model-based projections, for example, also attaches to projections about the societal effects of global warming.

In addition to this transfer of uncertainty, the kind of information developed on the basis of model-based projections is often not the most useful information for assessing the societal impacts of atmospheric changes. This is not a defect of the models. GCMs were developed in order to assist with basic research in atmospheric science. In recent years, they have been put to new uses. It is not surprising that they are not altogether suited for purposes for which they were not designed.[17]

GCM output tends to focus on means and averages rather than extremes. It is also more accurate with respect to temperature than precipitation, and provides more insight into global than regional climate patterns. These are all problems from the point of view of assessing the societal impacts of climate change.

Consider the importance of understanding climate variability versus knowledge of means and averages. Earlier in this section we saw how difficult it is to distinguish the "signal" of climate change from the "noise" of variability. Suppose that we want to know, for example, whether citrus groves will be an economically viable investment in central Florida in the twenty-first century. Predictions about mean or average temperatures over the next century would not be very useful. We need to be able to assess the probability of extremely cold winters and to have some idea of how extreme these winters might be. This information is not revealed by focusing on mean temperatures.

This case also suggests that societal impacts are essentially diverse and local. The social, economic, and political impacts of global warming matter greatly on how the physical effects are distributed and on what form they take. If the American high plains heats up and dries out, the impacts of this will be very different than if the deserts of the Southwest become even hotter. Unfortunately, while there is a great deal of agreement about a future rise in global mean temperature, there is much less agreement about regional impacts.

The final problem with assessing societal impacts that I shall mention is conceptually the most interesting. The global warming that we may already be experiencing is anthropogenic in origin. It is not something that is happening to people, but it is something that people are doing. Interaction between the physical effects of climate and societal responses is continuous and ongoing. Physical effects cause societal effects, which cause physical effects, and so on. These modulations do not occur sequentially, but often simultaneously. It is not like a chess game: First the physical side makes a move, then the societal side, then the physical side, and so on. The feedback between climate and human behavior is both constant and continuous.

The final stage of the model sketched in the previous section involves transferring information from physical and social scientists to policymakers and their advisers. We have already seen that there are severe problems with the quality of the available information. It is not clear how reliable the models are; our knowledge of regional impacts is sketchy; and there is constant, continuous feedback between physical effects and societal responses. Two other difficulties that appear in this stage of the model should be mentioned.

First, there is a problem with the communicability of the information produced by physical and social scientists. It is well known that ordinary people and even scientists have difficulty reasoning about probabilistic events. The same is true of policymakers. Moreover, GCM output and statistical profiles of anticipated behavior are not the currency of policymaking. Scientific vocabularies, though perhaps precise both in conveying what is and what is not known, are often regarded as arcane and obfuscatory by policymakers. They are often much more responsive to stories, metaphors, analogies, adages, homilies, and so on.[18] This is not surprising, and perhaps not even deplorable. Policymakers have backgrounds and education different from those of scientists, and their political survival depends on judgments whose grounds are very difficult to quantify and rationalize.

The final problem I wish to focus on concerns the time constraints within which policymakers must operate. For the purposes of scientific inquiry, it might make sense to have very strong standards of proof, and to pursue a research project in orderly stages. But if there is anything to the Greenhouse Effect, we will be experiencing its consequences long before rigorous science has been able to prove its existence. Even if this were not the case, we would still be committing future generations to dramatic climate changes while waiting for definitive scientific results.

There are many things wrong with the attractive model sketched in the previous section, but for present purposes the major problems are these. First, information about the extent and physical effects of global warming is uncertain and incomplete. Second, information about the societal effects is even less certain and complete because it depends on information from the physical sciences, because it involves difficult problems of its own, and because there is continuous feedback between societal and physical effects. Third, the information-transfer process cannot be as linear and sequential as the model specifies. If we face a serious problem, and if policy is to be effectual, then we must make policy while we continue to investigate the physical and societal effects of global warming. But this means that policy will also enter the feedback loop, influencing societal responses and physical effects. Instead of a pyramid with the physical sciences forming the foundation for social knowledge and policy interventions, we have something much more like the hermeneutic circle.[19]

It is beyond the scope of this chapter to sketch an alternative way of thinking about the relation between science and policy. Instead, what I try to do in the next two sections is to identify some salient considerations that should be taken into account when making policy relating to the Greenhouse Effect and then to suggest some policy prescriptions.

Some Important Considerations

As I have tried to show, there are many uncertainties surrounding the Greenhouse Effect. Yet some things are clear, and they need to be taken into account in formulating policy. This section discusses five such considerations.

First, there will continue to be substantial increases in atmospheric carbon dioxide. North America and Europe are responsible for most of the anthropogenic increases thus far. China, the Soviet Union, and the developing countries will be responsible for a much greater proportion of the future increase. Already this shift is occurring. During 1960, the United States was responsible for more than 36 percent of carbon dioxide emissions from fossil fuels. By 1985, the American share had dropped to little more than 26 percent. Over this twenty-five-year period, emissions by the United States increased by slightly more than 400 million tons. During the same period, emissions from China, the Soviet Union, and the developing countries, taken together, went from about the same to nearly twice the American share. Their absolute increase was nearly 1500 tons. During this period, the developing countries increased their emissions by about 450 percent.[20]

Second, increases in greenhouse gases will probably cause climate change. There will be longer, more frequent spells of extreme heat and drought, and perhaps more episodes of extreme wintertime cold. There will be more monsoons, typhoons, hurricanes, and other extreme events.

Third, there will be important biological and ecological impacts. These will be especially severe with respect to "unmanaged" ecosystems, causing increases and decreases in various populations of plants and animals, as well as some extinctions. There may be some tendency toward biotic simplification.

Fourth, economically there will be "winners" and "losers" both within and among nations.[21] Although it is difficult to tell which countries or regions or segments of societies will benefit and which will not, we can say with confidence that sea-level rises and shifting patterns of agriculture and other economic activities will be felt differentially.

Finally, although we are not in a position to predict what they may be, there will be effects on the political stability of some countries and on the pattern of international political and economic relations.

This much seems clear and important. The Greenhouse Effect threatens to be not only an issue of concern for environmentalists but one that has implications for economic policy and national security as well. In June 1988, an international conference attended by delegates from forty-six countries and fifteen international organizations was held in Toronto, Canada. The theme of the conference was "The Changing Atmosphere: Implications for Global Security." In its final statement the delegates declared that anthropogenic atmospheric change constitutes a threat to the planet that is second only to global nuclear war.[22] Despite the uncertainties I have identified, the Greenhouse Effect is a serious threat. The question is what should we do about it.

Advice for Policymakers

The first thing we should do is to give up the idea that all problems can be "managed." We are at the beginning of a new era in our relation to the environment. Fundamental global systems are being modified by human activity. The impacts will be felt for decades or even centuries. The effects are potentially devastating. Unsurprisingly, we are woefully ignorant of the consequences of what we have done. The usual techniques of policy analysis are not adequate to "managing" problems of this scale and magnitude. The beginning of wisdom is the acknowledgment of our limits.[23]

Second, it is very important to be clear about what problem global warming is supposed to pose. Two different conceptions have been articulated, though they have not always been distinguished. On one conception, the problem is the fact of the warmer world; what we should fear is the warmer world itself. On the other conception, the problem is not the fact of the warmer world but the transition to it. It is important to clarify the nature of the problem, since what interventions would count as successful depends on what the problem is supposed to be. Delaying the warming so that it occurs over a long period of time would be a solution to the second problem, but not to the first.

Third, for the purposes of societal assessment, we should disaggregate the effects of global warming. We are not in a position to assess many very different impacts on a global scale. We are in a position to assess the impacts of rising sea levels on Boston harbor, drought in northeastern Brazil, and floods in Bangladesh. Indeed, we have a great deal of experience in assessing these kinds of impacts. Our best chance of understanding what a warmer world would be like is from the "bottom up" rather than from the "top down."[24]

Fourth, since so little is known about the societal effects of global warming, and even less about what policies might be successful in responding to it, we should act conservatively. This has two dimensions.

When we seek policies to mitigate or adapt to global warming, we should focus on incremental changes and select these changes for multiple reasons. For example, the Wirth bill calls for requiring the American auto fleet to reach 55 miles per gallon fuel efficiency by 2010. Such a policy makes sense environmentally, economically, and from the point of view of national security.[25] In addition, it seems to have a great deal of public support.[26] Similarly, there are multiple reasons to be concerned about deforestation. Deforestation contributes to global warming both because it removes a carbon sink and because it releases stored carbon. There is also reason for concern on grounds of cultural preservation, species preservation, land degradation, and long-term economic sustainability. Policies that swap rain-forest preservation for debt, for example, can be recommended on all these grounds.[27] Even if the Greenhouse Effect turns out to be a chimera, we will not regret having preserved the rain forests and stimulated the production of more fuel-efficient cars.

Acting conservatively also means incorporating a concern for global systems into environmental impact assessments. Coal mining, for example, does not just scar landscapes; it also contributes to global warming. If we were to take the full effects of our projects into account, we would tend to favor those that are small in scale and decentralized over those that are large and "glitzy." We might, for example, focus on the development and marketing of energy-efficient lightbulbs and refrigerators rather than on building new power plants or developing new energy sources. Conservative policies may not permit us to win big, but they would minimize our chances of suffering devastating losses.

Fifth, in pursuing our policies we should act through cooperation and consensus to the greatest extent possible. This cooperation must be local, national, and global in scope. Any effective long-term policy will need to enlist those who stand to win from global warming (or think they do) as well as those who stand to lose. As we have seen, the excess carbon dioxide that is now in the atmosphere was injected mainly by Europeans and North Americans. Although these people continue to inject greenhouse gases into the atmosphere, the developing countries are becoming equally important sources.

Some regional scenarios suggest that the anticipated warming will result in more precipitation in the African Sahel and less in the American and Soviet grain belts.[28] This could benefit some poor African nations at the expense of the industrialized nations. Bandyopadhyaya has argued that rich nations enjoy many natural advantages over developing nations and that trying to preserve the global climate status quo is an attempt to preserve that advantage.[29] If there is to be progress on this issue, the rich nations must avoid pressuring the poor nations to remain poor so that the rich nations do not suffer. Real progress must be international and inclusive.

Finally, scientific research should be continued and accelerated. The reasons for this are obvious, but two cautionary notes are worth sounding. First, we should not think that additional scientific research will necessarily resolve our current uncertainties. Indeed, it may increase them. Just as a little light may make one only more confused when stumbling around in the dark, so more science may only increase our perplexities. We are dealing with enormously complicated issues that we are nowhere near understanding fully. Second, since there is such uncertainty, a number of different methods and approaches should be supported. When ignorance is as great as ours, especially about the societal effects of global warming, the best strategy is to encourage diverse and various lines of research.[30]

Conclusion

I have provided an overview of what may be an important environmental problem: the increasing concentrations of carbon dioxide and other gases in the atmosphere that result from human activities. I applied an influential model of the relation between science and policy to this problem and tried to show that it provides a distorted picture. I went on to identify some salient facts about the Greenhouse Effect and to suggest some policy prescriptions.

Many aspects of this problem have not been explored. Some of them, no doubt, are of more philosophical interest than the ones I have discussed. Still, by my lights, the issues are more important than the disciplines supposed to encompass them; if applied philosophy is to be worth doing, it must take real-world issues on their own terms rather than use them as props for philosophical discussion.[31]

Notes

Acknowledgments: I am indebted to Michael H. Glantz of the National Center for Atmospheric Research (NCAR) for his comments on an earlier draft, and to Richard W. Katz (NCAR) for helpful discussion of some of the issues addressed in the section "Some Flaws in the Artwork." I gratefully acknowledge support from the Ethics and Values Studies Program of the National Science Foundation, which has made this research possible. I alone am responsible for the views expressed in this essay.

1. World Meteorological Organization, *Report of the International Conference on the Assessment of the Role of Carbon Dioxide and of Other Greenhouse Gases in Climate Variations and Associated Impacts: Report of an International Conference Held at Villach, Austria, 9–15 October 1985* (Geneva, Switzerland: WMO, 1985).

2. For historical background, I have relied on J. Ausubel, "Historical Note," in Board on Atmospheric Sciences and Climate, Commission on Physical Sciences, Mathematics and Resources, National Research Council, *Changing Climate: Report of the Carbon Dioxide Assessment Committee* (Washington, D.C.: National Academy Press, 1983), 488–91; and William M. Kellogg, "Impacts of a CO_2-induced Climate Change," in *Carbon Dioxide: Current Views and Developments in Energy/Climate Research* (Dordrecht: Reidel, 1983); and on original sources.

3. G. S. Callendar, "The Artificial Production of Carbon Dioxide," *Quarterly Journal of the Royal Meteorological Society* 64 (1983): 236.

4. R. Revell and H. E. Suess, "Carbon Dioxide Exchange between Atmosphere and Ocean and the Question of an Atmospheric CO_2 during the Past Decade," *Tellus* 9 (1957): 19.

5. United Nations Environmental Programme, *The Greenhouse Gases* (Nairobi: UNEP, 1987).

6. Graham J. MacDonald, "Scientific Bases for the Greenhouse Effect," *Journal of Policy Analysis and Management* 7 (1988): 425–44.

7. V. Ramanathan, R. Cicerone, H. Singh, and J. Kiehl, "Trace Gas Trends and Their Potential Role in Climate Change," *Journal of Geophysical Research* 90 (1985): 5547–66.

8. Irving Mintzer, "Living in a Warmer World: Challenges for Policy Analysis and Management," *Journal of Policy Analysis and Management* 7 (1988): 445–59.

9. It should be noted that Ruckelshaus himself was acutely aware of the difficulties involved in keeping risk assessment and risk management distinct. He once wrote that "risk assessment data can be like the captured spy: if you torture it long enough, it will tell you anything you want to know." William Ruckelshaus, "Risk in a Free Society," *Risk Analysis* 4 (1984): 157–58.

10. This is documented in various reports issued by the U.S. Department of Agriculture and in the *Weekly Weather and Crop Report* issued jointly by the National Weather Service and the National Agricultural Statistics Service and World Agricultural Outlook Board.

11. William Koellner, "Climate Variability and the Mississippi River Navigation System," in *Societal Responses to Regional Climate Change: Forecasting by Analogy*, ed. Michael H. Glantz (Boulder, Colo.: Westview, 1988), 243–78.

12. Richard W. Katz, "Statistics of Climate Change: Implications for Scenario Development," in Glantz, *Societal Responses to Climate Change*, 95–112.

13. D. Freedman, R. Pisane, and R. Purves, *Statistics* (New York: Norton, 1978), 494.

14. John W. Tukey, "Some Thoughts on Clinical Trials, Especially Problems of Multiplicity," *Science* 198 (November 18, 1977): 679–84.

15. MacDonald, "Scientific Bases for Greenhouse Effect." It is not clear, however, that these studies are really independent. Only a few different models are employed in these studies, and it is common to discard model runs whose results fall outside the range of expected values.

16. For a discussion of these and other limitations of atmospheric models, see R. E. Dickenson, "How Will Climate Change?" in *The Greenhouse Effect, Climate Change, and Ecosystems*, ed. B. Bolin, B. Doos, J. Jager, and R. Warrick (New York: Wiley, 1986), 207–70.

17. Katz, "Statistics of Climate Change."

18. Dale Jamieson, "Grappling for a Glimpse of the Future," in Glantz, *Societal Responses to Climate Change*, 116–38.

19. For a clear account of the hermeneutic circle, see David Couzens Hoy, *The Critical Circle: Literature, History, and Philosophical Hermeneutics* (Berkeley: University of California Press, 1978).

20. Mintzer, "Living in a Warmer World."

21. Michael H. Glantz, "Politics and the Air around Us: International Policy Action on Atmospheric Pollution by Trace Gases (CO_2/Trace Gases-Induced Warming)," in Glantz, *Societal Responses to Climate Change*, 41–72.

22. "Toronto Delegates Call for a 'Law of the Atmosphere,'" *New Scientist*, July 7, 1988, 24.

23. Peter Brown, "Policy Analysis, Welfare Economics, and the Greenhouse Effect," *Journal of Policy Analysis and Management* 7 (1988): 471–75, argues that microeconomic tools are useful for certain purposes, but that "they are of little or no value in helping to decide what kind of world we should try to create" (p. 475). Thomas C. Schelling, "Climatic Change: Implications for Welfare and Policy," in Board of Atmospheric Sciences and Climate et al., *Changing Climate*, reminds us of how difficult it would have been for people a century ago to even imagine a world like ours: "Electronics was not dreamed of. Electric light would have been new in our lifetime and unknown to most of our countrymen.

"There was telephone but no radio. . . . Anesthesia was by ether, there were no antibiotics, bedbugs were a scourge. . . . Electric street railways were transforming our cities. . . . Only a third of the U.S. population lived in places with more than 5,000 inhabitants" (pp. 453–54).

24. Glantz, *Societal Responses to Climate Change*.

25. W. Chandler, H. Geller, and M. Ledbetter, *Energy Efficient: A New Agenda* (Washington, D.C.: American Council for an Energy-Efficient Economy, 1988).

26. According to a survey by the Analysis Group of New Haven, Connecticut, 77 percent of a randomly selected group of registered voters favor requiring automobiles to average 45 miles per gallon by the year 2000, even if such a requirement increases the price of a car by $500. See *Rocky Mountain News*, October 4, 1988, 7B.

27. H. Whelan, "Proposed 'Debt for Conservation Plan,'" *Environmental Conservation* 15 (1988): 78–79.

28. Kellogg, "Impacts of Climate Change."

29. J. Bandyopadhyaya, *Climate and World Order* (New Delhi: South Asian Publishers, 1983).

30. I sketch an alternative approach to thinking about the societal impacts of global warming in Jamieson, "Grappling for a Glimpse of the Future," 73–93. The volume in which the article appears (Glantz, *Societal Responses to Climate Change*) is devoted to exploring the possibilities of this approach.

31. For more on this last point, see Dale Jamieson, "Is Applied Ethics Worth Doing?" in *Theoretical and Applied Ethics*, ed. D. Rosenthal and F. Shehadi (Salt Lake City: University of Utah Press, 1988), 116–38.

Chapter 4

Models, Scientific Method, and Environmental Ethics

How we answer important questions of environmental ethics is often a function of the environmental risks associated with particular actions and policies. And the nature of the environmental risks, in turn, is often a function of the legitimacy of the scientific models used to predict hazards. Obviously, if we use poor scientific models, we shall make poor predictions of environmental risk. And if we make poor predictions of environmental risk, then the ethical imperatives based on those predictions may be equally poor. This suggests that, if we wish to do environmental ethics in a methodical and critical way, we need to be able to evaluate the legitimacy of the models giving us information about the environment. When those models go wrong, we have environmental catastrophes like Maxey Flats.

Maxey Flats, Kentucky, located in a poverty-ridden rural area in the Appalachian foothills, is the site of the world's largest (in curies) commercial radioactive waste dump.[1] Containing more plutonium than any other commercial facility, Maxey Flats is known as "the world's worst nuclear dump."[2] The corporate leaseholder, Nuclear Engineering Company (NECO), which opened the site in 1963, also manages two of the three existing U.S. low-level radwaste facilities. NECO said that it would take plutonium 24,000 years to migrate one-half inch at the Maxey Flats facility.[3]

NECO was wrong, by six orders of magnitude. Less than ten years after Maxey Flats opened, plutonium and other radionuclides had left their shallow earthern trenches and migrated two miles to streams and groundwater offsite.[4] This represents permanent contamination, since the half-life of plutonium 239 is approximately 25,000 years; a millionth of a gram of plutonium is sufficient to cause lung cancer.[5] Kentucky closed the facility in the mid-1970s after the Environmental Protection Agency (EPA) documented the plutonium migration.[6] Yet, despite NECO's lease violations and repeated unsafe waste-management practices, NECO forced the state to pay them millions of dollars for breaking the lease. In addition, the taxpayers of Kentucky, among the poorest in the nation, are now paying approximately a million dollars annually to maintain the site in perpetuity. Despite these maintenance costs, the radwaste is migrating farther and farther offsite,[7] and scientists say it is a potential public health hazard.[8]

Apart from the interesting political questions raised by the Maxey Flats catastrophe, there is the scientific issue: How could scientists be wrong, by six orders of magnitude, in their predictions about the waste migration? Obviously, the predictors' hydrogeological model was wrong. But this raises the question of *how we know* whether to accept or reject a given scientific model. This question is particularly troubling because, if the situation we are modeling were fully understood, we would not have to use a model of it in the first place. Presumably we use models only when complete, specific empirical data are not available or when the relevant processes are not fully understood. In such a situation, our models have a typically hypothetical character.

The question whether and when to use a given model is not easily answered, because different scholarly traditions dictate different responses. On the one hand, the epistemological answer, as articulated by philosophers of science like Larry Laudan, is that we ought to use a scientific model until a better one is available. On the epistemological view, it makes no sense to reject a model until we arrive at a better one.[9]

On the other hand, the ethical answer to questions of model selection, as articulated by moral philosophers who do environmental ethics, is that even if a better one is not available, some models ought to be rejected, especially if they could lead to undesirable public policy or dangerous environmental consequences. On the ethical view, even the best model may not be good enough to be accepted.[10]

Given these opposed positions on model selection, philosophers of science and environmental ethicists could well have made different decisions about whether to use the Maxey Flats predictive models, the models that proved to be wrong by six orders of magnitude. If philosophers of science and scientists examined the hydrogeological models employed at Maxey Flats, they may well have assented to their use, provided that they were the best models available. If environmental ethicists examined the same models, they may well have rejected their use, even if they were the best available.

How is it that our philosophy of science can be at apparent odds with our environmental ethics? At least one reason is that the goals of the moral philosopher and the philosopher of science are quite different. Another reason is that our criteria for model choice, in situations of environmental policymaking, are not clear. As a step in remedying this second deficiency, I attempt to establish at least three important points. First, applied philosophy of science, as practiced in environmental policymaking, requires one to heed the advice of the moral philosopher, not merely the epistemologist or philosopher of science. Second, the Maxey Flats situation reveals a number of important ways in which scientific modeling can go wrong. More generally, the case suggests that there are at least six important criteria for assessing the suitability of scientific models to be used for prediction, especially for predictions at the service of public policy.

Hydrogeological Models

To determine what the Maxey Flats case might tell us about where scientific models go wrong, or conditions under which they ought or ought not be used, we need to know something about hydrogeological models generally. Since the wastes were buried in shallow earthen trenches, the main guarantor of immobility is the site geology—in this case, shale. If the wastes migrate, it would be through leaching and water transport. Hence the need for examining hydrogeological models of site stability.

Most of the models used in hydrogeology are simulation models, mathematical expressions that attempt to describe or explain some physical phenomenon (e.g., dispersion of a subsurface liquid throughout the underlying geological strata). Development of a simulation model of some aspect of hydrogeology involves the use of many mathematical functions to express the interrelationships between the many processes involved. The major objective in building these models is to integrate these processes within a complete descriptive or explanatory structure capable of accounting for the time and space variability of various hydrogeological components.[11]

Although there is a variety of uses for hydrogeological models, at least three are dominant: for prediction, for detection, and for sensitivity analyses. Before most hydrogeological models can be used for any of these purposes, however, they must be calibrated. Calibration involves manipulating a specific model in such a way that, given input values, the model can reproduce (within a given range of accuracy) the response or output of the system under study. The range of accuracy is set by some criterion for the match between the value of some of the model parameters and the observed, measured, or field value of the same parameters.[12]

Of course, the Achilles heel of the whole calibration and modeling process is the fact that no model, either in terms of its system assumptions or in terms of particular values for its parameters, can be validated. This is because of the inadequacy and inaccuracy of the data that are supposed to act as checks on the accuracy of the model.[13]

The First Difficulty with Models: Unreliable Components

Let us look in more detail at exactly why some important parameters, variables present in hydrogeological models, cannot be known with accuracy. In general, the problem of accurate knowledge of these variables is a result of the fact that scientists must sample and disturb the environment about which they wish to obtain knowledge. Without unearthing an entire area, to a very great depth, and hence rendering it unsuitable for storing hazardous wastes, it is impossible to know exactly the characteristics of the underlying hydrology and geology.

Consider, for example, the problems associated with getting a fix on the parameter of soil moisture. Problems with this particular variable very likely figured in the erroneous predictions about groundwater movement at Maxey Flats. When the EPA did its review of the Maxey Flats facility, immediately after the plutonium was discovered offsite, it noted problems with seventeen types of data needed for accurate modeling of the hydrogeology at the Kentucky location. It named soil moisture among the variables for which it was most difficult to obtain accurate values.[14]

Soil Moisture

Understanding how soil moisture applies to particular empirical situations is absolutely crucial if one is to predict future infiltration capacities of waste sites and amounts of runoff and hence to know the potential volume of leachate that might post a problem at a facility like Maxey Flats, where earth covers the land-buried radwaste. Yet once one begins to analyze this concept, it is clear that a number of highly questionable assumptions are built into it and that its unavoidably value-laden use in field situations is likely to lead to a number of undesirable consequences.

When they were asked to name the greatest single parameter that consistently causes trouble with forecasts and predictions, a group of Kansas City hydrologists quickly responded, "soil moisture."[15] This is because a moisture-saturated soil will absorb no rainfall but will permit high runoff, and a dry soil will usually absorb a great deal of rainfall and permit little runoff. This means that if the soil-moisture variable is wrong, then the values for absorption and runoff are also wrong.

Soil-moisture determinations are problematic, in part, because they face all the typical difficulties associated with sampling. The variability of soil moisture, in both time and place, makes it hard to obtain an accurate basinwide measurement. Athough this problem can be minimized by selecting periods of water-storage change in which the amount of water in unsaturated zone storage (above the water table) at the beginning and end of the period is nearly equal, the problem of accurate knowledge of soil moisture persists. In field situations, soil-water characteristics for retention and transmission are frequently highly variable, with coefficients of variation approaching 70 percent.[16]

On the practical side, obtaining reliable values for soil moisture is also problematic. Point sampling methods are the usual approach, but these techniques, including neutron probes, can furnish detailed information over a large area only at prohibitive expense.

Because of a variety of problems associated with the neutron moderation method, overestimation or underestimation of soil moisture occurs because of calibration errors, sampling errors, or second-order errors. Moreover, because of the impossibility of obtaining an accurate measure of any sort for soil moisture, it would be difficult to tell how large an error was being made. Instead, one would know only that the results obtained from this value-laden method might be inconsistent with the results of another equally, but differently, value-laden means of measurement.[17] This, in turn, means that, to the extent that waste-siting issues focus on soil-moisture content, then to that degree are they likely to be the focus of scientific and political controversy.

Apart from the difficulties associated with direct measurement of soil moisture, through neutron probes for example, there are several problems with indirect measurement. It is not always desirable to determine the hydraulic conductivity (the power of conducting water) of a soil sample in the laboratory and then apply the results in measuring soil moisture or moisture movement in the field. For one thing, the values of hydraulic conductivity determined for small samples in the laboratory may not be representative of the soils in the field, where fissures and cracks between peds (natural aggregates of soil particles, usually between 1.3 and 15 centimeters) usually have a great effect.

Second, the relationship between soil moisture and hydraulic conductivity frequently exhibits hysteresis. Hysteresis is the name given to time-lag effects that are partly dependent on the previous *history* of the wetting and drying of the soil. The moisture content of a drying soil is greater than the moisture content of a soil being wetted through infiltration; in other words, hysteresis entails that the moisture content of a soil is a function of whether it is being wetted or dried, apart from what point sampling tests reveal. Moreover, many clays appear to exhibit hysteresis even though they remain saturated. Because of the phenomenon of hysteresis, the moisture content of a soil is "in a continual state of flux."[18]

CARDIFF

UWCC LIBRARY

Even the alleged soil-moisture "constants," for example, "wilting point" and "field capacity," "are not constants but rather subjectively determined variables whose magnitude depends upon a variety of changing climatic, vegetation, and soil-hydrological characteristics."[19] Because the values of soil-moisture constants rely on a number of interpretative judgments of a qualitative character, the concept of soil moisture is fundamentally dependent on cognitive or epistemic value judgments (see note 17).

This value-laden and interpretative concept of "soil moisture" typically leads to problematic consequences in applications involving waste siting. Parameter values for the crucial (water) infiltration (into the dumps) equations are provided by measurements of the soil hydraulic properties, such as soil moisture. Once one knows several of these properties, then water retention and transmission properties may be generated for the sample by analogy with a standard soil whose soil and water relationships are known. In other words, the various data on values such as soil moisture need to be combined in a simulation program. But if the soil-moisture values are highly interpretative, and if they are used in infiltration equations, and if the infiltration results are used to determine site suitability, then conclusions about the acceptability of an area for waste storage could be highly suspect.[20]

The chief alternative to using poor measured values for soil moisture would be model calibration, manipulating a specific model to reproduce the response of the watershed or catchment under study within some range of accuracy. But this, too, can lead to highly interpretative results. The fitting or calibration procedure involves adjusting the values of the process parameters such as infiltration and soil-moisture capacity, which cannot be readily determined by measurement. The problem, however, is that this range of accuracy is fixed by establishing a criterion of fit between the model's simulated response and the recorded catchment or watershed response. Establishing such a fit is highly value laden and interpretative, requiring numerous cognitive or epistemic value judgments (see note 17), since the model's response is judged on the basis of the field response; the field response, as was already argued for soil moisture, is almost impossible to determine with complete accuracy (see note 13). If so, then both direct and indirect determination of soil moisture is highly evaluative, making the results of the infiltration equations in which it is used highly evaluative. And if these equations are part of the basis on which decisions about site acceptability are made, then those decisions are likely to be highly evaluative and therefore questionable.

Conclusions Regarding Measuring Model Parameters

What this brief conceptual analysis of a representative parameter (e.g., soil moisture) reveals is that the reliability of hydrogeological models is undercut in several characteristic ways because of the lack of accuracy of values for the component parameters of the models. If we can come to understand the reasons behind these characteristic unreliabilities, then we may be able to approach the development of necessary and sufficient conditions for trusting a specific hydrogeological model in a particular situation.

The overview of soil moisture and hysteresis, for example, suggests that models whose parameters rely on unknown historical precedents (e.g., previous wetting or drying of the soil) are particularly problematic because knowing initial and boundary conditions is not sufficient for prediction. Instead, the actual values are a function, not of universal generalizations, but of a particular hydrogeological history. Much the same problem exists with ecological models; one cannot merely experiment or observe, in a particular ecosystem, in order to predict future species interactions; instead, future occurrences are a function of a prior history that is typically unknown and is not amenable to generalization.[21]

The "history problem" with modeling is related to a second difficulty illustrated by the analysis of soil moisture and its attendant problems with hysteresis. Many hydrogeological situations are unique; particular combinations of geological strata and moisture patterns, for example, are so complex and so heterogeneous that no other hydrogeological situation is similar. Hence, when one models a complex, heterogeneous, and therefore unique hydrogeological situation, it is impossible to know if the predictions are accurate, in part because it is impossible to *replicate* the situation. As with the "history problem," a similar problem exists in ecology. Particular species groupings, climate patterns, and resource configurations are unique; this means that prediction is undercut by the inability to replicate the situation.[22]

Admittedly the "uniqueness problem" would not occur in situations that are hydrogeologically uniform, for example, completely sandy soils with little or no rainfall, rather than (as at Maxey Flats) bedding planes of shales, erratically fractured, in an area of high rainfall. In uniform situations, replication of experiments or observations, as well as generalizations, would be much more plausible. This is in part because the number of relevant hydrogeological parameters would likely be fewer in number, and in part because the uniform field situations could more easily be represented by uniform laboratory situations. This suggests that site heterogeneity is a third modeling problem. To the degree that a proposed site for hazardous waste is hydrogeologically heterogeneous, to that same extent are modeling and predictions based on models questionable.

Another Modeling Problem: Assessing Field Conditions

In addition to the modeling problems associated with use of problematic values for parameters like soil moisture, a second class of difficulties arises because the systematic representations of processes and interactions presupposed by a given model either do not obtain in the field or are not known to obtain. In other words, modeling runs into problems not only because of inaccurate components but also because of unknown or inaccurate representations of the interactions among the components.

To illustrate this second difficulty with hydrogeological modeling, consider one type of model that is of utmost importance in siting a hazardous waste facility; those of groundwater flow. Groundwater has typically been studied by means of models because it is a hidden and largely inaccessible resource. In his recent study of groundwater hydrogeology, Todd organizes groundwater models into four classes: porous media models, miscellaneous analog models, electrical analog models based on the similarity between Ohm's Law and Darcy's Law, and digital computer models for numerical solution of aquifer-flow equations.[23] Brief examination of the assumptions built into each of these models should provide some insight into the degree to which groundwater modeling is value laden and therefore limited in its ability to represent and predict subsurface processes.

Groundwater-Flow Models

Porous media models are physical scale models of an acquifer in which the boundaries are scaled down and the permeability or hydraulic conductivity is modified. A typical class of porous media models consists of the same-tank models. These are constructed in watertight boxes, and the water table often serves as their upper boundary. Piezometers are tapped into the models to obtain piezometer levels, and the flow fields can be determined from dye added to the sand at certain points. (Piezometers are instruments for measuring the pressure of a substance or the compressibility of a substance when subjected to a given pressure.)[24]

Miscellaneous analog models are physical scale models whose applicability rests on the analogy between laws of water flow through porous media and laws governing laminar flow of fluids, heat, and electricity.[25] Electric analog models are physical models built on the similarity between Ohm's Law and the Darcy equation, $v = -K\, dh/dx$. Electric current in Ohm's Law is analogous to velocity in the Darcy equation; specific conductivity is analogous to hydraulic conductivity; and voltage is analogous to heat.[26]

Digital computer models are mathematical models of aquifers. Three of the main types of digital computer models are finite-difference models, finite-element models, and hybrid computer models that combine a resistance network with a digital computer. Finite-difference models rely on the computational procedure of dividing an aquifer into a grid and analyzing the flows associated within a single zone in terms of partial differential equations.[27]

Like the finite-difference models, finite-element models solve differential equations governing flow by means of discretization, where a continuous domain is represented as a number of adjacent subareas. That is, finite-element models rely on the computational procedure of dividing an aquifer into "finite elements" whose size and shape are arbitrary. In the finite-difference model, approximations to a continuous solution are defined at isolated points by finite differences; in the finite-element model, however, the approximate solution is defined over the entire domain, and it is not necessary to apply additional interpolations to obtain a solution at some point in the domain.[28]

Hybrid computer models have been developed to reduce the lengthy computer time required for iterative finite-difference solutions. In this model, imput data are expressed in electric form by a digital–analog converter and connected with the resistance network by means of a distributor. Node voltages are fed back to the digital computer.[29]

Problems with Groundwater-Flow Models

As was already noted, one of the main problems with all these models is that they depend on accurate input data. Because accurate input data are lacking, especially for parameters like soil moisture, infiltration, and the coefficient of dispersion, the reliability of the output of the model can be questioned, apart from whether the model itself is based on correct presuppositions.

A second problem with many of these groundwater-flow models is that they sometimes presuppose field conditions that do not obtain. For example, a number of the models depend on Darcy's Law, which applies to laminar flow (flow through thin layers) in porous media. Darcy's Law is not applicable to turbulent flow, such as can be found in basalt and limestone rocks that contain large underground openings. Other groundwater-flow models depend on presuppositions that are often counterfactual: that the acquifer in question is homogeneous and isotropic (having the same properties, e.g., conductivity, in all directions); or that it has impermeable boundaries at the side and bottom; or that the flow region is rectangular (even though it is known, for example, that the shape and size of a plume depends on local geology and may be highly variable).[30] None of these modeling conditions is met at the Maxey Flats site.[31]

A third problem with many groundwater-flow models is that they govern idealized and oversimplified situations whose applicability to the real world simply is unknown. For example, groundwater flow is obviously a function of whether or not the underlying rock beds are fissured. Yet it is impossible to know the nature and location of all the fissures and fractures that may be present below the surface. That is why one expert noted that only rough estimates of groundwater flow in fissured and fractured rocks are possible.[32] Another unknown in models is how to deal with nonuniformity of geological structures through which groundwater flows. In the unglaciated Appalachian region, for example, the highlands have varying geological structure, and the groundwater flow can be small, moderate, or erratic.[33] It is not certain either that one could know whether the flow was erratic or not in a particular location. Moreover, even if one did know that it was erratic, obviously no model could be relied on too extensively, especially a model that assumes that the aquifer is uniform. At the Maxey Flats site, the aquifer is not uniform, and the groundwater is perched (existing in small amounts, here and there, in the soil/shale above the water table or saturated zone). The groundwater comes and goes in various areas at different times, since all flow is through hairline fractures occurring at unpredictable intervals.[34]

Consequences of Using Problematic Groundwater-Flow Models

Because of all these problems with groundwater-flow models, it is evident that they require considerable judgment and evaluative skill in setting up the problem and applying the model to the field situation. When the model is applied to a particular problem, perhaps one involving siting waste facilities, it is likely that many of the caveats and conditions on the limits of validity of the model are forgotten.

For example, geologists might cite the number of feet to the water table, and note that the proposed waste would be above this level and protected by an impermeable bottom layer (e.g., of shale). They might forget that saturation extends slightly above the water table, because of capillary attraction, and that the subsurface flow can occur above the water table.[35] They might also forget that depth to the water table has been confirmed only at the spots sampled, not for the whole area. Or, in being comforted by the "fact" of the number of feet to the water table, those who use various hydrogeological models to determine site acceptability might forget that the upper and lower values of the depth to the water table can vary by 500 to 600 percent or more, that the zone of saturation is not flat, and that the water table does not always rise uniformly.[36] In the presence of relatively uniform measures at a geologically heterogeneous site, scientists would be likely to forget some of these possibilities for error in their modeling.

Another consequence of applying groundwater-flow models to particular potential waste sites is that one is likely to make much of the fact that different sites have relatively different rates of flow, and then to draw conclusions about site suitability, for the present and the future, on the basis of this alleged fact. In reality, however, these alleged differences in rates of flow should not be taken as sacrosanct, for a number of reasons. For one thing, past fluvial environments are known to have been highly variable in time and space. Second, the present estimates of groundwater properties, on the basis of models, are likely to be highly inaccurate, for all the reasons already mentioned. Third, there is little evidence to support the claim that flow rates are the direct response to immediate processes, since the system state is often so transitory in the case of groundwater. Fourth, human activities have often had a great effect on fluvial processes.[37]

Moreover, as was already mentioned, no model based on Darcy's Law can be meaningfully applied to flow rates in limestone.[38] With several low-level radwaste sites and numerous toxic waste sites in limestone areas of the southeastern United States, it is probable that this dictum has often been forgotten. Likely also to be forgotten is the fact that springs often occur in limestone areas and that such areas can include vast underground caverns and rivers,[39] all of which present problems that can lead to waste transport offsite.

Making too much of the allegedly different rates of groundwater flow predicted at different proposed waste sites, and therefore forgetting the extremely simplistic and inaccurate conclusions yielded by the models, one is apt to have a false sense of security about the safety of waste deposits at certain locations. It is often said of certain radwastes, for example, that "by the time" they travel offsite through groundwater, they will be harmless. Obviously, however, the accuracy of such a statement is a function of the accuracy of the flow rates obtained from a particular model, all of which have been shown to be value laden (see note 17). When toxic wastes were deposited underground at a New York site recently, policymakers must have relied on a geological conclusion either that the leachate would travel slowly enough through the groundwater that it would not harm anyone or that, if it traveled quickly, the pollution would be so diluted and dispersed that it would not present a problem. Yet, a short number of years later, the leachate plume from this site was 3 kilometers long.[40]

All these difficulties with groundwater-flow models suggest a fourth criterion for evaluating the suitability of using a particular model. To the degree that one cannot determine whether the idealized model constraints fit the actual situation, to that extent should we question use of the model. Or, to the degree that one is unable to know the consequences resulting from the poor fit between model and reality, to that extent should we question use of the model.

In the Maxey Flats situation, use of this fourth criterion for assessing models very likely would have resulted in skepticism about our ability to model the proposed radwaste site. As mentioned, NECO argued that it would take the plutonium 24,000 years to move one-half inch. Yet EPA geologists, in assessing the site, specifically noted that modeling problems, associated with assuming that groundwater flow on site was through intergranular porous media, could result in grossly underestimating the groundwater velocities.[41] Because the Maxey Flats situation is not perfectly represented by groundwater-flow models that assume geological homogeneity and a porous media, use of such models "could cause the channelling and movement of groundwater at unexpectedly high velocities" through the fractures in the shales.[42] Something like these "unexpectedly high velocities" must be the case, since contaminated wastes moved two miles offsite in nine years.[43]

A Third Difficulty with Hydrogeological Models: Testability

In addition to having contraints that are not known to fit the field situation, another difficulty with hydrogeological models is that they typically are not testable and are rarely even falsifiable. The problems associated with testing groundwater-model predictions by means of tracer methods provide a good illustration of this point. Some of the most important field data for testing groundwater-flow models, especially predictions about velocity and dispersion, are obtained from tracer tests, auger-hole tests, and pumping tests.

Tracer tests measure hydraulic conductivity and are made by measuring the time interval for a water tracer to travel between two observation wells or test holes. Auger-hole tests involve the measurement of the change in water level after the rapid removal of a volume of water from an unlined cylindrical hole. Pumping-test methods are based on observing water levels near pumping wells in order to obtain an integrated value of hydraulic conductivity over an aquifer section. Because of its importance in determining the permeability or hydraulic conductivity of the underground terrain and therefore its importance in siting waste facilities, let us examine the tracer method. Its assumptions, and the consequences likely to follow from its use.

To trace underground water flow, at least three types of tracers may be used: particulate tracers, chemical and dye tracers, and radioactive tracers. The basic principles involved in the use of all three tracers are the same. The tracer is injected into a well at a desired spot and then output wells are monitored for the reappearance of the tracer.

Some of the problems associated with use of tracer methods arise from the nature of the tracers used. All known tracers face difficulties of one sort or another. The ideal tracer should be susceptible to quantitative determination in minute amounts, should not react chemically with the natural water, should be absent from the natural water, should be safe in terms of human health, and should be inexpensive and readily available. No known tracer meets all these requirements. Although particulate tracers (e.g., moss spores) move at approximately the same rate as the groundwater, they tend to be filtered out of the water by underground sediment. On the practical side, they are expensive and difficult to use.[44]

Theoretically, tritium, one of the radioactive tracers, is the best form of water tracer. It is the only form that, for example, can be used in situations where adsorption losses are likely to occur, as in clays with high ion-exchange properties. Unlike tritium, the other radioactive tracers are subject to varying degrees of loss under field conditions. The two main handicaps to the use of radioactive tracers is that they are expensive and that safety precautions are stringent. Regarding the use of tritium as a tracer, another disadvantage is that its use in a groundwater study can invalidate the interpretation of natural tritium measurements over a considerable area. For this reason, tritium has not been widely used as a tracer.[45] At Maxey Flats, tritium is one of the most common radioactive isotopes released from the site operations.[46] Hence it would be difficult to evaluate which tritium levels came from the dump and which came from the tracer.

Apart from the difficulties with the tracers themselves, a number of problems are associated with tracer methods. First and most obviously, one needs to observe wells over a long period of time, since groundwater movement is often such a slow process.[47] Second, results from the use of tracers in wells require one to discount the effect of drilling on the hydrogeology and the effect of the drill hole or well on the natural flow and dispersion of the water. It may not be reasonable to discount these effects of measuring and observation.[48]

A third (and perhaps the most serious) problem with tracing methods is that, unless the flow direction is accurately known, the tracer may miss the downstream hole entirely. Multiple sampling holes can help solve this problem, but they add to the cost and further disrupt the hydrogeological environment that one is attempting to monitor.[49] A fourth difficulty is that because of diffusion, tests must be conducted over short distances in order to have detectable concentrations at the downstream well. Even then, it is difficult to determine a representative time of arrival.[50]

Problems analogous to those facing tracer methods of testing predictions clearly beseiged the geologists at Maxey Flats. Perhaps the crucial difficulty with tracer methods is knowing where to check for the presence of a tracer; particularly in a situation of fractured shale, as at Maxey Flats, the patterns of flow would be quite erratic. For this reason, determining a good checkpoint would be virtually impossible. Ian Walker, one of the first geologists to study the site, as well as the scientist on whose findings the decision to site the facility was based, explicitly noted this difficulty:

> It would be extremely difficult if not impossible to monitor
> contamination of groundwater at Maxey Flats by wells located
> outside of the burial pits. Nondischarging wells monitor a
> stream of groundwater at a width, at most, only twice their di-

ameter. . . . At Maxey Flats it would be impossible to predict
the path of a ribbon of contaminant in order to locate monitoring wells as the contaminated water would tend to undu-
late to seek permeable joints in the shale and to avoid the
impervious solid matrix.[51]

Hence, even the location of monitoring wells, such as those used by
health physicists working for the state of Kentucky, for NECO, for the
U.S. Geological Survey (USGS), or for the EPA, involved researchers
in highly evaluative judgments. Given these evaluative judgments, it is
difficult to conceive even of the possibility of testing the predictions
issuing from their hydrogeological models.

All these difficulties with testability, as illustrated in the discussion
of tracer methods, suggest that use of such models is less defensible to
the degree that they cannot be tested. Particularly in the case of assessing a potential site for hazardous waste, the testability criterion is
important, since the periods for which such wastes need to be stored
are so long. This suggests a fifth criterion for models: that their utility
be assessed in terms of the degree to which they can be subjected to
long-term tests.

A Fourth Difficulty with
Hydrogeological Models

Of course, if hydrogeological models cannot be tested, or if they fail
the relevant tests, this suggests that they are inadequate, at least in
part, because they may not have identified all the relevant parameters.
After all, one could not expect a model to enjoy predictive success
unless it had correctly incorporated all the relevant variables responsible for the phenomena under consideration.

At Maxey Flats, it seems that at least one of the reasons why initial
site predictions failed, by six orders of magnitude, is that the hydrogeology of the site was so poorly understood that all the relevant variables were not incorporated into the models. This point is clear if one
examines one of the earliest hydrogeological studies of the Kentucky
site, a study that was by far the most influential in the decision to
locate the radwaste facility in northeastern Kentucky. This is the fa-

mous Walker study, done in 1962. In his analysis, Walker assumed that he need take no account of any parameter associated with lateral movement of the groundwater through the rock or shale. He specifically assumed that there were only two variables relevant to the groundwater movement out of the proposed burial trenches: lateral movement through the soil zone and vertical movement through the fractures in the shale. He wrote: "Water will leave a burial pit either through near-vertical joints in the New Providence formation or . . . through the soil zone."[52]

Walker was not alone in his predictions that ignored the potential for lateral movement of water, especially between bedding planes of shale or rock. Six EPA geologists likewise ignored the significance of such lateral movement. They claimed that "if lateral migration of radionuclides from the trenches occurs, it is very slow."[53] Two other EPA geologists specifically stated that if water left the trenches, then it would have to be through vertical movement, lateral movement, lateral movement through the soil, or surface runoff. They completely ignored the possibility of lateral movement through the shale.[54] Because the horizontal movement was perceived as either impossible or very slow, their analyses did not take account of it.

USGS geologists, however, did take account of the lateral or horizontal movement through the rock and shale. Moreover, they claimed that the "preferential movement" of the water would be in a horizontal direction, because the fractures in the shale terminated in bedding planes.[55] It is clear that the USGS geologists were correct to include the horizontal component, since later radionuclide data proved that there had to be lateral movement through the rock. The models used to predict flow at the site, however, assumed vertical flow.[56]

Apart from the fact that the hydrogeological models were wrong in ignoring the horizontal-flow parameters, the important fact is that existing groups of scientists did not agree on what were the relevant parameters necessary to explain the hydrogeology of the site. Their disagreement suggests a sixth criterion for using a particular model: Scientists need to have arrived at some sort of consensus about the relevant parameters that need to be included in the model, apart from whether the model turns out to be accurate in more specific ways.

Inability to determine even the relevant parameters in the Maxey

Flats case is illustrated not only by the problem with lateral-flow components but also by analogous difficulties with failure to check for particular radioactive isotopes in well tests; with determining levels of gamma radiation, rather than merely alpha and beta; and with deciding where the sampling stations needed to be located. For example, Bud Zehner, the USGS Project Director at Maxey Flats, indicated that the main vehicle for obtaining hydrogeological information, vertical wells, could not provide the information needed about underlying flow patterns, since such wells might or might not intersect the fractures along which radwaste transport could occur.

All these difficulties (not obtaining gamma measurements, not taking account of significant lateral movement through the shale, not sampling at some spots deemed crucial by USGS and EPA scientists, not checking for particular radioactive isotopes, and not knowing where to monitor for tracers) indicate that the scientists did not agree on what parameters were necessary for the predictive success of their models. The difficulties also indicate that they did not agree on what might constitute a falsification of predictions from their model, at least in part because they did not agree on the parameters relevant for assessing the situation.[57] All this suggests that necessary conditions for responsible use of a model were not met at Maxey Flats.

Apart from whether a model can in fact be falsified or confirmed, the situation ought to be well enough understood so that scientists can agree on what variables ought be included in the model, and what a falsification might be like. Otherwise, use of the model makes little sense in a situation with empirical consequences.

Some Suggestions for Modeling in Applied Science

If this "Monday-morning quarterbacking" regarding the causes of the Maxey Flats errors is at least partially correct, then the problems encountered by hydrogeologists in that case suggest at least six criteria for when models ought not be used, or at least ought to be used only with extreme caution. These include situations in which

1. knowing current measured parameters is inadequate for prediction, since processes depend on earlier *historical* events not amenable to generalizations (this means, perhaps surprisingly, that some allegedly natural sciences, like geology, may have some of the same shortcomings as the more historical social sciences);

2. the combination of phenomena being investigated are *unique* and hence incapable of being *replicated*;

3. the site is so *heterogeneous* and *complex* that normal measures of uniform values of hydrogeological parameters are not likely to be representative and therefore are questionable;

4. the *empirical fit* of the models, with their idealized conditions, is unknown;

5. the predictions generated by the model admit of no realistic *testing* or rarely admit of *falsification*;

6. scientists knowledgeable about the phenomena do not even agree on the *relevant parameters* that ought to be included in a model.

If these six criteria are at least partially correct, then they suggest conditions under which one might disagree with the majority of scientists, epistemologists, and philosophers of science who argue for using the best models we have to evaluate alternative sites. The moral of the story: In some situations, even the best models might not be good enough for environmental policymaking.

Objections to the Analysis

If even the best scientific models might not be able to provide a sound basis for environmental policymaking, this raises a number of objections: First, in the absence of good scientific models, what, practically speaking, are we to do with hazardous waste? Second, if science cannot help us with environmental policy choices, then decision makers and industrialists are likely to choose whatever site they wish, perhaps for the wrong reasons. Third, because my analysis is critical of hydrogeological methods, it seems to be erroneously "antiintellectual." Moreover, contrary to the claims made earlier, why would the best scientists or philosophers of science, in a situation (like Maxey Flats) with potentially catastrophic public policy consequences, be likely to condone the use of imperfect hydrogeological models? Would they really say that scientists should use the best models that they have, regardless of the practical context in which the models might be used?[58]

How Do We Make Policy If Scientific Models Are Unreliable?

The first objection to this analysis raises an important and practical question. If even the best hydrogeological models are not good enough for environmental policymaking, then how are we to make decisions about siting hazardous waste facilities? In other words, if scientific models cannot help us in our public decision making, then, practically speaking, what are we to do? How are we to make policy?

The response to this objection, based on the difficulties encountered in the Maxey Flats case, is that we should choose a hazardous waste site that is amenable to hydrogeological modeling, so that we know the likely consequences of opening a particular facility. In the situation discussed earlier in this analysis, hydrogeologists persisted in modeling a site that was not amenable to modeling, that was geologically heterogeneous. The moral of Maxey Flats is not that one ought not use hydrogeological models but that, *if one has alternative waste sites that can be modeled effectively*, one ought not use even the best hydrogeological models in cases (1) where the site does not fit the contraints of the model, and (2) where the margin of error in the model cannot be determined.

In other words, to the degree that a given scientific model, even the best model, fails to fit the site at hand, to that extent ought one to be wary of using the model (since its results would be misleading); instead, one ought to seek alternative sites that do fit existing models. The devil you know is better than the devil you don't know.

But if the devil you know is better than the devil you don't know, then my analysis of the Maxey Flats case would dictate modeling a more permeable, more predictable site over a less permeable but less predictable one. That is, it would be better to model, and hence to consider, a hazardous waste site that was hydrogeologically uniform and susceptible to easy and reliable prediction, even if the underlying strata were more permeable (like the homogeneous sandy soil under-lying the Savannah River, South Carolina, radwaste depository), than to model or consider a site whose underlying strata were virtually impermeable, but heterogeneous and therefore difficult to predict, like Maxey Flats. Admittedly, it would make no sense, if one had no *alternative* radwaste sites, to avoid using the best available models for the one available site. This means that the purpose of my analysis of hy-drogeological models is to draw a conclusion about the *relative* desir-ability of modeling alternative sites, based on modeling contraints; my purpose is not to proscribe use of the best models when only one site is available. Moreover, it would make no sense to proscribe use of the best models in any single case because there is never merely a single-case situation; hydrogeological modeling for the purpose of siting waste facilities must be inherently comparative; otherwise, one would beg the question of choosing the best available site.

If Policymakers Cannot Use Scientific Models, Then Their Decisions Are Likely to Be Arbitrary and Subjective

Yet another objection to my analysis is that, in the absence of good scientific models, and therefore in the absence of compelling scientific proof that a particular policy action is harmful, industrialists and deci-sion makers are likely to do whatever is in their interests. They might use scientific ignorance as a cover for whatever actions serve their own economic welfare. In other words, this objection is that my criticisms of hydrogeological models could lead to dangerous consequences: *laissez-faire* siting decisions.

The most obvious response to this objection is that *not* criticizing hydrogeological models also leads to dangerous consequences, such as poor siting decisions, with their resultant offsite migrations of haz-ardous wastes and serious public health threats, as at Maxey Flats. Not to recognize the limits of predictive environmental science is to take false comfort in persuasive, but erroneous predictions like those at Maxey Flats.

In the absence of a "smoking gun" showing site unsuitability for hazardous wastes, it is true that the tendency of waste industries would be to assume the best, to assume that absence of known harm is the same as safety. That this self-serving assumption occurs, however, is not the fault of those who rightfully criticize scientific models but the fault of those who allow waste industries to seek refuge in a fallacious argument from ignorance. The absence of scientifically demonstrated harm does not prove safety, any more than the absence of scientifically demonstrated safety proves harm. Both modes of argument are fallacious because ignorance proves nothing one way or the other. Hence, if one blames the critic of hydrogeological methods for arbitrary, self-serving industry siting decisions (decisions made in the absence of good scientific studies), then one commits at least two errors: (1) ignoring industrial appeal to some form of an argument from ignorance, and (2) "blaming the bearer of bad news" (the hydrogeological critic), rather than the persons who misuse that "news" to serve their own ends.

Are the Criticisms of Hydrogeological Models Antiintellectual?

A third, and related, objection is that my criticism of hydrogeological models appears antiintellectual and antiscientific. Good intellectuals and good scientists, goes the objection, use the best information and best models they have (see note 9). To criticize the best scientific information and models, claims the objector, is to engage in antiintellectual "science bashing."

This objection has particular force because so much science bashing is now fashionable. There are a number of reasons, however, why the science-bashing charge does not hold in this particular case. First, I have not argued against the best hydrogeological models per se, but against using the best hydrogeological models in situations in which they do not apply, in which the limits of their errors are unknown, and in which there are alternative sites that admit of accurate modeling. Hence, the preceding analysis is not broadside science bashing, but a criticism of the misuse of science. Second, if one's concern is to safeguard the credibility of science, against its bashers, then one of the best ways to do so would be to criticize poor applications of particular models, as has been done here; not to criticize such applications is to run the risk that these applications will lead to catastrophe and to science bashing arising out of failed science.

Third, criticisms of hydrogeological models are not themselves anti-intellectual, just because they can be misused by those who are antiintellectual. For example, S. J. Gould was not antiintellectual when he detailed some of the problems with the Darwinian theory of evolution. The fact that his criticisms were misused by creationists seeking to discredit evolution proves only that they, not he and other biologist critics, were antiintellectual.

Fourth, what this analysis suggests is not that hydrogeological models ought not be used (an antiintellectual claim) but that their use ought to be determined in part by the situation, not merely by the quality of the model itself. What is an acceptable use of a model in pure science might not be desirable in applied science. Likewise, what might be acceptable in a Bayesian situation of scientific *risk* might not be desirable in a Bayesian situation of *uncertainty*. Our use of models might need to be far more conservative in cases of uncertainty, especially if there were great potential for public harm.[59]

Do Scientists Support the Best Available Model?

This raises the question whether scientists and philosophers of science in fact fail to be conservative in their use of models in cases like Maxey Flats. A fourth objection claims that I misrepresent the opposition between scientists/philosophers of science and moral philosophers when they discuss criteria for use of models.

First, is it misleading to claim that scientists/philosophers of science, in a problematic situation of environmental policymaking, would recommend using the best available scientific model? Although many of them, like Larry Laudan, might be personally sensitive to the dangers associated with naively using the best of a set of poor scientific models, there are several reasons why many scientists/philosophers of science might not demonstrate this sensitivity. For one thing, most policymakers and scientists probably accept the Bayesian rule to maximize expected utility, rather than the Rawlsian rule to avoid the worst possible consequence.[60] This suggests that they would choose *in favor of* the best alternative, rather than *against* the worst one. It also suggests that they would not allow contractarian or deontological ethical constraints to have precedence over the decision to opt for the best alternative, as defined in terms of expected utility.

Moreover, in situations of scientific uncertainty, like that of Maxey Flats, where precise modeling was impossible, the dominant Bayesian school also supports maximizing utility rather than following a more conservative approach to societal risk acceptance. In fact, when probabilities of hazardous consequences are unknown, Bayesians support using the assumption that all such probabilities are equal.[61] This means that situations of scientific uncertainty, for them, present no in-principle obstacles to modeling and decision making. Bayesians, in such a situation, are required simply to use the best model their analysis generates; scientific uncertainty does not require them ever to say that they know too little to employ a given model; if it did, they would not use the equiprobability assumption. Hence, to the degree that scientists and philosophers of science accept the dominant Bayesian position, to that extent are they likely to ignore scientific uncertainties and simply employ the best model they have.

A second reason why scientists and philosophers of science appear likely to use the best available scientific model, apart from dangerous consequences associated with doing so, is that American scientists working in policy contexts are required by law to keep pollution and other dangerous consequences of technological/industrial activity "as low as is reasonably achievable" (ALARA). What is reasonably achievable is determined on the basis of a favorable benefit–cost analysis.[62] Hence government regulations sanction using the best achievable standards, whatever they are, not the standards that might be necessary to protect people or to avoid disaster. This suggests that the best standards and the best scientific models are both defined pragmatically, apart from what standards or models our ethics might dictate. The pragmatic definition of acceptable ALARA standards and the Bayesian definition of acceptable environmental risk, even in cases of uncertainty, both allow policymakers to avoid important ethical issues. Hence it seems reasonable to claim that scientists and philosophers of science—indeed, anyone not specifically trained in moral philosophy—might be likely merely to use the best available scientific model, in situations of environmental policymaking, and therefore likely to avoid important ethical considerations. This analysis has outlined some of the hazards of following such a procedure.

Notes

Acknowledgments: The author is grateful to Mike Bradie, Ray Frey, and Alan Gewirth for constructive criticisms of an earlier, oral presentation of this essay. Whatever errors remain are the responsibility of the author.

1. P. S. Zurer, "U.S. Charts Plans for Nuclear Waste Disposal," *Chemical and Engineering News*, July 18, 1983, 23. See also Henry Eschwege, U.S. General Accounting Office, testimony in U.S. Congress, House of Representatives, *Low-Level Radioactive Waste Disposal, Hearings before a Subcommittee of the Committee on Government Operations*, 94th Cong. 2nd sess., February 23, March 12, and April 6, 1976 (Washington, D.C.: Government Printing Office, 1976), 4. See also Frank Browning, "The Nuclear Wasteland," *New Times* 7, no. 2 (July 1976): 43–47, esp. 45. See also G. Lewis Meyer, *Preliminary Data on the Occurrence of Transuranium Nuclides in the Environment at the Radioactive Waste Burial Site, Maxey Flats, Kentucky*, EPA-520/3-75-021 (Washington, D.C.: Environmental Protection Agency, 1976), 1.

2. W. F. Nadele, "Nuclear Grave Is Haunting Kentucky," *Philadelphia Bulletin*, May 17, 1979, 1–3, in U.S. Geological Survey (USGS), "Maxey Flats—Publicity," vertical file, Water Resources Division, Department of the Interior, Louisville, Kentucky, 1962. (The Louisville office of the USGS is responsible for monitoring the Maxey Flats radioactive facility.) F. Browning, "The Nuclear Wasteland," *New Times* 7, no. 2 (July 1976), 43–47.

3. Herbert Hopkins, USGS, "Ground-Water Conditions at Maxey Flats, Fleming County, Kentucky," USGS report in the files of the USGS office, Department of the Interior, Louisville, Kentucky, 1962. See also A. Weiss and P. Columbo, *Evaluation of Isotope Migration—Land Burial*, NUREG/CR-1289, BNL-NUREG-51143 (Washington, D.C.: Nuclear Regulatory Commission, 1980), 5. (Although this document refers to NECO by its original name, it should be noted that, in part because of adverse publicity, NECO has changed its name to U.S. Ecology, Inc.)

4. G. Meyer, "Maxey Flats Radioactive Waste Burial Site: Status Report," Advanced Science and Technology Branch, Environmental Protection Agency, February 19, 1975, 9.

5. Environmental Protection Agency, *Considerations of Environmental Protection Criteria for Radioactive Waste* (Washington, D.C.: EPA, February 1978), 9. J. M. Deutch and the Interagency Review Group on Nuclear Waste Management. *Report to the President*, TID-2817 (Springfield, Va.: National Technical Information Service, October 1978), iv; see also Environ-

mental Protection Agency, *Protection Criteria*, 23, where it is explained that many of the radioactive wastes will have to be isolated "permanently" (for a million years) from the biosphere. For more information regarding the necessity of permanent containment, see Energy Research and Development Administration, *Final Environmental Statement: Waste Management Operations, Hanford Reservation, Richland, Washington*, vol. 1, ERDA-1538 (Springfield, Va: National Technical Information Service, October 1975), X-179.

6. For details about the history and closing of the facility, see Meyer, "Maxey Flats Radioactive Waste" 1975; P. Hyland et al., Legislative Research Commission, *Report of the 1978–1979 Interim Special Advisory Committee on Nuclear Waste Disposal* Research Report 167 (Frankfort, Ky.: Legislative Research Commission, 1980). See also P. Hyland et al., Legislative Research Commission, *Report of the Special Advisory Committee on Nuclear Issues*, Research Report 192 (Frankfort, Ky.: Legislative Research Commission, 1982); hereafter cited as LRC.

7. LRC, 36.

8. This is the opinion of the EPA and of the Kentucky radiologists who monitored the site. See, for example, D. T. Clark, "Personal Comments Concerning Revision of the Six Month Study Report," NECO Files, through C. Hardin and R. Fry, Memo from the Department for Human Resources, Commonwealth of Kentucky, Frankfort, December 17, 1974. Clark writes: "The only conclusion that can be reached is that 'the potential for a public health hazard exists in the Maxey Flats area'" (p. 3). In a site project report, B. M. Wilson wrote, with his co-worker: "The potential for a public health hazard exists in the Maxey Flats area due to migrated radioactivity." See D. T. Clark and B. M. Wilson, Radiological Health Program, "Project Report, Kentucky Radioactive Waste Disposal Site," Memo to Stanley Hammons, M.D., Commissioner, Bureau for Health Services, State of Kentucky, October 21, 1974, 14.

9. Many epistemologists and philosophers of science would maintain that we always ought to use the best model we have because it makes no sense to reject a scientific model until a better one is available. Indeed this claim is central to the current criticism of classical or traditional philosophy of science. To understand why this is so, consider the argument for this claim given by L. Laudan, *Progress and Its Problems* (Berkeley: University of California Press, 1977), 26–44. Laudan maintains that thinkers from Bacon and Mill through Grunbaum and Lakatos have stressed the importance of refuting instances; he says that, on their classical view, the occurrence of even one anomaly in a theory or model is sufficient for the rational scientist to abandon it (p. 26). On

the contrary, L. Laudan (with P. Duhem, O. Neurath, and W. Quine) holds that in any empirical test, it is an entire network of theories that is assessed; for this reason, the occurrence of an anomaly need not compel the abandonment of a theory (p. 27). He argues, therefore, "that a problem can only count as *anomalous* for one theory if it is *solved* by another," and hence argues "against the common view that one sort of anomaly, *the refuting instance, poses a direct cognitive threat to a theory*, even if it is unsolved by any competitor" (p. 30).

If Laudan means what I suspect, then no model or theory has any refuting instances or fatal flaws. Only if a competitor model or theory is able to solve the refuting instance, or improve upon the flaw, does the flaw pose a cognitive threat to the original theory. My argument in this essay is that such flaws can pose *practical* and *ethical* threats, apart from their alleged cognitive liabilities.

10. Even the best scientific models (e.g., in welfare economics) might not be "good enough," might not be ethically defensible or acceptable in a given situation. For a moral philosopher who defends this point of view, see Mark Sagoff, *Risk Benefit Analysis in Decisions Concerning Public Safety and Health* (Dubuque: Kendall/Hunt, 1985); and Mark Sagoff, *The Autonomy of the Earth* (New York: Cambridge University Press, 1988).

11. G. Fleming, *Computer Simulation Techniques in Hydrology* (New York: Elsevier, 1975), 180.

12. Ibid., 180.

13. Ibid., 237, 257.

14. S. S. Papadopulos and I. Winograd, "Storage of Low-Level Radioactive Wastes in the Ground: Hydrogeologic and Hydrochemical Factors," EPA-520/3-74-009 (Washington, D.C.: Environmental Protection Agency, 1974), 17–18.

15. D. R. Wiesnet, "Remote Sensing and Its Application to Hydrology," in *Facets of Hydrology*, ed. J. C. Rodda (New York: Wiley, 1976), 50. See also Thomas Dunne and Luna Leopold, *Water in Environmental Planning* (San Francisco: W. H. Freeman, 1978), 177–78.

16. F. X. Dunin, "Infiltration: Its Simulation for Field Conditions," in Rodda, *Facets of Hydrology*, 215. See D. K. Todd, *Groundwater Hydrology* (New York: Wiley, 1980), 362. Another geologist who points out that soil moisture capacity "cannot readily be assessed by measurement" is George Fleming. See Fleming, *Computer Simulation Techniques*, 237.

17. For a discussion of the role of cognitive or epistemic value judgments in science, see K. Shrader-Frechette, *Science Policy, Ethics, and Economic Methodology* (Boston: Reidel, 1985), 67–98.

18. R. C. Ward, *Principles of Hydrology* (London: McGraw-Hill,

1975), 142. See also T. C. Atkinson, "Techniques for Measuring Subsurface Flow on Hillslopes," in *Hillslope Hydrology*, ed. M. J. Kirkby (New York: Wiley, 1978). For a discussion of the coefficient of variation, see R. G. Barry, "Precipitation," in *Water, Earth, and Man*, ed. R. J. Chorley (London: Methuen, 1969), 120–21.

19. Ward, *Principles of Hydrology*, 143.

20. Dunin, "Infiltration," 215; Fleming, *Computer Simulation Techniques*, 237.

21. See M. B. Davis, "Climatic Instability, Time Lags, and Community Disequilibrium," in *Community Ecology*, ed J. Diamond and T. Case (New York: Harper & Row, 1986), 269–84. See also R. W. Graham, "Response of Mammalian Communities to Environmental Changes during the Late Quaternary," in ibid., 300–313; and S. P. Hubbell and R. B. Foster, "Biology, Chance, and History and the Structure of Tropical Rain Forest Tree Communities," in ibid., 314–29. See also note 22.

22. See, for example, D. R. Strong, "Natural Variability and the Manifold Mechanisms of Ecological Communities," *American Naturalist* 122, no. 5 (November 1983): 636–60; E. F. Connor and E. D. McCoy, "The Statistics and Biology of the Species–Area Relationship," *American Naturalist* 113, no. 6 (June 1979): 791–833; and E. F. Connor and D. Simberloff, "The Assembly of Species Communities: Chance or Competition," *Ecology* 60, no. 6 (1979): 1132–40.

23. Todd, *Groundwater Hydrology*, 384.

24. For a discussion of porous media models, see ibid., 384–87.

25. For a discussion of miscellaneous analog models, see ibid., 387–93.

26. For a discussion of electric analog models, see ibid., 393–99.

27. For a discussion of finite difference models, see ibid., 399–400; and G. F. Pinder and W. G. Gray, *Finite Element Simulation in Surface and Subsurface Hydrology* (New York: Academic Press, 1977), chaps. 1–2.

28. For a discussion of finite element models, see Todd, *Groundwater Hydrology*, 401–2; and Pinder and Gray, *Finite Element Simulation*, chaps. 3–8.

29. For a discussion of hybrid computer models, see Todd, *Groundwater Hydrology*, 402–3.

30. See ibid., 67–68, 93, 101, 342. For a discussion of Darcy's Law, see D. B. McWhorter and D. K. Sunada, *Ground-Water Hydrology and Hydraulics* (Fort Collins, Colo.: Water Resources Publications, 1977), 27, 65ff.

31. H. H. Zehner, *Hydrogeologic Investigation of the Maxey Flats Radioactive Waste Burial Site, Fleming County, Kentucky*, USGS Open File Re-

port 83–133 (Louisville, Ky.: Department of the Interior, USGS, 1981), 132–34, 153, 157, 175, 181. See also Eberhard Werner, *Joint Intensity Survey in the Morehead, Kentucky, Area,* report prepared for the USGS, 1980, on file at the USGS office, Water Resources Division, Room 572, Federal Building, 600 Federal Place, Louisville, Kentucky 40202. See also note 34.

32. H. Schoeller, "Analtyical and Investigational Techniques for Fissured and Fractured Rocks," in *Ground-Water Studies,* ed. R. H. Brown, A. A. Konoplyantsev, J. Ineson, and V. S. Kovalevsky (New York: UNESCO, 1974), 4.

33. See Todd, *Groundwater Hydrology,* 59.

34. Zehner, *Hydrogeologic Investigation* 1, 3, 73–77, 112, 119–26. See also note 31.

35. See Todd, *Groundwater Hydrology,* 31; and R. Z. Whipkey and M. J. Kirkby, "Flow within the Soil," in Kirkby, *Hillslope Hydrology,* 121–44, esp. 123.

36. Todd, *Groundwater Hydrology,* 1–2, 221. See also J. P. Waltz, "Ground Water," in Chorley, *Water, Earth, Man,* 265; and Ward, *Principles of Hydrology,* 133, 193, 194, 241. See also T. Dunne, "Field Studies of Hillslope Flow Processes," in Kirkby, *Hillslope Hydrology,* 246; and D. T. Currey, "The Role of Applied Geomorphology in Irrigation and Groundwater Studies," in *Applied Geomorphology,* ed. J. R. Hails (New York: Elsevier, 1977), 69. Finally, See L. B. Leopold, *Water* (San Francisco: Freeman, 1974), 21.

37. J. B. Thornes and D. Brunsden, *Geomorphology and Time* (New York: Wiley, 1977), 103.

38. See D. I. Smith, "Applied Geomorphology and Hydrology of Karst Regions," *Applied Geomorphology,* 93–94.

39. Todd, *Groundwater Hydrology,* 40.

40. D. H. Miller, *Water at the Surface of the Earth* (New York: Academic Press, 1977), 401.

41. Papadopulos and Winograd, "Storage," 34.

42. Meyer, "Maxey Flats Radioactive Waste," 9.

43. See note 4.

44. Smith, "Applied Geomorphology," 95–96.

45. Ibid., 97–99. See also D. B. Smith, "Nuclear Methods," in Rodda, *Facets of Hydrology,* 67. See also T. C. Atkinson, "Techniques for Measuring Subsurface Flow on Hillslopes," in Kirkby, *Hillslope Hydrology,* 93.

46. R. L. Blanchard, D. M. Montgomery, H. E. Kolde, and G. L. Geis, *Supplementary Radiological Measurements at the Maxey Flats Radioactive Waste Burial Site,* EPA-520/5-78-011 (Montgomery, Ala.: Environmental

Protection Agency, 1978), esp. 29–30. See also R. L. Blanchard, D. M. Montgomery, and H. E. Kolde, *Radiological Measurements at the Maxey Flats Radioactive Waste Burial Site*, EPA-520/5-76-020 (Cincinnati, Ohio: Environmental Protection Agency, 1977), esp. 5–70, 71–72, 79 ff.

47. Thornes and Brunsden, *Geomorphology and Time*, 104.

48. Smith, "Nuclear Methods," 71.

49. Todd, *Groundwater Hydrology*, 75.

50. Ibid.; R. K. Linsley, M. A. Kohler, J. L. Paulhus, *Hydrology for Engineers* (New York: McGraw-Hill, 1975), 203. See also note 47.

51. I. Walker, "Geological and Hydrologic Evaluation of a Proposed Site for Burial of Solid Radioactive Wastes Northwest of Morehead, Fleming County, Kentucky, USGS, Kearney, New Jersey, September 12, 1962, 2. On file in the Louisville, Kentucky, office of the USGS.

52. Ibid., 2.

53. Blanchard et al., *Supplementary Measurements*, 4.

54. Papadopulos and Winograd, "Storage," 40.

55. *Hydrogeologic Investigation of the Maxey Flats Radioactive Waste Burial Site, Fleming County, Kentucky*, Open File Report 83–133, 129; see also 19, 21, 112, 114, 131.

56. Ibid., 114.

57. See Papadopulos and Winograd, "Storage," 9–16, 35–36, 40–42; Blanchard et al., *Radiological Measurements*, 58, 68–69, 74.

58. All three of these objections were raised by Michael Bradie, Ray Frey, and Alan Gewirth in response to an oral presentation of my analysis on September 9, 1988. I am grateful to them for formulating these problems so precisely.

59. See the next section of this analysis for a brief discussion of Bayesian decision making.

60. John Harsanyi, "Can the Maximin Principle Serve as a Basis for Morality? A Critique of John Rawls's Theory," *American Political Science Review* 69 (1975): 594–606, explicitly affirms that the Bayesian position is currently the dominant one.

61. Ibid., 594, 598–601.

62. See, for example, *Code of Federal Regulations* 10, pt. 20 (Washington, D.C.: Government Printing Office, 1978), 182; and Nuclear Regulatory Commission, *Issuances* 5, bk. 2 (Washington, D.C.: Government Printing Office, June 30, 1977), 928.

Daniel Barstow Magraw

James W. Nickel

Chapter 5

Can Today's International System Handle Transboundary Environmental Problems?

Environmental problems that are international in their dimensions and required solutions have become common. International rivers face devastating pollution, as can be seen in the Sandoz chemical spill in the Rhine and in the pollution that would flow into the United States along the western boundary of Glacier National Park from a proposed coal mine in Canada.[1] Oceans face pollution from polluted rivers, sewage flows, dumping at sea, and tanker and pipeline leaks. Atmospheric pollution across national boundaries is common. Examples include nuclear radiation from the Chernobyl disaster, ozone depletion as a result of human-made chemicals such as chlorofluorocarbons, global warming caused by greenhouse gases, and acid deposition caused by emissions of sulfur dioxide and nitrogen oxides.

Several factors are likely to increase the number, seriousness, and complexity of international environmental problems. The world will continue to industrialize, with greater pollution as the result. Increasingly complex technology will probably be used, with resulting increases in risks of accidents and costs of remedying them. Population growth will place great stress on existing resources, especially because such growth will be accompanied by demands for better standards of living for the world's poor.

The international dimension of transboundary environmental problems often makes them difficult to solve. Managing transboundary pollution typically requires joint action by the source country and the receiving country. The receiving ("downstream") state cannot unilaterally regulate the cause of the pollution because that cause is located outside its territory, in another country. The source ("upstream") state has an incentive not to regulate adequately because the harm done in another country is an "externality": Its costs are felt downstream, but not by the source state. Bilateral or multilateral action involving cooperation between upstream and downstream countries is needed. Frequently, as with ozone depletion, action on a global scale is necessary; bilateral or regional measures will not suffice. States with widely varying characteristics, values, and interests will or should be involved in arriving at solutions.

Cooperative action between states is a key link—and sometimes a weak one—in our ability to deal with international environmental problems. In this chapter we examine the prospects for such action and try to show that great pessimism is not warranted. Our discussion has two aspects. One argues that familiar claims about the inherent limits of the international system are exaggerated. The second points to some areas where successful cooperative action on international environmental problems has already occurred.

The International Political and Legal System

The habitable areas of the earth are divided into approximately 167 countries. The government of each state exercises sovereignty (with some limitations) over its territory and the people therein. The international system is decentralized because the strongest centers of power are at the national or subnational levels. It is, however, a much more centralized system than humans started with; it incorporates within 167 units diverse peoples whose ancestors were divided into thousands of linguistic and cultural groups.

At least since the end of World War II, a state's right to exercise sovereignty over its territory has implied duties on other states to refrain from invasion and certain other forms of interference. The International Court of Justice held recently in the *Nicaragua* case that norms proscribing the aggressive use of force are embodied not only in the UN Charter (to which almost all states are parties) but also in customary international law (described below).[2] Like many norms, the duty not to invade or interfere in other countries is both widely subscribed to and frequently violated. Other broad principles operative within the international system are that agreements should be kept and that warfare should be limited.

The formation of the United Nations and the accompanying recognition of the right of states to be free from the use of force by other states are of great importance for environmental management. The United Nations, for example, provides an ongoing forum available for raising and discussing issues, and the UN Environment Programme (UNEP) is specifically engaged in attempting to solve international environmental problems, as evidenced by its important role in the negotiations leading to the 1987 Montreal ozone protocol.[3] The United Nations also is a means of transforming environmental disputes into non-zero-sum games, as occurred with the bitter Indus River dispute between India and Pakistan. In that dispute, which had important strategic and nationalistic implications as well as natural-resource ramifications, the two countries initially faced a zero-sum-game situation, that is, any gain by one country resulted in a roughly equivalent loss by the other country. The International Bank for Reconstruction and Development (the World Bank) facilitated a settlement by offering additional resources (money and expertise) for developing the disputed watershed if the countries resolved the dispute. By providing that incentive, the World Bank effectively transformed the controversy into a non-zero-sum game and made it tractable.

The development of the right to be free from the use of force by other states has strengthened the right to be free from environmental interference by other states. Other major developments since World War II include the focus on the environment itself, the application of international law to an ever expanding range of activities, the expansion in the number and role of international organizations, massive decolonization with its focus on the rights of the new states and the need to improve the standard of living of people in developing countries (LDCs), rapid improvements in worldwide telecommunication, and the growth of international human rights standards.

Multilateral cooperation of the kind necessary to manage international environmental problems occurs within the framework of the international legal system. Negotiations often take place within existing international institutions (e.g., the UN International Law Commission, which currently is studying international liability and international watercourses,[4] both of which have environmental implications) or ones created for the occasion (e.g., the Third UN Conference on the Law of the Sea described later in this chapter). Negotiated solutions, or common standards that otherwise evolve, are embodied in international law.

The international legal system differs from the typical national legal system (e.g., the legal system of France) in ways that hinder international cooperation and place constraints on the world's ability to deal with transboundary environmental problems. For example, the international legal system does not contain any centralized rulemaking, dispute settlement, or law enforcement authorities. Lacking them, it is sometimes difficult or impossible to determine what environmental standards exist, what they mean, or whether they have been violated, and to force compliance with such standards.

The two primary sources of international law are international agreements and customary international law, with the former probably more important in the environmental area. Determining the existence and normative authority, in terms of international law, of an international agreement (referred to by various terms, such as *convention, treaty,* and *protocol*) is usually straightforward, although that is not always the case. Difficulties often arise in interpreting such agreements; the problem can become quite complicated when there are oral agreements and, as often happens, official texts are in more than one language.

Customary international law is even more complicated. Like law stemming from treaties, customary law can be on a less than global basis, applying only to two countries, countries in a geographical region, and possibly even countries that are not geographically proximate but nevertheless share some common characteristic. A country can exempt itself from the application of a global customary norm only by persistently objecting to that norm during its formation. The test to determine whether a particular rule of customary international law exists asks whether there has been general and consistent state practice, done in the belief that the practice was required or permitted by international law (*opinio juris*).[5] Unfortunately, the vagueness of notions of *opinio juris* and general and consistent practice often makes it difficult to determine whether a standard exists or applies to a particular country.[6]

The Statute of the International Court of Justice (ICJ) provides for a third source of international law, namely, "general principles of law recognized by civilized nations."[7] Although it is thus clear that the ICJ must apply such principles, it is not settled either what such principles consist of or whether such a source exists more generally, that is, whether principles from this source are relevant to the decisions of other bodies.[8] The international legal status of a principle of municipal environmental law that might be identified in each of the world's developed legal systems (civil, common, Islamic, socialist, etc.), such as a "polluter pays" principle, is thus unclear, outside the unusual situation of a case in the ICJ.

Other issues regarding sources of law arise from the existence of *jus cogens*, that is, peremptory norms of international law, and from the problematical, but potentially very important, effect of declarations of international organizations, such as UN General Assembly declarations. Moreover, states with various legal and political systems have different views about the sources of international law. Soviet and some Third World theorists, for example, emphasize state sovereignty and the importance of consent more than do U.S. writers. These differences complicate the process of determining whether an international norm, environmental or otherwise, exists.

Questions also arise concerning whether an international norm is effective as municipal law so that, for example, it can be enforced by municipal courts. In some countries, such effectiveness occurs automatically. In the United States, customary international law—at least customary law that does not conflict with existing municipal law—is effective; but an international agreement is effective only if it does not contravene the U.S. Constitution, has not been superseded by a subsequent federal law, and has either been enacted into federal law or is "self-executing." Making the last-mentioned determination, in particular, is not always an easy task. For some other states, international agreements cannot be self-executing and can be effective only if embodied in municipal law through, for example, a statute.

In spite of the problems, international law serves a variety of useful functions in today's world, ranging from providing norms to making available negotiation or dispute-settlement mechanisms to defining available remedies. Matters covered by the international legal system are varied and cover an extremely broad range, as indicated by even a cursory review of UN activities. More than 30,000 international agreements have been registered with the United Nations since World War II, with perhaps 2000 of them multilateral; the remainder have been bilateral or among only a small number of states.[9] The United States is party to approximately 7500 international agreements currently in force.[10] More than 125 international agreements exist that deal directly with international environmental problems.[11]

Most international law is obeyed. Consider, for example, income tax treaties, which define the jurisdiction of countries to tax activities and persons in order, *inter alia*, to avoid double taxation and tax evasion. States occasionally differ on the application of particular treaty provisions, but it is clear that the treaty will be followed once that difference is resolved. Still, we are all familiar with instances where international law has not been honored, such as U.S. activities in Nicaragua.

Theoretical Accounts of Obstacles to International Action

Pessimism about the prospects for needed joint actions on transboundary environmental problems within the international system is stimulated both by experience of international failures (e.g., the two world wars of this century, the failure of the League of Nations, and the weakness of the United Nations in at least some situations) and by theoretical accounts of the difficulties of cooperation between sovereign states. In this section we consider and evaluate some of these theoretical accounts.

Many views of why cooperative action is difficult or impossible within the international system are based on accounts of the disadvantages of being without a strong central authority found in the early modern political philosophers Thomas Hobbes and John Locke.¹² These accounts suggest that an international system of sovereign states with no central authority is closely analogous to people living together in a territory without a government. Since these people (or states) recognize no central authority, they experience the disadvantage of the "state of nature." The case for government made by Hobbes is significantly different from the one made by Locke, but both are worth considering in this context.

Hobbesian Problems

According to Hobbes (1588–1679), competition is inevitable but extremely dangerous in the state of nature because it is likely to lead to distrust, violence, and escalating conflict.¹³ Without government, people need not recognize any authority superior to themselves and are free to use any means to preserve their lives and advance their interests. Some people are likely to engage in aggression and violence in pursuit of their interests, and this will lead others to be generally distrustful and prepare to protect their interests. The result will be hostility and distrust, with escalating preparations for conflict. In these circumstances, Hobbes alleges that civilized life will be impossible. The only solution, Hobbes claims, is for people to give up most of their sovereignty and submit themselves to a strong central authority that can impose a system of regulation backed by force.

It is obvious that this story of competition, distrust, and escalating preparations for conflict bears some similarity to what often happens in the international system. Hobbesians can point to numerous instances in the international sphere of competition for power, influence, and resources; of simmering distrust; of escalating military buildups; and of wars large and small.

A Hobbesian account of these problems in the environmental area might point to competition between nations for natural resources on land and water, the use of air and water within the territories of other countries as free disposal zones for industrial wastes, and unresolved international conflicts over environmental policies. Environmental disputes, after all, are just a particular variety of dispute over how territories and resources—on earth and in outer space—should be controlled and used.

A more detailed account might point to some specific features of the international system that lead to conflict over environmental matters. *Different Values and Interests.* Differing values, interests, and perspectives are often a problem in trying to deal with international environmental problems. We need to distinguish at least three different kinds of value conflicts.

First, countries may have *conflicting interests.* For example, the United States may wish to continue to allow its emissions from Ohio Valley power plants to drift into Canada because it will be extremely expensive to equip all these plants with cleaner ways of burning coal. Canada has an interest in stopping these emissions because of the bad environmental consequences for Canadian lakes, forests, and buildings of acid deposition. Conflicts of interest can arise when countries have the same values. Canada and the United States both value pollution-free environments, but the United States does not want to spend the large sums required to reduce its contribution to Canada's acid deposition problem.

Second, countries may have *genuinely different values.* For example, some Brazilian officials during the 1980s attached little value to the preservation of Amazonia's forests, while many people in other countries were intensely concerned about saving them.

Third, countries may share the same values but have *different priorities.* A clear example of this is Brazil's policy during the 1970s and 1980s of building large hydroelectric dam projects and of encouraging agricultural development in tropical forests. The attitude of the Brazilian government has been—at least until recently—that economic development and the jobs it brings are of higher priority than preservation of the gene pool existing only in tropical forests and that it is unfair for more developed countries to insist on preservation measures that stand in the way of Brazil's development. As often happens, this case is one of different priorities rather than totally different values. The claim of the Brazilian government has not been that environmental preservation is of no value but that it is of lower value than economic development for a country with many hungry people.

These types of disagreement over values can lead to international conflict and to being unable to agree on joint action to manage environmental problems. Conflicts between countries over acid rain, for example, might arise because their interests conflicted (as upstream and downstream countries), because their values were genuinely different (as when one country attaches no value to preventing the acidification of lakes), or because their priorities were different (as when one country takes noninterference with private industry to have higher priority than diminishing acid deposition in a neighboring country).

No Central Authority Is Available to Enforce Standards and Agreements. Suppose that two or more countries are able to overcome disagreements in interests and values; they agree that joint action to deal with a transboundary environmental problem would be a good thing. Each party may worry, however, that the other parties will not fully comply. Each knows that an agreement at the international level between diplomatic representatives is not easy to convert into effective action at the practical level within each country. Implementing legislation, executive follow-through, and public cooperation are usually also needed. Without any central authority to ensure that other parties will actually take the complicated and costly measures needed to comply, they may worry that an agreement on cooperative action will not be worth the paper it is written on. Given this worry, they may assign a low priority to proceeding with negotiations.

Distrust Makes Coordinated Action Difficult. Another way of telling the same story emphasizes the riskiness of cooperative action when one party is uncertain whether to trust the other party. If an effective international enforcement mechanism existed, one might be able to trust the other party; but without such a mechanism, costly or dangerous forms of cooperation may seem too risky.

Contemporary Hobbesians like to pose this problem by recounting the Prisoners' Dilemma. A prosecutor has strong reason to believe that two prisoners are both guilty of a serious crime, but is not sure that this can be proven without a confession. The prisoners are kept from communicating with each other, and the prosecutor communicates the following to each prisoner: "I am making this offer to both of you. Study it, and you will see that it is clearly in your interest to confess to this crime. If both of you confess, I will get the judge to give each of you a light sentence, namely, five years in prison. If one of you confesses and the other doesn't, I'll make sure that the one who confesses gets a very light sentence of only one year and that the one who doesn't confess gets a heavy sentence of ten years. If neither of you confesses, I'll get both of you convicted on a lesser charge and you'll each serve two years."

Suppose that the prosecutor's statements about likely jail terms are believed to be true by the prisoners, and that each prisoner wants to serve as few years in prison as possible. Each prisoner will therefore rank the possibilities as follows:

Best option: I confess and the other prisoner doesn't (one year in prison for me).

Second best: Both prisoners refuse to confess (two years in prison for me).

Next-to-worst: Both prisoners confess (five years in prison for me).

Worst: The other prisoner confesses and I don't (ten years in prison for me).

The first choice is not available because neither prisoner can assume that one prisoner will be willing to make a large sacrifice for the other. The second choice is attractive, but is very risky. If one prisoner cannot be sure that the other prisoner will refuse to confess, refusing to confess could lead to the worst option. The next-to-worst option, which involves confession, is safe, since at worst a confession yields five years and at best yields only one year. Seeing this, each prisoner decides to confess, and each gets five years in jail. Had they been able to cooperate by both refusing to confess, they could have gotten only two years. The riskiness of cooperation leads to a nonoptimal outcome for both prisoners.[14]

One might claim that this dilemma does not arise in international diplomacy because diplomats have full freedom to talk to one another. But trust, not communication, is the issue. Suppose that the two prisoners are able to send messages. One receives a message from the other, saying, "Let's both refuse to confess; it's best for both of us." The prisoner receiving the message now has to make a decision: Does the sender intend to comply with the offer, or is this a self-interested attempt to fool one prisoner into not confessing while the other prisoner confesses? If it is the latter, the prisoner who receives the message gets ten years, while the prisoner who sent the message gets only one year. Because deception is a real possibility (and assuming that the prisoner who receives the message has no way of imposing costs on the other prisoner if the latter engages in such deception), cooperation is too risky. The prisoner decides to confess in spite of the message received.

Before proceeding to the Lockean account of the problems arising from lack of a central authority, we offer some evaluations of the Hobbesian problems. Our general claim here is that these problems are seldom as insuperable as Hobbesians suggest because the abstract terms of the Hobbesian story ignore many important features of the international system.

The first set of difficulties pertains to differences in interests, values, and priorities. There is no denying that these frequently pose obstacles to international action on transboundary environmental problems. But there is no reason for thinking that they will pose insuperable obstacles in most cases. There usually are important shared values between countries (e.g., preserving human health or rich fisheries against environmental hazards), and these are sometimes of sufficiently high priority to lead to joint action that entails substantial costs or sacrifices of other values. The United States and Canada, for example, have a record of extensive cooperation in managing shared lakes and rivers.

The second set of difficulties pertains to the unavailability in today's international system of a central authority to enforce standards and agreements. Experience with international agreements, however, shows that the vast majority of them *are* complied with. A threat of retaliation by other parties to the agreement is often effective in helping countries resist the temptation to freeload. Retaliation may be in kind ("If you continue polluting us in violation of our agreement, we'll turn off our emissions controls and do the same to you"), or they may be in another area ("If you continue violating our environmental agreement, we'll refuse to accept future agreements that you want"). Self-help can be effective in the international arena, just as it is in domestic legal systems (e.g., the reliance in the United States on private tort or antitrust actions). Further, blatant hypocrisy tarnishes the reputation of countries as well as of individuals who speak for countries. In particular, a country's noncompliance with an international norm tends to weaken the force of its subsequent complaints that another country is violating international law. In addition, many environmental issues arise between countries in close proximity to one another. Physical proximity between states, especially a common border, increases the likelihood that a norm will be followed: States cannot move away if they are dissatisfied with one another, and the frequency and variety of interactions (private and governmental, formal and informal) between the two countries tends to be high. The possibility of interfering with such interactions raises the costs of noncompliance with a treaty, even when the treaty governs another activity. Finally, the likelihood of a state's complying with a particular international norm generally diminishes as the state perceives that compliance would compromise its vital security interests. Solutions to most, but not all, transboundary environmental problems fall outside the security area. Atmospheric pollution from nuclear testing may be an exception, as may radiation from some nuclear power production: The Chernobyl nuclear reactor was part of the Soviet backup system for producing plutonium for nuclear weapons. Attempts to deal with the Greenhouse Effect may also cut close to the bone because of the role of fossil fuel burning in the energy plans and practices of most countries. But those examples are exceptions. Most treaties negotiated to alleviate environmental problems can thus be expected to receive general compliance.

The third set of problems arises from the fact that distrust makes many forms of cooperation risky. The first point to make here is that many forms of action do not involve all-or-nothing measures like confessing or refusing to confess. It commonly takes time, and many steps, to implement an international environmental accord. This allows one party to observe the extent to which the other party is proceeding in good faith and to act accordingly. If measures of compliance proceed at a reasonable rate on both sides, confidence can be built. Further, considerable trust already exists between many countries. To see that total distrust does not prevail everywhere in the international sphere, compare the different levels of mutual confidence between the governments of the United States and, respectively, Canada, Spain, Poland, North Korea, and Iran. The existence of considerable stability and trust in the international system can be seen in the large investments in the economies of other countries that are common today.

Moreover, analyses such as the Prisoners' Dilemma assume that one party cannot impose additional costs on the other party if the latter breaches an agreement (i.e., the agreement not to confess). Transboundary environmental problems do not necessarily satisfy this assumption. For example, the United States once threatened to return to Mexico contaminated Mexican-origin water, by piping it to a different point on the border and allowing it to flow back into Mexico.

Finally, two countries typically do not face only one environmental dispute, but interact with respect to a number of issues—environmental and other—over a long time frame. In such a situation, in contrast to the one-shot Prisoners' Dilemma, there are a number of equally possible equilibria. Other factors will thus determine whether cooperation occurs.

In sum, the Hobbesian analysis is too pessimistic, and the Prisoners' Dilemma offers no predictive assistance. The Prisoners' Dilemma does highlight the importance of trust and communication and thus the desirability of maintaining ongoing working relations and steady and substantial information streams between states.

Lockean Problems

John Locke's (1632–1704) account of the deficiencies of the state of nature is considerably less severe than Hobbes's.[15] The state of nature has a number of "inconveniences," but social life and civilization are not held to be impossible in the absence of a central authority that can impose laws. The inconveniences of the state of nature, which have civil government as their remedy, are these:

> First, there wants an established, settled, known law received
> and allowed by common consent to be the standard of right
> and wrong and the common measure to decide all controver-
> sies between them. . . .

Secondly, in the state of nature there wants a known and indifferent judge with authority to determine all differences according to the established law. . . .

Thirdly, in the state of nature there often wants power to back and support the sentence when right, and to give it due execution.[16]

It is easy to find these same problems in an international system that lacks a supreme central authority. Lockeans can point to weaknesses in international law stemming from the absence of legislators, clearly identified legal standards, international tribunals with compulsory jurisdiction to interpret and apply international law, and police forces to ensure compliance. In fact, the discussion of international law presented above noted that international law is distinctive in lacking these features. We next discuss each of these "Lockean" problems with international law in more detail—with the exception of the enforcement problem, which has already been discussed as a Hobbesian problem.

No Central Lawmaker Is Present. No person or body, including the General Assembly of the United Nations, currently has authority to make laws that are binding on countries independently of their consent. Members of the United Nations have consented to give this kind of authority to the UN Security Council under some circumstances, but that authority has been effectively enervated by the veto power enjoyed by five nations that are politically at odds.[17] One result of this is that general law is often unavailable in matters where it is most needed (e.g., to provide an international framework for action on the global warming issue). Another result is that outmoded customary norms may be difficult to change.

The Existence of Law Is Often Unclear. As noted above, there are several sources of international law. Some of these—for example, "consistent state practice" and "general principles of law recognized by civilized nations"—embody vague criteria for the existence of law. The result is that it is often unclear whether law relevant to a problem really exists. If a lawmaking body were available to make international law, and to clarify the sources of international law, uncertainty about whether a binding international legal norm exists could often be avoided.

The Meaning and Proper Application of Law Is Often Unclear.
This problem may arise in particular cases where conflict occurs between countries, or it can arise when countries try to figure out exactly
what their obligations are in a particular area, as indicated by the
disputes between the United States and Canada that have arisen with
respect to boundary-water pollution and acid deposition. If tribunals
with compulsory jurisdiction were available to decide cases and to
give binding interpretations of the meaning of international law, countries subject to that law would be better able to guide their own conduct and anticipate the conduct of others.

Once again, it is useful to offer some evaluations of the seriousness
of these problems as barriers to effective international action on transboundary environmental problems. The Lockean account does not
present the problems as impossible to live with; it simply views them
as substantial inconveniences. The point not recognized by the Lockean perspective is that it is possible to ameliorate these problems substantially by measures falling far short of introducing a central political authority. This is well illustrated by today's international system.

The first set of problems pertains to the absence of a lawmaker.
This absence is no barrier to the evolution of customary law, and
international law makes substantial use of customary norms. More
important in the environmental area, because of their greater ability to
define precise rules of behavior and specify reciprocal obligations in
the event of particular circumstances, are international agreements between two or more countries, such as the 1967 treaty on outer space.[18]
These agreements are clear sources of relevant law, they can be created to deal with new problems (e.g., ozone depletion),[19] and they can
be modified when circumstances change—although modification is
often far from easy, as is evidenced by the seriatim attempts to amend
the Hague Rules regarding carriage of goods by sea.[20] This source of
law is not binding on a state unless that state consents to its provisions, which often makes it hard to create law that is universally binding. Nevertheless, a large body of law exists that is binding on all or
most states. The role of UN General Assembly declarations in fostering the formation of norms and in explicating them is also very important, as evidenced in the *Nicaragua* case.[21]

Problems about the existence of law are ameliorated by the creation of clearly binding treaties. Once a country becomes a party to a treaty, uncertainty about the existence of norms relevant to particular behavior or to a dispute often disappears. Disagreements about whether some aspect of customary law is relevant to future behavior or to a dispute can be resolved by negotiating a treaty making clear what norms are relevant to that dispute. This occurred in the 1958 Geneva Convention on the Continental Shelf and to some degree in the agreement leading to the *Trail Smelter* arbitration, described below.

The third set of Lockean problems stems from the absence of tribunals with compulsory jurisdiction to interpret and apply international law. Three practical means are available within international law for dealing with this problem. One is that states with conflicting views on what their legal duties are can negotiate a treaty that offers a clear answer. Examples include the Canada–U.S. agreements following nonbinding proceedings in the International Joint Commission, described below. A second possibility is that states can refer the dispute to a binding tribunal,[22] as occurred in the *Trail Smelter* and *Gulf of Maine* cases, also described below. Another means of dealing with this problem is to specify within a treaty how disputes about the meaning or application of the treaty are to be adjudicated or arbitrated. This occurred in both the 1909 Boundary Waters Treaty and the 1982 Law of the Sea Convention, described later in this chapter.

The Hobbesian and Lockean obstacles we have described have been taken by many to suggest that a new sort of international system is needed: If we do not have the kind of international system required to deal with international environmental problems, perhaps we should change it to something that would work better. It has sometimes been urged that some sort of world government is needed because a strong global authority would have the power to impose everywhere the environmental measures necessary to deal with, say, climate change or acid rain. Such a system might be the answer for the distant future, but it is highly implausible anytime soon.

First, such a system would surely take a long time to create. Action on international environmental problems should not be delayed while we try to create a world government. Second, the obstacles to the creation of such a system would surely be worse than the obstacles to multilateral environmental measures. This approach proposes the nearly impossible as a way of dealing with the very difficult. Third, this approach would convert the problem of dealing with large-scale environmental problems from a difficult international problem to a difficult regional problem. Agreement between New York and Ohio on measures to control acid rain has been nearly as difficult to obtain as agreement between the United States and Canada. Indeed, it might even exacerbate managing some problems that are now amenable to regional resolution by superimposing another level of authority and political considerations. Of course, the opposite might result in some circumstances. The point is that global government would not be a panacea. Finally, a decentralized system allows useful experimentation that would be less likely in a global system.

Other Problems

Here we present some obstacles to effective international action on transboundary environmental problems not associated with any general philosophical critique of the international system.

Differing Levels of Development. International action to combat environmental problems has to cope with an extremely wide range of levels of national development and wealth. Brazil, China, and Mexico, for example, have severe air pollution problems, but the control measures they can afford or have the administrative and technical sophistication to implement, monitor, and enforce, given their resources and other problems needing attention, are much more limited than those affordable by, say, Japan or West Germany. More generally, North–South conflict (not to mention East–West conflict) over a variety of matters can impede international action to deal with environmental problems.[23]

The question whether LDCs should bear the same burdens as more developed countries in remedying transboundary environmental problems is vexing and crucial. One might make a Lockean argument that LDCs are not entitled to special treatment. The Lockean principle of acquisition from a commons permits one to appropriate or use a resource provided one does not take more than one can use without waste and that after one's acquisition there is "enough, and as good left in common for others."[24] How much it is permissible to take will depend on how many others want to use the resource and on how much they are likely to need or want. Presumably the Lockean principle covers, for example, using the sea as a disposal site. If only a few other polluters are around the area, and if they are likely to put only small amounts of pollutants into the sea, then country A may be able to put in a large amount of pollutant (call this amount N) without violating the Lockean condition. Later, when many more countries put pollutants into the same area, another country, B, may not be able to dispose of an amount as large as N without running afoul of the Lockean proviso. Country B then has no complaint that country A used to be able to dispose a greater amount or that A was able to dispose a greater aggregate amount over time by having an earlier need for disposal.

The Lockean proviso cuts in the other direction as well. Suppose that country A continues to dispose of amount N every year, even while new polluters, in order to avoid violating the Lockean proviso, have to dispose of less than N per year. Here the newer polluters have grounds to complain that there is no longer any basis for country A's claim that it is entitled to dispose of amount N. Country A, like the other polluters, is entitled to contribute only an amount that takes into account the number of parties wanting to make use of the commons.

Consider this problem in a real case. Some scientists think that uncontrolled forest burning in the western part of Brazil contributes a significant amount to the climate change problem. Suppose that this amount is 25 percent. Countries that industrialized earlier than Brazil and whose fossil fuel use contributes much of the rest of the problem might complain that Brazil cannot make this large deposition of carbon dioxide into the atmosphere without violating the Lockean proviso. Surely this would be correct. But Brazil would also be correct in responding that other countries can no longer put as much carbon dioxide into the atmosphere as they were once free to do. Brazil would be correct, that is, in appealing to the Lockean proviso in demanding that cuts be multilateral, rather than limited to Brazil alone.

This chapter is not the appropriate place for a full exploration of either the problems of fairness between more and less developed countries in distributing the burdens of dealing with transboundary environmental problems or of the possible legal bases for treating less and more developed countries differently in that respect. But it is appropriate to assert that fairness and legal issues will have to be taken seriously and that it will not be plausible for more developed countries to insist that they should be allowed to continue contributing as much pollution as they once did just because they started doing it first. The 1982 Law of the Sea Convention (described below) has an elaborately negotiated set of provisions specifying the rights and duties of LDCs, including rights and duties in respect to the environment.[25] Other international agreements will have to make similar efforts to deal with this issue.

The Environmental Values States Can Agree upon Are Not Necessarily the Right Ones. Any system of law or policy can embody values or approaches that are ineffective or worse as solutions to common problems. A national regulatory agency, for example, may fall "captive" to the industry it regulates and thus create regulations that are more noteworthy for their low cost of compliance than for their effectiveness.

A frequent theme of environmentalists, and of philosophers writing about environmental issues, is that environmental decision making has been and still is guided by an inadequate conception of relevant values. It is often claimed that the values that guide environmental decision making are too oriented toward short-term consequences,[26] too strongly focused on economic considerations or on values that can be represented in monetary terms,[27] and too oriented toward the value that environmental features have for humans as opposed to the value that they might have in themselves. A related claim is that humans have important but neglected moral obligations in the environmental sphere, for example, obligations to future generations[28] or to respect the rights of nonhuman animals.[29]

John Dryzek's *Ecological Rationality* argues that systemic changes can be made in the contemporary political order—national and international—that will make it give greater weight to environmental concerns (in his terms, move it toward greater "ecological rationality"). His proposals include moving away from large states to "small autonomous communities," greater reliance on mediation and "practical reason," and participatory procedures for devising policies for specific functional areas (e.g., acid rain, nuclear wastes) that involve representatives from all affected parties.[30] This proposal, like the opposite idea of creating a world government, proposes to deal with the difficult (international environmental problems) by doing the nearly impossible (radically altering the boundaries of most states).

More practical, but perhaps less glamorous, ways of improving the "ecological rationality" of states involve ongoing environmental research, education, consciousness raising, and lobbying. Political structures are most likely to embody sound environmental values if the people who vote and hold public office in them have been influenced by these activities. A recent, relatively successful example of this kind of coordinated international program is the set of U.S. activities leading to the Montreal ozone protocol. Among other things, the United States organized a series of nonpublic workshops at which governmental representatives from around the world could get to know one another and study and discuss the ozone-depletion issue without having to take positions or make public statements. Another example, the success of which is still in question, is Canada's attempt to educate and influence public opinion in the United States about transboundary acid rain.

Examples of International Action on Transboundary Environmental Problems

Canada–U.S. Environmental Issues

Canada and the United States have a relatively long and generally successful history of dealing with environmental disputes. In 1909, the two countries entered into the Boundary Waters Treaty, which provides that neither nation should pollute the waters that flow into the other nation.[31] The treaty also established the International Joint Commission (IJC), a binational body to which the states can jointly refer environmental disputes for binding or nonbinding resolution. No disputes have been referred for the former, but more than 100 disputes have been sent to the IJC for nonbinding consideration. The IJC's recommendations normally have been followed in spirit, thus resolving difficult disputes in an amicable and timely manner.[32]

The IJC typically proceeds by forming an advisory board composed of equal numbers of technical experts from each nation. The board is directed to investigate and report on the factual basis of the dispute. Making policy recommendations normally is not part of the board's mandate. Nevertheless, the board's findings (which usually are unanimously endorsed by the board) have frequently eliminated much of the controversy by removing factual misunderstandings or disagreements that had interfered with developing bilateral consensus.

The most recent controversy to go before the IJC involves a proposed coal mine at Cabin Creek, British Columbia. The United States has argued that the coal mine will pollute the North Fork of the Flathead River, killing fish, harming the recreational value of the area, and causing other damage. The dispute is especially troublesome because eastern British Columbia is not very developed economically and because the North Fork of the Flathead River constitutes the western boundary of Glacier National Park—a part nominated by the United States as a World Heritage Site pursuant to the World Heritage Convention[33] and one that operates joint activities with Canada's adjoining Waterton Lakes National Park as part of UNESCO's Man and the Biosphere Program.[34] The dispute was referred to the IJC; the IJC appointed an advisory board, which engaged in a fact-finding inquiry of the type described above and issued several reports. In December 1988, the IJC adopted the final report of the advisory board.[35] The IJC concluded that the coal mine should not be approved as proposed and recommended that the governments consider a joint management regime for the entire upper Flathead River basin, perhaps along the lines of the successful cooperation in jointly managing the Skagit River Valley, which also straddles the Canada–U.S. border.[36] The ultimate resolution is up to the two countries' governments. But there is no reason to think the dispute will not be successfully resolved.

Pollution of the Great Lakes presented an issue too large for the 1909 Boundary Waters Treaty. Two subsequent treaties, in 1972 and 1978, established a regime to control the problem—a problem of great significance to both nations and to which both nations contributed.[37] That regime, which utilizes the IJC, has worked relatively well since its inception.

Another Canada-U.S. dispute involving the environment concerned the maritime boundary between the countries in the Gulf of Maine area. The two nations disagreed vigorously about the proper location of the boundary, which was to determine rights to resources both on the continental shelf (such as oil) and in the adjoining water (such as fish). The richest fishery at issue was the Georges Bank, which would have been split between the two nations if the boundary urged by Canada had been adopted. The United States countered that the Georges Bank is a single ecosystem that can be protected adequately (e.g., from overfishing) only by being located entirely within one nation.

After years of unsuccessful negotiations, the two nations submitted the dispute to a designated panel of the International Court of Justice for binding adjudication. The panel arrived at a boundary different from those proposed by either nation, which split the Georges Bank between them. In rejecting the U.S. argument that protection required control by one state, the panel remarked on the long history of effective environmental cooperation between the two countries and stated that there was no reason to assume that cooperation would not continue.[38]

Casting an apparent pall over the successes Canada and the United States have achieved with respect to freshwater and marine environmental issues is the question of atmospheric pollution and, more specifically, acid deposition. Interestingly, the first encounter with this problem by these two countries not only led to an amicable dispute settlement but also to an arbitral opinion that still stands as the primary beacon of international environmental law: the *Trail Smelter* case.[39]

The dispute arose because the sulfur dioxide plume from a private smelter in Trail, British Columbia, migrated to the United States and damaged private and public property in Washington State. Judicial remedies were unavailable in both nations. The United States pursued a diplomatic claim on behalf of the injured U.S. nationals against Canada, and after an unsuccessful attempt at utilizing the IJC, the two nations eventually agreed to submit the case to binding arbitration. After extensive scientific investigation, the tribunal held in 1941 that Canada should pay the United States a certain amount (Canada eventually paid about $350,000) for past damage, that Canada could allow the smelter to continue operating only if it imposed a specified regulatory regime on the smelter, and, perhaps most significantly, that

Canada would have to pay for any future damage that occurred *even after* the smelter was in compliance with the specified regulatory regime. The tribunal stated:

> Under the principles of international law, . . . no state has the right to use or permit the use of its territory in such a manner as to cause injury by fumes in or to the territory of another or the properties of persons therein, when the case is of serious consequence and the injury is established by clear and convincing evidence.[40]

The *Trail Smelter* case has become the most frequently cited and quoted individual environmental law case (often appearing in tandem with the *Corfu Channel*,[41] *Lac Lanoux*,[42] and *Nuclear Tests*[43] cases), for the simple reason that there are no other individual cases like it. That the case was submitted to arbitration and that the tribunal's decision was obeyed undoubtedly have to do in part with the two nations' leadership at the time, but they also reflect other factors. The two nations share the same dominant language, a Western European cultural and colonial background, a primarily common-law legal tradition, democratic forms of government, relatively equivalent standards of living, the world's largest bidirectional trading relationship, a large number and variety of other interactions by private persons and governments, and a long border. These commonalities increase the probability of reaching and keeping agreements, although it is not clear how important any individual feature has been.

The early success in the atmospheric pollution area has been overshadowed during recent years by the controversy over broad-scale, bidirectional acid deposition. In 1966, the IJC was directed to study and report on bilateral air pollution along the border, and it established the International Air Pollution Board to do so. The board has not been funded adequately to function effectively. The IJC was also directed to monitor implementation of the 1974 Michigan–Ontario Air Pollution Agreement. An advisory board was formed, but was disbanded in 1983.[44] Meanwhile, the two countries' awareness of internal air pollution problems was increasing. The United States passed the Clean Air Amendments in 1970,[45] and Canada passed a Clean Air Act in 1971.[46] As a result of these and other measures, Canada reduced its sulfur dioxide emissions between 1970 and 1984 by approximately 41 percent, and the United States reduced its by approximately 24 percent. In 1978, recognition of the international dimension of this problem led the two nations to form a Bilateral Research Consultation Group (BRCG) on the long-range transport of airborne pollutants (LRTAP) in order to facilitate information exchange, coordinate research activities, and develop an agreed-upon scientific data base from which the two nations could develop solutions. Following congressional pressure on the U.S. government, the BRCG was specifically requested to investigate transboundary pollution caused by each nation. The BRCG reported that the Ohio Valley was the principal source of emissions affecting eastern Canada.

On August 5, 1980, the two nations entered into a Memorandum of Intent Concerning Transboundary Air Pollution.[47] The Memorandum stated the two nations' intentions to enforce vigorously their existing air pollution laws and to work toward a bilateral agreement on air quality, and it established five joint working groups to investigate various aspects of LRTAP. At about the same time, an interesting development occurred on the legislative front. Section 115 of the U.S. Clean Air Act required (and still requires) the Administrator of the Environmental Protection Agency to require state plans to be modified whenever there is reason to believe that pollutants originating in the United States "may reasonably be anticipated to endanger public health or welfare in a foreign country." Section 115 applies, however, only if the United States has reciprocal rights. Canada granted those rights in 1980.[48]

On June 23, 1981, formal negotiations began to develop a bilateral agreement on LRTAP. Most of the working groups formed under the Memorandum of Intent subsequently issued reports that were referred for peer review in each of the two nations. In 1983, both nations' peer review groups concluded that scientific evidence was sufficient to conclude that emissions should be reduced and abatement measures undertaken.

On January 25, 1984, however, President Ronald Reagan announced in his State of the Union address that the United States would not take action to reduce emissions but would intensify research into the causes and effects of acid deposition. Despite further scientific consensus on the most significant facts relevant to the acid deposition problem, the U.S. position in this regard remained essentially unchanged throughout the Reagan administration. The two nations appointed two special envoys in March 1985 in an attempt to reinstitute negotiations. The special envoys issued their report in January 1986, concluding that acid deposition was a serious environmental hazard in both nations and a transboundary problem. This report was endorsed by President Reagan and Prime Minister Brian Mulroney in a March 1986 summit meeting.[49]

A Bilateral Advisory and Consultative Group was subsequently established to oversee implementation of the special envoys' recommendations, to facilitate consultations between the two countries, to prepare a scientific update, and to review emission-reduction opportunities. The United States also agreed to undertake a five-year, $5 billion research program for removing sulfur from coal, to be jointly funded by the U.S. government and private industry. Because of good U.S.–Canada relations, what makes this problem hard is not its international dimension but the extremely high cost of remedying it. Substantial progress would be very hard to achieve even if Ontario were a province of the United States.

Although various actions have been taken since that time, the Reagan administration's position remained that the United States is prepared to negotiate a bilateral agreement limited to joint monitoring, research, and evaluation, but one that does not include reductions in emissions. The Canadians feel strongly that the transboundary flux must be reduced, which requires reducing U.S. emissions. More specifically, the Canadian position is that acid deposition should be reduced to or below a critical load level of 20 kilograms per hectare (about 18 pounds per acre), which in turn requires that the transboundary flow from the United States to Canada be reduced by about 50 percent from the 1980 level.

In legal terms, the Canadians claim the United States is violating obligations expressed in cases such as *Trail Smelter* and *Corfu Channel*.[50] The United States responds that it is not in violation of its duties because it is negotiating in good faith, because the question whether U.S. emissions are causing significant harm has not been shown by "clear and convincing" evidence (language used in the *Trail Smelter* case), and because a balancing test is required about the legality of LRTAP and U.S. actions to date satisfy that test.[51] Canadian officials are considering requesting that the controversy be referred to binding arbitration, but they prefer to settle the matter via negotiation.

In the most recent development, President George Bush stated in spring 1989 that he supports reducing sulfur dioxide emissions by 10 million tons (about one-half the total) over ten years and reducing nitrous oxides by 2 million tons over the same period, using a market-based approach that would be less costly than some other alternatives.[52] A major shift in U.S. policy is thus evident, one that could lead to resolving the controversy.

The Chernobyl Disaster

On April 26, 1986, a nuclear power reactor at Chernobyl in the Ukraine malfunctioned during a test of emergency procedures. Fuel overheated and disintegrated. Ensuing chemical reactions led to steam and then thermal explosions that blasted a hole in the reactor's roof, casting aside in the process a 1000-ton concrete shield. The explosions started many fires, including one in the graphite core (used as the reactor's moderator), and led to the immediate release of large amounts of radioactive material from the reactor.

Altogether, it is estimated that approximately 18 million curies were released into the atmosphere by the Chernobyl accident. About one-quarter of that amount, over 4 million curies, was released the day of the explosion. (For a comparison, the accident at Three Mile Island released a total of approximately 18 curries.)

As a result of the emission of radioactive materials, thirty-one people died in the days and months following the accident, most of them from radiation burns, and many more people were hospitalized. Estimates vary widely regarding medical difficulties that will arise in the future as a result of the exposure. Everyone agrees that cancer, leukemia, and genetic mutation rates will increase, but it is not clear by how much. One widely quoted mid-range figure is that the death toll will rise by 20,000 over the next seventy years. That figure does not include the many people who will experience painful and debilitating illnesses that do not result in premature death. Approximately 1000 square kilometers in the Soviet Union, in which 135,000 people formerly resided, have been evacuated as uninhabitable. The damage in the Soviet Union is officially stated as about $3 billion, though Western observers put the figure much higher.

Damage also occurred outside the Soviet Union. During the first two days after the accident, radioactive clouds drifted in a northwestern direction to Sweden and Finland, turned southeast across Polish territory, Czechoslovakia, southern Germany, and north again to the Netherlands. On the following days, the pollutants went directly southeastward, thus affecting Austria and northern Italy (as well as Kiev and other portions of the Soviet Union that had theretofore been relatively untouched). After several days, the radioactive pollutants reached the western United States and Japan.

The USSR did not notify potentially affected countries of the accident or the drift of the clouds. The first public indication of danger came from Sweden. Affected states were essentially left to their own devices to detect the pollutants, including both their nature and their amount, during the critical period during which precautionary measures were possible. The Soviet Union did not even acknowledge the accident until two days after it occurred.

The Chernobyl tragedy raised a multitude of legal questions, including whether the Soviet Union was strictly liable to other states because the damage to those states resulted from an ultrahazardous activity, whether the Soviet Union was liable for negligent operation of the plant (the plant's operators intentionally disabled the plant's emergency backup systems in the crucial hours before the test), and whether the Soviet Union was liable for failure to warn other states. Space does not permit a complete analysis of those complex issues.[53] We focus on the question of notification and warning.

At the time of the Chernobyl disaster, there apparently was no international agreement requiring the Soviet Union to notify other countries of the potential harm and inform them of the details of that harm. The Soviet Union is a party to the Convention on Long-Range Transboundary Air Pollution of 1979, whose definition of air pollution would include the effects of Chernobyl. The convention's obligations to prevent and inform, however, primarily aim at reducing continuous transboundary air pollution from ordinary sources. Some provisions apply only to sulfur dioxide emissions.

Whether customary international law included a duty to inform at the time of Chernobyl is subject to dispute. Most Western commentators would contend that there was such a duty. The Soviet Union, with its more positivist view of law, argued the contrary position and thus that the Soviet Union did not violate international law in not warning potentially affected states.

In the case of Chernobyl, warning clearly would have made a difference. For example, radioactive materials can affect people via a number of routes including direct skin contact from and inhalation of materials lying on the ground and kicked up as dust; and ingestion of food or water contaminated by radioactive materials. A state warned of the imminent arrival of airborne radioactive materials can instruct its residents to stay indoors and avoid ingesting certain foods that are likely to be contaminated (e.g., milk or leafy vegetables). In addition, more aggressive steps may be taken, such as providing iodine pills to minimize the intake of radioactive iodine 131, which has a half-life of only eight days and which, together with cesium 137 and strontium 90, is one of the three most common and dangerous radioactive elements emitted at Chernobyl.

The Soviet Union's failure to warn was morally abhorrent. It seems certain that there will be a greater incidence of cancer, leukemia, and genetic mutation as a result of that failure than would have happened if timely notification had occurred—and notification could have been accomplished easily and inexpensively. In spite of this, there may not be a legal remedy if the Soviet Union did not violate international law.

In order to deal with the notification questions highlighted by the Chernobyl experience, a new treaty on notification was drafted at a special August 1986 meeting of the International Atomic Energy Agency (IAEA).[54] That convention has been signed by fifty-eight states, including the United States and the Soviet Union, and is now in force. The Soviet Union agreed to comply with the convention provisionally, pending ratification. Consistent with that, the Soviet Union complied with the notification provisions when a Soviet nuclear submarine foundered in the Atlantic in the fall of 1986. This shows that it is relatively easy to produce a new international agreement if (1) the need is clear (especially from a recent "lesson"), (2) an appropriate institutional structure is available, and (3) the costs of compliance are relatively low (e.g., mere notification of other states in possible cases in the future).

The convention applies to any "accident involving [nuclear facilities] from which a release of radioactive material occurs or is likely to occur and which has resulted or may result in an international transboundary release that could be of radiological safety significance for another State." The scope of the convention is thus quite broad. The convention provides two duties: (1) In the event of a nuclear accident covered by the scope provision just quoted, the state has a duty to notify "forthwith" states of the accident, its nature, the time of its occurrence, and its exact location where appropriate; (2) the state also has a duty to provide "promptly" a variety of specified "available" information relevant to minimizing the radiological consequences of the accident in those states. The convention also contains a provision for dispute settlement, but many states, including the United States and the Soviet Union, have indicated that they will refuse to be bound by that provision.

Many questions remain about the convention. For example, is there any implied national security exception? What do the requirements of "forthwith" notifying and "promptly" providing information actually entail? And what does "available" information imply with respect to a possible duty to collect pertinent information? Moreover, the convention could and should be strengthened in certain ways—regarding dispute settlement, for example. The Notification Convention is an important step in the right direction, but it should not be allowed to impede other, more forceful action in the future.

Related to the possible duty to warn on the part of the source state is a possible duty of a downstream state to assist the source state in the event of a nuclear accident. A duty to assist is a concomitant to the duty to warn and the duty to prevent because those duties exist in part in order to protect the interests of the potentially assisting state. No such duty is currently established by international law with respect to nuclear power, although states were relatively quick to offer assistance to, and respond to requests for assistance from, the Soviet Union. International organizations and private persons also became involved, especially in the provision of medical care.

A convention to address this need, referred to as the Assistance Convention, was adopted at an International Atomic Energy Agency meeting in September 1986.[55] The convention has been signed by fifty-seven states, including the United States and the Soviet Union. It provides a general obligation to cooperate to facilitate prompt assistance in the event of a "nuclear accident or radiological emergency to minimize its consequences and to protect life, property and the environment from the effects of radioactive releases." The convention also specifies various procedures for such things as providing assistance and being reimbursed.

The 1982 Law of the Sea Convention

The law of the sea has been a major focus of the international legal system since at least the time of Hugo Grotius (1583–1645). Customary law developed first and was quite sophisticated by the beginning of the present century. The four 1958 conventions on the high seas, continental shelf, maritime fisheries, and territorial sea, drafted initially by the UN International Law Commission and finalized at the First UN Conference on the Law of the Sea, were quite extensive but left open several questions, the most important of which concerned the breadth of the territorial sea. That issue came within one vote of being resolved at the Second UN Conference on the Law of the Sea (1960), but ultimately was not decided.

The Third UN Conference on the Law of the Sea (1973–82) began with the territorial sea issue and a few others, but quickly turned into a total reexamination of the law of the sea, including some new and very sensitive issues, such as deep-seabed mining. To the astonishment of many, the Third Conference eventually resulted in a comprehensive treaty acceptable to nearly every country in the world—the only real exceptions were the United States (under the Reagan administration) and several of its allies.

The 1982 Law of the Sea Convention[56] is remarkable in several respects. First, it is widely believed that the reason agreement was possible on so many critical and divisive issues—including such vital national security issues as the right of transit by military vessels through narrow straits—was precisely that there were so many of them; they cut so many ways and so differently that voting blocs could not and did not materialize. Allies on one issue were opponents on another. And creative statesmanship and negotiating, rather than chaos, resulted.[57] Certain combinations of environmental issues may have this potential, as well, for example, a comprehensive law of the atmosphere.

Second, the convention met squarely the issue of how to treat LDCs with respect to the environment. Basically, with the exception of one aspect of land-based pollution,[58] the result was that LDCs and more developed countries must meet the same standard of care, but the more developed are obligated to assist LDCs in meeting that standard.[59] The standards are phrased, however, so that the economic status and capabilities of the state in question might affect the precise behavior required by the standard.[60] This may be a model for other environmental treaties, although the Montreal ozone protocol took a different approach.[61]

Third, the convention dealt with a global commons and established, *inter alia*, a new institution to govern part of that commons (i.e., deepseabed mining), as well as a specialized body to settle disputes. These steps are unprecedented and bode well for future attempts to deal with environmental problems.

Finally, although the convention is not yet in force, the process of drafting and finalizing it had the result of crystallizing many norms of customary international law. Even the United States takes the position that the convention, for the most part, states customary international law. The potential significance of such conferences in this respect should be kept in mind because it may make possible progress on otherwise intractable issues.

Conclusion

We have tried to show that there are neither theoretical nor practical reasons for thinking that international solutions to transboundary environmental problems are impossible or extremely unlikely. This is not to suggest, of course, that such solutions will come easily, particularly when dealing with problems that require large expenditures for success. Unfortunately, both acid deposition and climate change—two key transboundary environmental problems—are likely to require very large expenditures for amelioration. The Hobbesian and Lockean problems of the international system, among others, clearly make cooperative action more difficult. We have seen, however, that these problems can often be circumvented even in the absence of a central political authority at the international level. Sidestepping these problems is not just a theoretical possibility; it actually occurred in the three examples presented in the previous section. It is important not to be naively optimistic about the prospects for international action on environmental problems. But it is also important that the alleged impossibility of international action on transboundary environmental problems not be used as an excuse for failing to initiate and support such action.

Notes

1. International Joint Commission (Canada–United States), *Impacts of a Proposed Coal Mine in the Flathead River Basin* (December 1988), 11; Flathead River International Study Board, *Flathead River International Study: Board Report* (July 1988); Flathead River International Study Board, *Flathead River International Study: Board Supplementary Report* (June 1988).

2. *Military and Paramilitary Activities in and Against Nicaragua* (*Nicaragua v. United States*), Merits, 1986 ICJ 14 (Judgment of June 27). Hereafter cited as *Activities, Nicaragua*.

3. *Montreal Protocol on Substances That Deplete the Ozone Layer*, September 16, 1987, reprinted in *International Environment Reporter* 21 (1988): 3151. Hereafter cited as *Montreal Protocol*.

4. Daniel Magraw, "Transboundary Harm: The International Law Commission's Study of 'International Liability,'" *American Journal of International Law* 80 (1986): 322.

5. *North Sea Continental Shelf* (*West Germany v. Denmark; West Germany v. Netherlands*), 1969 ICJ 3 (Judgment of February 20).

6. Moreover, the test has recently been applied in the *Military Activities* case; see note 1, at para. 186 and 207, in a manner suggesting that it may have changed.

7. ICJ Statute, Art. 38.

8. But cf. *Restatement (Third) of the Foreign Relations Law of the United States*, sec. 102(d) (1987) (describing this as a "subsidiary" source of law).

9. Louis Henkin, Richard Pugh, Oscar Schacter, and Hans Smit, *International Law, Cases and Materials*, 2d ed. (St. Paul, Minn.: West, 1987), 70.

10. See Congressional Research Service, Library of Congress, *Treaties and Other International Agreements: The Role of the United States Senate* (study prepared for the Senate Committee on Foreign Relations), S. Pvt. 205, 98th Cong., 2d sess. 39 (Comm. Print 1984).

11. See, e.g., *Survey of State Practice Relevant to International Liability for Injurious Consequences Arising out of Acts Not Prohibited by International Law* (prepared by UN Secretariat), 14–18, 30, 211, UN Doc. ST/LEG/15 (1984).

12. The idea of associating familiar problems in the international system with the philosophies of Hobbes and Locke was suggested by Oran R. Young, "On the Performance of the International Polity," *British Journal of International Studies* 4 (1984): 315–30.

13. Thomas Hobbes, *Leviathan* (1649), chap. 13 An accessible edition is *Leviathan*, ed. M. Oakeshott (New York: Oxford University Press, 1947).

14. This version of the Prisoners' Dilemma is adapted from David Gauthier, *Morals by Agreement* (New York: Oxford University Press, 1986), 79–80 For a more elaborate discussion of the Prisoners' Dilemma in the context of international relations generally, see Kenneth Abbot, "Modern International Relations Theory: A Prospectus for International Lawyers," *Yale Journal of International Law* 14 (1989): 701.

15. John Locke, *The Second Treatise of Government* (1690). A contemporary edition is edited by Thomas P. Peardon (New York: Macmillan, 1952).

16. Ibid., chap. 9.

17. UN Charter, Arts. 33–51. That the authority was used once (in Korea) occurred because the USSR boycotted the meeting, an event that is not likely to be repeated.

18. *Treaty on Principles Governing the Activities of States in the Exploration and Use of Outer Space, Including the Moon and Other Celestial Bodies*, Art. IX, January 27, 1967, 18 U.S.T. 2410, T.I.A.S. No. 6347, 610 U.N.T.S. 205.

19. *Montreal Protocol*.

20. Nelson Horn and Clive Schmitthoff, *The Transnational Law of International Commercial Transactions* (Kluwer Law Netherlands, 1982), 25.

21. *Activities, Nicaragua*, para. 188, 191, 203.

22. Even mediation might resolve some disputes. See John Dryzek and Susan Hunter, "Environmental Mediation for International Problems," *International Studies Quarterly* 31 (1987): 87.

23. See, generally, The World Commission on Environment and Development, *Our Common Future* (1987); Independent Commission on International Development Issues, *North–South: A Programme for Survival* (Cambridge, Mass.: MIT Press, 1980).

24. Locke, *Second Treatise*, chap. 5, sec. 27. For a discussion of the "enough and as good" proviso, see Robert Nozick, *Anarchy, State and Utopia* (New York: Basic Books, 1974).

25. See, e.g., *UN Convention on the Law of the Sea*, opened for signature December 10, 1982, Arts. 151(2), 207(4), reprinted in *International Legal Materials* 21 (1982): 1262.

26. John Dryzek, *Rational Ecology* (Oxford: Basil Blackwell, 1987).

27. Mark Sagoff, "At the Shrine of Our Lady of Fatima, or Why Political Questions Are Not All Economic," *Arizona Law Review* 23 (1981): 1283.

28. E. Brown Weiss, *In Fairness to Future Generations: International Law, Common Patrimony, and Intergenerational Equity* (Dobbs Ferry, N.Y.: Transnational, 1989).

29. Tom Regan, *The Case for Animal Rights* (Berkeley: University of California Press, 1983); Christopher D. Stone, *Should Trees Have Standing? Toward Legal Rights for Natural Objects* (Los Altos, Calif.: William Kaufman, 1974).

30. John Dryzek, "Ecological Rationality," *International Journal of Environmental Studies* 21 (1983): 5. See also Dryzek and Hunter, "Environmental Mediation" (advocating mediation of transboundary environmental problems).

31. *Treaty Relating to the Boundary Waters and Questions Arising Along the Boundary between the United States and Canada*, January 11, 1909, United States–Canada, 36 Stat. 2448, T.S. No. 548. For a discussion of the United States–Mexico environmental relationship, see Stephen McCaffrey, "Transboundary Environmental Relations between Mexico and the United States," in *Transatlantic Colloquy on Cross-Border Relations: European and North American Perspectives*, ed. S. Ercmann (Zurich, 1977).

32. For a more detailed description of the IJC, see Richard B. Bilder, "When Neighbors Quarrel: Canada–U.S. Dispute-Settlement Experience," Institute for Legal Studies, University of Wisconsin–Madison Law School, May 1987, 54–60. The Claude T. Bissell Lectures, University of Toronto 1986–87. Disputes Processing Research Program, Working Papers Series 8. There are now more than a dozen binational commissions or other joint bodies established by Canada and the United States to resolve disputes. Ibid., 54.

33. *Convention Concerning the Protection of the World Cultural and Natural Heritage*, November 16, 1972, 27 U.S.T. 37, T.I.A.S. No. 8226.

34. See UNESCO, "Action Plan for Biosphere Reserves," *Nature and Resources* 20 (October–December 1984).

35. International Joint Commission, *Proposed Coal Mine in the Flathead River Basin*.

36. See Joint News Release of British Columbia Ministry of the Environment and City of Seattle, "Skagit Details Released," April 14, 1983.

37. *Agreement Relating to the Establishment of a Canada–United States Committee on Water Quality*, September 21, 1972, United States–Canada, 23 U.S.T. 2813, T.I.A.S. No. 7470; *Agreement on Great Lakes Water Quality*, November 22, 1978, United States–Canada, 30 U.S.T. 1383, T.I.A.S. No. 9257.

38. *Delimitation of the Maritime Boundary in the Gulf of Maine Area* (*Canada* v. *U.S.*), 1984 ICJ 246 (Judgment of October 12).

39. *Trail Smelter* (*U.S.* v. *Canada*), 3 R. Int'l Arb. Awards 1905 (1938 and 1941). The United States and Canada have submitted approximately twenty disputes of various types of binding arbitration. Bilder, "When Neighbors Quarrel," 43.

40. *Trail Smelter*, 1965.

41. *Corfu Channel* (*U.K.* v. *Albania*), 1949 ICJ 4 (Judgment of April 9).

42. *Lac Lanoux* (*France* v. *Spain*), 12 R. Int'l Arb. Awards 281 (1957) (French), reprinted in *International Law Review* 24 (1957): 101 (English).

43. *Nuclear Tests* (*Australia* v. *France*), 1974 ICJ 253 (Judgment of December 20); *Nuclear Tests* (*New Zealand* v. *France*), 1974 ICJ 457 (Judgment of December 20).

44. Gunther Handl, *Transboundary Resources in North America: Prospects for a Comprehensive Management Regime*, in *Transboundary Air Pollution*, ed. C. Flinterman, B. Kwiatkowska, and J. Lammers (Martinus Nijhoff, 1986), 72–73.

45. Clean Air Amendments of 1970, 42 U.S.C. sec. 1857 (1982) (amending 42 U.S.C. sec. 1857 [1967]).

46. Clean Air Act (Canada, 1971), chap. 47.

47. *Memorandum of Intent Concerning Transboundary Air Pollution*, August 5, 1980, United States–Canada, 32 U.S.T. 2521, T.I.A.S. No. 9856.

48. See *Thomas* v. *New York*, 802 F. 2d 1443 (D.C. Cir. 1986); Handl, *Transboundary Resources*, 75–76.

49. Drew Lewis and William Davis, *Joint Report of the Special Envoys on Acid Rain* (Washington, D.C.: U.S. Department of State, January 1986).

50. Remarks by Edward Lee, Legal Adviser and Assistant Deputy Minister for Legal, Consular, and Immigration Affairs, Canadian Department of External Affairs, August 7, 1988.

51. Remarks by Scott Hajost, Deputy Associate Administrator for International Activities, U.S. Environmental Protection Agency, "Legal Implications of U.S. Policy on Acid Deposition," August 7, 1988.

52. Tom Wicker, "Who'll Stop the Rain?" *New York Times*, June 16, 1989, A15; "Economic Watch: Sale of Air Pollution Permits Is Part of Bush Acid Rain Plan," *New York Times*, May 18, 1989, A13.

53. For discussions of the legal issues raised by Chernobyl, see Richard Levy, "International Law and the Chernobyl Accident: Reflections on an Important but Imperfect System," *Kansas Law Review* 36 (1987): 81; and Linda Malone, "The Chernobyl Accident: A Case Study in International Law Regulating State Responsibility for Transboundary Nuclear Pollution," *Columbia Journal of Environmental Law* 12 (1987): 203. See also Anthony D'Amato and Kirsten Engel, "State Responsibility for the Exportation of Nuclear Power Technology," *Virginia Law Review* 74 (1988): 1011

54. IAEA, *Convention on Early Notification of a Nuclear Accident*, September 26, 1986, reprinted in *International Legal Materials* 25 (1986): 1369; Andronico Adede, *The IAEA Notification and Assistance Conventions in Case of a Nuclear Accident* (1987).

55. IAEA, *Convention on Assistance in the Case of a Nuclear Accident or Radiological Emergency*, September 26, 1986, reprinted in *International Legal Materials* 25 (1986): 1377. In a sense, the converse of the duty to assist—if and when it exists—may be a duty to accept help on the part of the state in which the nuclear accident occurs. International law has made few strides in this area, but this is a topic that deserves attention.

56. *UN Convention on the Law of the Sea.*

57. For a description of the events leading up to that conference and the negotiating process at the conference, see William Wertenbaker, "A Reporter at Large: Law of the Sea," *New Yorker*, August 1, 1983, 38, and *New Yorker*, August 8, 1983, 56.

58. See *UN Convention on the Law of the Sea*, Art. 207 (in endeavoring to establish regional and global approaches to land-based marine pollution, states shall "take into account characteristic regional features, the economic capacity of developing States and their need for economic development").

59. Ibid., Arts. 203, 204.

60. See, e.g., ibid. "States shall take . . . all measures . . . necessary to prevent, reduce and control pollution of the marine environment from any source, using for this purpose the best practicable means at their disposal with their capabilities."

61. See *Montreal Protocol*, Arts. 2, 5.

Chapter 6

Takings, Just Compensation, and the Environment

"The power vested in the American courts of justice of pronouncing a statute to be unconstitutional," Alexis de Tocqueville wrote, "forms one of the most powerful barriers that have ever been devised against the tyranny of political assemblies."[1] Judges apply this power to environmental law in many ways, but especially when they review zoning ordinances and statutes that restrict the uses of property.

Everyone who owns property has the duty, of course, to exercise his or her property rights in ways that respect the similar rights of others. In addition to this basic duty, political assemblies have gone far—perhaps too far—in obliging landowners, for example, to maintain the integrity of landmarks and scenic areas,[2] to refrain from filling wetlands,[3] to preserve open space,[4] to restore mined land to its original contours,[5] to maintain habitat for endangered species,[6] to allow public access to waterways and beaches,[7] to leave minerals in place to support surface structures,[8] and so on.[9] Landowners often ask judges to review these statutes on constitutional grounds.[10]

State and local governments, in general, impose these duties on landowners by regulation rather than by exercising eminent domain. States prefer regulation to condemnation so that they do not have to compensate landowners for the substantial losses in market value that often accompany the duties and restrictions statutes place on them. Governments may attempt to dedicate property to public use, then, not by taking property rights through eminent domain, but by regulating those rights away and, therefore, without compensating owners for the market value of those rights.

Courts are then called on to decide whether a statute that imposes public-spirited duties on property owners complies with the Fifth Amendment of the Constitution, which provides that "private property [shall not] be taken for public use, without just compensation."[11] When courts sustain these statutes and ordinances on constitutional grounds, as they frequently do,[12] local governments gain an important legal weapon for protecting the aesthetic, cultural, historical, and ecological values that often attract people and, therefore, subdividers and developers to a region. If the courts sheathe this legal weapon, however, society may have to kiss these values good-bye, since it can neither afford to exercise eminent domain to purchase the property in question nor can it depend, except in a limited way, on private action in common-law courts to protect these values.

When does a regulatory "taking" of property require the state to pay compensation, and when not? Justice Oliver Wendell Holmes, in a leading case decided in 1922, asserted that "this is a question of degree—and therefore cannot be disposed of by general propositions."[13] The absence of such propositions, that is, the lack of a theory on which to decide cases, has characterized "just compensation" jurisprudence for more than half a century. Commentators generally describe this area of law as a "muddle,"[14] a "crazy quilt,"[15] "unilluminating,"[16] "ad hoc,"[17] "confused,"[18] "baffling,"[19] "mystifying,"[20] and "chaotic."[21] In 1987, Justice John Paul Stevens summarized: "Even the wisest lawyers would have to acknowledge great uncertainty about the scope of this Court's takings jurisprudence."[22]

In recent years, several academic lawyers have analyzed takings law to try to define a theory on which future jurisprudence might be based.[23] Such an analysis could succeed, I think, if it (1) rests on acceptable normative and constitutional principles and (2) is not so inconsistent with existing case law that it requires a dramatic rescission of environmental statutes and ordinances now generally thought to be constitutionally sound.

In this chapter, I want to suggest a line of analysis that will satisfy these conditions. I argue that compensation need not attend a regulation that takes property rights unless it also burdens some individuals unfairly to benefit other individuals or the public as a whole. The "takings" question, in other words, may not depend fundamentally on an analysis of property rights; instead, it may depend on a conception of justice.

Pragmatic versus Theoretical Decision Making

Zoning is ubiquitous. Every state restricts the ways in which property owners can develop their land, especially in sensitive areas such as in flood plains, coastal zones, and agricultural districts. When such a restriction causes the market value of parcels of land to fall, the owners may believe that their land is being dedicated to a public use, for which the public ought to pay. They may then go to court to seek damages under the Fifth Amendment of the Constitution.

In one such case, *Just* v. *Marinette County*, the Supreme Court of Wisconsin upheld a zoning ordinance that prevented owners of a coastal marsh from using landfill on their property and thus from developing it for commercial purposes. The court held that the "takings" clause of the Constitution does not protect an interest, however profitable, in "destroying the natural character of a swamp or a wetland so as to make that location available for human habitation."[24] Citizens have no claim for compensation, the court reasoned, when an ordinance restricts their use of their land "to prevent a harm from the change in the natural character of the citizens' property."[25]

Ellen Frankel Paul, in her timely and well-argued book *Property Rights and Eminent Domain*,[26] points out that decisions such as *Just* strike "at the very heart of the property rights conception—that what is mine may be used by me as I see fit provided only that I not use it in a manner that violates the like right of other owners" (p. 138). Paul notes that by filling in his wetland, Mr. Just did not threaten the rights of others; he merely set about improving the economic utility of his land, just as many others had done up and down the coast.

Paul accepts common law, particularly tort, as the test for determining when a person uses his or her property in a way consistent with the rights of others. As she says, the concept of harm to others that limits the rights of landowners "would have to be comparable to a harm recognized in the tort law" (p. 139). Would filling the wetland cause an injury to anyone sufficient to give him or her standing to sue in common law? What sort of right could anyone assert as a matter of common law to enjoin Mr. Just from filling in his marsh?

Paul argues that nothing in nuisance, tort, or anywhere in common-law suggests a basis for such an injunction. For more than a century, the public, for aesthetic, sanitary, economic, and other reasons, encouraged landowners to fill in swamps. Now, the public (for the same reasons) wants to keep remaining wetlands wet. This may be a valid objective; the public may legitimately change its values. Society may correctly believe that it now benefits many localities more from scenic and open space than from condominiums and commercial strips.

The question is whether the state may legitimately force Mr. Just and others like him to provide *gratis* the scenic, ecological, and perhaps moral benefits the public gains from the presence of open and undeveloped land. Should the state instead compensate Mr. Just for his financial loss or, if the government cannot afford to pay, allow him peacefully to develop his wetland?

Richard Epstein, in *Takings: Private Property and the Power of Eminent Domain*, analyzes this case in the same way. He observes that the plaintiff, by filling in his wetland, might pollute his own property, but he threatens others with no harm cognizable in common law. Epstein argues that "the normal bundle of property rights contains no priority for land in its natural condition; it regards use, including development, as one of the standard incidents of ownership."

By building on their marsh, the plaintiffs do only what their neighbors had already done; no one would have a case against them in common law. Epstein concludes: "Stripped of its rhetoric, *Just* is a condemnation of these property rights, and compensation is thus required."[27]

Ellen Paul's *Property Rights and Eminent Domain* and Richard Epstein's *Takings* endorse a theory of natural property rights, at the heart of which is the principle that people may use their property as they see fit as long as they respect the same rights and liberties of others. Both authors deplore the legal doctrine dominant in "takings" cases for sixty years, since it fails to recognize the existence of "natural" property rights; in fact, it rejects that theory out of hand. In place of this theory, the dominant doctrine, formulated by Justice Holmes, has called for ad hoc, case-by-case decision making, an approach that attempts to determine a fair or just outcome in the circumstances of each suit, without relying or even speculating on a general theory or conception of property rights.

So both Paul and Epstein confront and oppose the pragmatic, case-by-case approach taken by the U.S. Supreme Court and many state courts. They are outraged that these courts routinely uphold legislation that plainly contravenes the theory of natural property rights they espouse. They argue that these courts should overturn their precedents to give legal force to that theory, especially the "core" freedom to do as one wishes with one's property as long as one remains within the constraints of common law. And they find thoroughly offensive the courts' refusal to advance a theory or conception of property—*any* theory—in cases brought under the Fifth Amendment of the Constitution.

Two questions arise, then, that Paul and Epstein must answer. First, is the pragmatic, case-by-case approach unworkable, unfair, or otherwise flawed in itself? In other words, does Paul or Epstein offer telling arguments against current practice per se and thus show that it must change to base itself on some theory of property? Or do they condemn it only because it does not accommodate the theory of "natural" property rights they believe to be correct?

Second, let us suppose that the courts reach principled and equitable, if pragmatic, resolutions of "takings" cases. Let us suppose that the principles on which the courts rely, while not unjust or unworkable in themselves, do not recognize but implicitly reject the theory of natural property rights Paul and Epstein espouse. Has this theory such a deep philosophical and constitutional basis that courts should adopt it, even if the pragmatic approach works well enough? The importance of these two books depends on how well they respond to these questions.

What Is Wrong with Current Practice?

The courts now follow a reasonably predictable course in "takings" jurisprudence—although not the one Paul and Epstein recommend. Courts at present view justice in this area as a privative virtue, which is to say, they overturn legislation only if it commits one of a list of specific injustices—for example, if it is intended (or plainly functions) to exclude racial groups from particular localities. Courts ask a series of ad hoc questions: Does the regulation physically remove the owner from the land? or deprive the owner of substantially all reasonable use of it?

Does the regulation fail to advance a legitimate public interest in a way rationally and closely related to the proscribed use? Does the restriction work unfairly to burden a few landowners to benefit a few others? Was the owner prevented from representing his or her interests in the political process? Has the government, through zoning, merely attempted to lower the market value of the land to make it cheaper to condemn?

Courts address "takings" cases with an ad hoc, pragmatic checklist of questions such as these—all of which are well known—reflecting a variety of moral, policy, and equity considerations. These questions go to the fairness and legitimacy of the statutes landowners challenge, but they pay little or no attention to any theory of property rights.

Courts rely on well-known ad hoc principles or rules of thumb, such as those these questions suggest, to determine whether the interests of the property owner have received a fair shake. The courts also take notice of the political and civil rights of various parties affected by a statute (e.g., the rights of minorities to live where they wish, the rights of individuals to political representation). In "takings" cases, courts mull over questions involving fairness, justice, and personal, civil, and political rights before making their decisions. But in answering these questions, the courts do not address or appear to want or need to address a theory of property rights.

Since lawyers know the kinds of questions the courts will ask—for example, whether a statute is "exclusionary," "extortionary," or "confiscatory"—they nearly always formulate zoning ordinances to survive this kind of review. As a result, the outcome of "takings" or "inverse condemnation" proceedings is generally predictable. Absent some special infirmity in the law (e.g., it may be plainly extortionary), the decision will go against the plaintiff.

Jurisdictions, then, through zoning and other ordinances, routinely succeed in vastly restricting the otherwise permissible ways landowners might use their land. And a good lawyer will tell aggrieved landowners not to bother to challenge a properly drafted statute because the courts will routinely and predictably uphold it, even though it makes a mockery out of the notion of natural property rights.

As Paul notes, "takings" jurisprudence, which routinely upholds zoning regulations in this way, strikes "at the very heart of the property rights conception." She is right. Should judges take the theory of natural property rights seriously? May they instead properly remain indifferent to that theory and, indeed, to all theorizing about property and property rights?

Professor Paul proposes that the case-by-case, pragmatic, ad hoc decision making that characterizes "takings" jurisprudence "has simply not worked" (p. 188). She offers three arguments to support this contention.

First, Paul proposes that current jurisprudence puts too much power in the hands of politicians, who may next decide, for example, where each citizen will live. "The slippery slope is real, and it is alarming" (p. 192). Paul relies on this "slippery slope" appeal to dispatch what she sees, correctly, as her main opponent, namely, pragmatic modern liberalism. "If liberals are absolutists about any political value, it is certainly not property." Paul adds: "Modern liberalism . . . holds that civil rights can be separated from property rights. For modern liberals like John Dewey, property rights are relatively unimportant. A democratic society can flourish by protecting civil rights while not unduly concerning itself with property rights" (p. 190). Paul fails to provide, however, a single example of the reality of this slippery slope—an instance in which a judge or other public official moved in practice from "takings" precedents to a denial of civil, political, or personal rights. On the contrary, while the U.S. Supreme Court in its "takings" jurisprudence, over the last sixty years, may have kicked property rights into a cocked hat, the same Court has greatly advanced political, civil, and personal rights and liberties against the government. Perhaps Paul believes that the latter rights are connected, logically or empirically, with rights, for example, to develop one's marsh for commercial use. But no argument in her book, or anywhere else, as far as I know, demonstrates such a connection.

The second argument appeals to authority: "Virtually everyone admits that this area of the law is in a chaotic state" (p. 188). The third argument asserts that the pragmatic approach fails "to develop a sound theoretical underpinning for property rights" (p. 185).

These last two arguments are correct as far as they go. Commentators on "takings" jurisprudence, including Supreme Court justices, describe it as chaotic. Yet "takings" doctrine has given predictable results: The property owner will lose unless some special injustice, from an ad hoc but well-known list, has been done. If it is predictable and consistent, how, then, has it failed? People describe it as chaotic—but why should they?

The principal reason Paul, Epstein, and others believe that pragmatic, ad hoc jurisprudence is chaotic, as far as I can tell, is that it is ad hoc and pragmatic. They think it is bad for an important area of constitutional property law to fail to develop a sound theoretical underpinning for property rights. But why? If "takings" jurisprudence relies on an ad hoc, pragmatic list of reasonable concerns, why do judges need to indulge in theorizing? Academics theorize as a condition of getting tenure, of course, but justices already have lifetime terms.

The answer to the question whether the pragmatic, case-by-case approach fails may depend on the answer to the second question, namely, whether a different basis—one residing in deep philosophical principles—can and should be found. "I will argue that natural rights provides a consistent theory of property rights," Paul says, "and that a theory of property rights is essential for extricating ourselves from this impasse" (p. 188).

Paul versus Epstein

I want to mention here reasons I believe Paul's *Property Rights and Eminent Domain* is not only an excellent book but is also better argued than Epstein's *Takings*. First, Epstein makes no attempt whatever to show that current jurisprudence has failed in its own terms, that is, failed to provide a workable, predictable resolution of controversies arising under the Fifth Amendment. Instead, Epstein merely reviews a large number of legal decisions, shows that they make mincemeat of the theory of natural property rights, and then rebukes the judges for being such jerks. If you, poor reader, are among the damned who have not seen the divine light of natural property rights theory, Epstein regards you—along with Congress, the courts, state legislatures, municipal authorities, and other sinners—with contempt. Contempt, however, is not argument, and that is the problem with Epstein's treatise.

Paul, on the contrary, does not preach only to the saved. She recognizes that her opponents may favor current jurisprudence for initially plausible reasons, for example, to prevent "irreversible loss of agricultural land, estuaries, wetlands, and open space, and the wasteful consumption of energy" (p. 192). Paul believes that it may be more important for the law to protect natural property rights than to protect nature beyond the limits of tort. Unlike Epstein, she recognizes, however, that the truth of this belief is not self-evident.

Second, Paul clearly recognizes what Epstein only occasionally glimpses, namely, the strict incompatibility and antagonism between utilitarian and libertarian approaches to property rights. The old utilitarians, such as Jeremy Bentham, thought that governments create and protect property rights for purposes of utility maximization; Bentham described talk of natural rights as "nonsense on stilts." When property rights get in the way of the aggregate public interest (as they presumably do in "takings" cases), then it is property rights rather than the general welfare that must give way. Any intellectually honest utilitarian or utility maximizer must agree with Bentham on this point.

Chicago School utilitarians, who would maximize a form of utility Richard Posner calls "wealth," are driven to Bentham's conclusion. They would defend property rights, not as a matter of principle or of basic justice (as Paul would), but only insofar as that policy might promote the efficient allocation of resources. Owing to market failures, bargaining costs, holdouts, and everything else, however, governments may generally achieve greater efficiency through cost–benefit planning than by allowing free exchange. Paul notes correctly that the "wealth-maximization" or "efficiency" view presupposes the communistic fiction that everyone wants the same thing, namely, efficient allocation, and thus it encourages experts to override individual rights to provide it. "It is ironic that a view that sincerely intends to be supportive of individualism and property rights, is actually collectivist, and just as aggregative as utilitarianism" (p. 217).

Paul has replied to Epstein in other places, showing that utilitarian goals, such as wealth maximization, conflict just as thoroughly as any other centralized statist program with a regime of natural property rights.[28] Her discussion of this issue (pp. 212–24), which includes a devastating reply to Posner's conception of *ex ante* compensation, may be the best in the literature.

Epstein, after a wave of the hand to Locke, assumes that every well-socialized individual knows that property rights are natural rights—and he is off and running. Paul, in contrast, recognizes that "the advocates of natural rights did fail to provide a logical, internally consistent, deductive defense of these rights. Bentham certainly has his point" (p. 188). Thus, Paul attempts to argue for the fundamental thesis that Epstein merely assumes, namely, that property rights are natural rights.

She attempts "to supply the natural rights theory of property with such a deductive defense," which, she hopes, will be persuasive to those, like Bentham, "who are highly skeptical of 'metaphysical rights'" (p. 188). How successful, then, is her argument for natural property rights?

The Argument for Natural Property Rights

Paul's argument for natural property rights, although at times hard to follow, seems to depend on two plausible principles. First, following Locke, she reasons that every human being has a natural right to acquire from the commons such commodities as are necessary to his or her survival. "Man must labor," Paul points out, "in order to attain the rudiments necessary for his survival" (p. 226). Second, following Locke, Paul argues that everyone has a fundamental property right to anything useful that person creates through his or her labor and ingenuity. She asserts "that the person who creates X ought to own X" (p. 232).

While both principles are familiar and plausible, they do not entail anything about compensation in "takings" cases. How does Professor Paul get from a natural right to own what one creates and/or needs for survival to a doctrine about just compensation in "takings" cases? Let us grant that individuals have a natural right to the products they create and/or need in order to survive. How does this show that the government should compensate Mr. Just when an ordinance against certain kinds of development lowers the market value of his land?

While the answer to this question is by no means evident, Paul introduces two further premises. First, she rejects as "artificial" any "distinction between necessities and luxuries" (p. 236). "After all, who is to judge which are goods necessary for survival and which are luxuries?" Paul asks. "Such a task would entail the existence of a godlike omniscience, or else the moral system would hinge on caprice" (p. 234).

Second, Paul emphasizes this principle: "All value is the artifact of some purposive activity on the part of the individual." She continues: "What I am arguing goes one step beyond Locke, who contended, alternately, that nine-tenths or ninety-nine hundredths of the value of any commodity was the handiwork of man rather than nature. *I maintain that 100 percent of the value of a good is the work of human activity*" (p. 230).

Any real estate agent will tell you that there are three determinants of the market value of real property: location, location, and location. None of these depends on the labor, ingenuity, or creativity of the property owner. Henry George adopted his radical views about land tenure in part because he saw the price of property go up tenfold overnight when the government announced its plan to extend the railroad to a section of California. The lucky owners, far from laboring for their survival, were asleep at the time. They woke up to find that the government, by creating a railroad, highway, park, or whatever, had instantly multiplied the price at which they might sell their land.

had instantly multiplied the price at which they might sell their land.

Paul counters such an objection in advance by writing: "I am not talking about market value (or price) and how it is determined on a free market" (p. 231). She adds, in words that might warm the heart of any defender of current "takings" practice:

> Each person has a perpetual property rights in that which he or she has created, that is, in the values produced. Your right, then, is to the object or process itself, and not to the market value or price, which is nothing more than the appraisal in the minds of others, at the margin, of the value to them of your good. The preference orders of others are beyond your control, and form no part of your entitlement (p. 234).

If Paul is not concerned with market value, then, it seems, she would have little to say on behalf of Mr. Just, who sued for the difference between the price he could get for his land before and after the zoning ordinance. He had made no use of his land—he had invested no labor or ingenuity in processing it—and he still possessed the object itself. The entire value of the land that Mr. Just sued to recover was market value: the value the land would have, as a matter of speculation, if it could be developed for commercial or residential purposes. On Paul's account, then, Mr. Just would have no entitlement to this value, since it is the creation not necessarily of his own action, but of the preferences of others.

All or nearly all zoning ordinances maintain the kind of property right that Paul defends. Statutes and regulations uniformly "grandfather" every existing use that cannot be construed as creating a nuisance. Current "takings" jurisprudence respects the sort of property right a person has to the products of his or her own labor—or at least Paul provides no evidence to the contrary. Accordingly, Paul's interesting defense of property rights seems to support, or at least not to undermine, current pragmatic, ad hoc, case-by-case approaches to "just" compensation under the Fifth Amendment of the Constitution.

Does the Right to Develop Imply
a Right to Destroy?

As we have seen, Professor Paul distinguishes between "use value (i.e., the utility of a thing) and market value (or price)" (p. 230). While Paul does not develop this distinction, there are familiar examples of it. Water and air, for example, have high use values, since life cannot go on without them. Yet air and water are so plentiful in most localities that they have a low market value or price.

Land also has value both as an object of use and an object of exchange and speculation. The use value of a wetland consists, for example, in the many services and benefits it provides to the public. These include its function in the tertiary treatment of wastes, in the control of floods, in providing habitat for fish and wildlife, and so on. Wetlands tend also to be beautiful ecosystems delighting those who experience intelligently the play of natural history, scenic landscapes, and open space.

The market value of a wetland, like that of any real estate, depends principally on its location. In a coastal area, a wetland, once filled in, may provide the site for profitable enterprises, especially if, as in Atlantic City, gambling casinos, massage parlors, bars, and discos can be built. Everyone knows what happened to land values in and around Atlantic City when the government allowed gambling. That is what the market value or price of land is all about.

Now, policy problems arise when the use value of a wetland conflicts with its market value. In order to preserve the uses of the wetland—the ecological and aesthetic values associated with it—we should have to forbid certain kinds of development. In order to maximize the market value of the wetland, however, we should have to develop it in ways that destroy the use value. This is essentially the choice that confronted the *Just* court.

The court may have framed this question in terms of another: Did the owner's destruction of the use value of the wetland—for example, its value as a habitat, aquifer, or whatever—constitute a "noxious" activity that the legislature may prohibit without paying compensation, even though that sort of destruction would not be recognized as a tort in private law? In other words, if legislatures, rather than common-law courts, become the arbiters of what counts as a "nuisance" for purposes of "takings" jurisprudence, the Wisconsin zoning ordinance was perfectly constitutional. If the notion of a nuisance, and therefore the extent of property rights, depend on what may be enjoined at private law, however, the ordinance would not be constitutional. And so the question might amount to this: May legislatures identify and prohibit public nuisances that extend beyond activities that would contravene private rights and therefore be enjoined in common-law courts?

The courts have held that state governments will not run afoul of the Fifth Amendment when they enact measures to protect the public from injurious uses of private property, even when the injuries in question are not cognizable in tort. For example, the U.S. Supreme Court in *Mugler* v. *Kansas* 1887, its first full consideration of regulatory takings, found against the plaintiff, a brewery owner, the value of whose property had been severely diminished when the Kansas legislature prohibited the sale of alcoholic beverages in the state. Justice John Harlan wrote:

> The power which the states have of prohibiting such use by individuals of their property as will be prejudicial to the health, the morals, or the safety of the public, is not . . . burdened with the condition that the state must compensate such individual owners for pecuniary losses they may sustain, by reason of their not being permitted, by a noxious use of their property, to inflict injury upon the community.[29]

It is clear in Harlan's majority opinion that the legislature has the power to declare as "noxious" or "injurious" uses that would not be identified as torts under common law.[30] Although the Supreme Court has held that "the legislature has no right to declare that to be a nuisance which is clearly not so,"[31] it has deferred to legislative findings as long as they met procedural due process requirements. Thus, when states justify regulations on the basis of a colorable "noxious use," the Fifth Amendment has no force beyond what the Fourteenth Amendment also guarantees, namely, that a person shall not be deprived of property without due process of law.[32]

One may surely argue, however, that the legislature should not be the judge of its own case, that is, that some "substantive due process" review is required to determine that the "noxious" use in question does involve a threat to the public health, safety, or welfare. How would this work out with respect to the Wisconsin ordinance? Does the ordinance simply benefit the public at the expense of the landowner? Or does it function to prevent the landowner from enriching himself at the expense of the public?

While it is notoriously hard to identify general principles by which to answer this question, courts have found that restrictions are not compensable when they stop a landowner from "engaging in conduct he ought, as a well-socialized adult, to have recognized as unduly harmful to others."[33] The conception of "undue harm" at work here is drawn not from common law alone but from the wider social and cultural standards of the community.[34] Since these standards change and evolve, "definition and redefinition of the institution of private property is always at stake."[35]

The decision in *Just* builds on this rationale, as one commentator writes, by denying that expectations of profit are legitimate if they "are inconsistent with widely prevailing standards of society."[36] To assume that one has an inherent right to develop one's land (e.g., to fill a marsh) "ignores or distorts an obvious relationship between such activity and interests of the public that have long existed, but that until recently have been taken for granted."[37]

This argument stands on the premise that the central incidents of property—the right to use, to exclude, and to alienate[38]—do not include the right to destroy.[39] Professor Paul correctly attributes this point to Locke. She writes that appropriation from the common is limited by two conditions: "that as much and as good remain in common for the like appropriation of others, and that spoilage must not occur. Indeed, Locke maintains that one's right to land extends not beyond what one can use, so that one does not possess a right to waste" (p. 204).

It is easy to show that a right to use property does not entail a right to destroy it. The right to use a car one has borrowed or hired, for example, does not involve a right to destroy it; similarly, the right to use by consuming food does not entail a right to waste or spoil it. Locke reasons that a person can "heap up" as many resources as he can use or cause to be used economically—"the *exceeding of the bounds of his* just *property* not lying in the largeness of his possession, but in the perishing of anything uselessly in it."[40]

One might reply that the right to use consumables, such as food or fuel, implies a right to "destroy" them, for to use is to consume these things. This reply, however, shows only that the right to use entails a right to use up—not necessarily a right to destroy. The difference between using up provisions and destroying them is too obvious to require examples. Environmental resources of the sort that wetland regulations protect, moreover, are generally not consumable goods but "renewable" services. They are not consumed but conserved through proper use.

Similarly, the right to transfer property does not on its face entail a right to destroy it. Thus the auctioneer has a right to transfer property to the highest bidder, but this does not give him a right to destroy it, even if it is not sold. To be sure, if an item is worthless, the possessor may have a right to toss it out. But the right to destroy does not attach, for that reason, to property that has a high use value. For this reason, courts sometimes impose a "law of waste" to prevent property owners from destroying scarce resources that are of great usefulness to others.[41]

Mr. Just has no valid claim to compensation, according to this argument, because he has no right or entitlement to destroy resources that have become scarce and are of great importance to society. The decision in *Just* is correct, on this view, because a regulation that prevents a landowner from destroying resources by filling a marsh does not take a right from him. He had no right to destroy those resources.

This result seems entirely consistent with a Lockean theory of property rights, which limits property not only to that which can be possessed without waste, was we have seen, but also to that which may be acquired from a commons without creating scarcity. As Locke puts this thought, a person can rightfully acquire an unowned resource from the commons only if there is "enough and as good left in common for others."[42]

The *Just* court argued that an owner may not validly claim compensation when he or she is prevented from "destroying the natural character of a swamp or a wetland . . . when the new use . . . causes a harm to the general public."[43] The contention may be that the prohibited development would destroy resources that the public owns in common, owing to "the interrelationship of the wetlands, the swamps and the natural environment of shorelands to the purity of the water and to such natural resources as navigation, fishing, and scenic beauty."[44] In the past, an individual may have been free to appropriate these resources without depleting the common unduly, but those times are gone. Mr. Just has come too late to the commons; there is no longer as much and as good for others.

One might argue that this famous Lockean proviso[45] covers aesthetic and ecological resources that belong as organic parts (or even as emergent properties) to larger systems and are destroyed when land is removed from its natural condition. Those who come to the commons early may legitimately appropriate these resources by consuming or destroying them; but when a common resource, such as natural beauty, becomes critically scarce, society may rule against further appropriations because they significantly worsen the social situation from that which would obtain if the proposed "improvements" were not made. As Professor Paul rightly concludes in another place, a natural rights theory that "embraces the Lockean proviso can be utilized to validate environmentalist land use legislation . . . without such regulations constituting a compensable takings."[46]

Conclusion

Courts should uphold environmental regulations, such as the Wisconsin ordinance, that prevent landowners from destroying natural resources the public has long enjoyed and in which it has a legitimate interest. The incidents of property include the rights to use, exclude, and transfer, but not the right to destroy. Destruction of resources that implicitly belong to the common, then, constitute a "noxious" use, which is not protected by the Constitution. This approach may leave landowners little protection in the Fifth Amendment that they do not find in the Fourteenth and in the larger, ad hoc, pragmatic approach to "takings" jurisprudence such as we have described. Absent a persuasive theory of natural property rights, however, this may be the most reasonable approach that does not squander use value for the sake of market value—that does not ruin the environment to make speculators rich.

Notes

Acknowledgments: This essay is a revised version of a paper read at a conference, "Upstream/Downstream: Issues in Environmental Ethics," at Bowling Green State University, Bowling Green, Ohio, September 10, 1988. Portions of the paper will also appear in a book review of *Private Property and Eminent Domain* to be published in *Environmental Ethics*.

1. Alexis de Tocqueville, *Democracy in America* (New York: Random House, 1981), chap. 6.

2. See, e.g., *Penn Central Transportation Co.* v. *New York City*, 438 U.S. 104, 107 (1978) (holding that the city could operate a "comprehensive program to preserve historic landmarks" without "effecting a 'taking' requiring the payment of 'just compensation'"); *Steel Hill Developers, Inc.* v. *Town of Sanbornton*, 469 F.2d 956, 959 (1st Cir. 1972) ("preserving [the] 'charm [of] a New England small town'"); and *County Commissioners* v. *Miles*, 246 Md. 355, 372, 228 A.2d 450, 459 (1967) (allowing "the preservation, in some manner, of existing conditions").

3. *Just* v. *Marinette County*, 56 Wis. 2d 7, 201 N.W.2d 761 (1972); *Sibson* v. *State of New Hampshire*, 115 N.H. 124, 336 A.2d 239 (1975). In dozens of similar court challenges to state prohibitions on filling or otherwise changing wetland and coastal environments, plaintiffs generally succeed in winning compensation under the "takings" clause of the Fifth Amendment (or under analogous provisions in state constitutions) only if they are able to show that they are deprived of all reasonable and viable economic use of their land. For an exhaustive survey showing a "trend" toward upholding the validity of wetland regulations, see Daniel R. Mandeleker, "Land Use Takings, the Compensation Issue," *Hastings Constitutional Law Quarterly* 8 (1981): 491, esp. 495–502; and Sarah E. Redfield, *Vanishing Farmland: A Legal Solution for the States* (Lexington, Mass.: D. C. Heath, 1984), chap. 2.

4. *Agins* v. *City of Tiburon*, 447 U.S. 255, 261 (quoting from the Cal. Gov't. Code Ann. sec. 65561(b) (West, 1983) (recognizing the legitimacy of open space plans to "discourage the 'premature and unnecessary conversion of open-space land to urban uses'").

5. *Hodel* v. *Virginia Surface Mining and Reclamation Association*, 452 U.S. 264 (1981) (sustaining the Surface Mining Control and Reclamation Act).

6. The Endangered Species Act of 1973 (16 U.S.C. secs. 1531–43) (1976 & Supp. I 1977 & Supp. II 1978 & Supp. III 1979) requires (sec. 1536) that all federal departments and agencies "insure that actions authorized, funded, or carried out by them do not jeopardize the continued existence of such endangered species." The act effectively makes the preservation of habitat a condition of any federal permit for development.

7. For discussion of litigation concerning ordinances expanding public access to waterfront property, see Carol Rose, "The Comedy of the Commons: Custom, Commerce, and Inherently Public Property," *University of Chicago Law Review* 53 (1986): 711, 713–23.

8. *Keystone Bituminous Coal Association* v. *DeBenedictis*, 55 LW 4326 (March 9, 1987).

9. For a discussion of environmental zoning for ecological purposes in the context of the "takings" problem, see "Developments in the Law: Zoning," *Harvard Law Review* 91 (1978): 1427, 1618–24.

10. A landowner who proceeds against the government in this way is said to assert a theory of "inverse condemnation" of his land because he, rather than the government, initiates the action. See *San Diego Gas and Electric Co.* v. *City of San Diego*, 450 U.S. 621, 638 n. 2 (1981) (Brennan, J., dissenting).

11. The Fifth Amendment to the Constitution of the United States. This provision is now applicable to the states through the Fourteenth Amendment. *Chicago, B. & O. R.R.* v. *City of Chicago*, 166 U.S. 226, 235–41 (1897). Almost all the states have analogous clauses in their constitutions. For documentation, see "Developments in the Law," 1463.

12. Thus, in the leading case, *Pennsylvania Coal Co.* v. *Mahon* (260 U.S. 393, 415), Justice Holmes stated "that while property may be regulated to a certain extent, if regulation goes too far it will be considered as a taking." It is difficult to predict how a "takings" will be decided. Ackerman notes that "recent wetlands regulation cases have divided approximately evenly on the issue of compensation." Bruce Ackerman, *Private Property and the Constitution* (New Haven: Yale University Press, 1977), 191 n. 7 and 217 n. 54.

13. *Pennsylvania Coal*, 260 U.S. 416.

14. Carol M. Rose, "*Mahon* Reconstructed: Why the Takings Issue Is Still a Muddle," *Southern California Law Review* 57 (1984): 561.

15. Allison Dunham, "*Griggs* v. *Allegheny County* in Perspective:

Thirty Years of Supreme Court Expropriation Law," *Supreme Court Review* 63 (1962): 105.

16. S. Van Alstyne, "Taking or Damaging by Police Power: The Search for Inverse Condemnation Criteria," *Southern California Law Review* 44 (1971): 1, 39. ("The judicial calculus involved in the balancing process is described in a variety of unilluminating ways.")

17. W. Oakes, "'Property Rights' in Constitutional Analysis Today," *Washington Law Review* 56 (1981): 583, 602–3 (characterizing takings decisions as "ad hoc line drawing").

18. W. B. Stoebuck, "Police Power, Takings, and Due Process," *Washington and Lee Law Review* 37 (1980): 1057, 1062–63 (referring to "extreme confusion about police power takings").

19. Comment, "Regulation of Land Use: From Magna Carta to a *Just* Formulation," *UCLA Law Review* 23 (1976): 904, 904–5 (takings decisions are "bafflingly" inconsistent).

20. Thomas Hippler, "Reexamining 100 Years of Supreme Court Regulatory Taking Doctrine: The Principles of 'Noxious Use,' 'Average Reciprocity of Advantage,' and 'Bundle of Rights,' from *Mugler* to *Keystone Bituminous Coal*," *Environmental Affairs* 14 (1987): 653–725 (describing "the rather mystifying nature of regulatory takings jurisprudence").

21. Fred Bosselman, David Callies, and John Banta, *The Taking Issue* (Washington, D.C.: Council on Environmental Quality, GPO, 1973), 322.

22. *Nollan* v. *California Coastal Commission*, 55 LW 5145, 5156 (Stevens, J., dissenting). Here Justice Stevens echoes Justice Brennan in *Penn Central Transportation* Co. (428 U.S. 123, 124) (stating that the question "of what constitutes a 'taking' for purposes of the Fifth Amendment has proved to be a problem of considerable difficulty" susceptible to no "set formula"). Cf. Joseph Sax, "Takings and the Police Power," *Yale Law Journal* 74 (1964): 36, 37 ("the predominant characteristic of this area of law is a welter of confusing and apparently incompatible results"). Cf. *Goldblatt* v. *Town of Hempstead*, 369 U.S. 590, 594 (1962). ("There is no set formula to determine where regulation ends and taking begins.")

23. See, e.g., Ackerman, *Private Property*; Frank Michelman, "Property, Utility, and Fairness: Comments of the Ethical Foundations of 'Just Compensation' Law," *Harvard Law Review* 80 (1968): 1165–1258; and Joseph Sax, "Takings, Private Property and Public Rights," *Yale Law Journal* 81 (1971): 149–86.

24. *Just* v. *Marinette* Co., 56 Wis. 2d 7, 201 N.W.2d 761, 768 (1972).

25. Ibid., 767.

26. Ellen Frankel Paul, *Property Rights and Eminent Domain* (New Brunswick, N.J.: Transaction Books, 1987), 138. Unless otherwise noted, all quotations attributed to Paul in this chapter are taken from this work.

27. Richard Epstein, *Takings: Private Property and the Power of Eminent Domain* (Cambridge: Harvard University Press, 1985), 123.

28. See, for example, Paul's comments in "A Reflection on Epstein and His Critics," *Miami Law Review* 41 (1986): 235.

29. 123 U.S. 623, 669 (1887).

30. Ibid., 671–72.

31. *Lawton* v. *Steele*, 152 U.S. 133, 140 (1894).

32. See, for example, *Powell* v. *Pennsylvania*, 127 U.S. 678 (1888).

33. Ackerman, *Private Property*, 102.

34. Courts may meet their constitutional obligation as long as they apply these standards consistently in all cases. For discussion of this point, see ibid., 14.

35. C. Haar, *Land-Use Planning* (Boston: Little, Brown, 1959), 410. Justice Holmes may have had the centrality of evolving community standards in mind when he said in *Mahon* that "this is a question of degree—and therefore cannot be disposed of by general propositions." This seems to be consistent with the view sometimes attributed to Holmes that judges apply standards of good taste and reasonableness and not simply formal legal prescriptions.

36. P. Soper, "The Constitutional Framework of Environmental Law," in his *Federal Environmental Law* (St. Paul, Minn.: West, 1974), 67.

37. Ibid.

38. Epstein, *Takings*, 20, endorses this analysis of property rights, citing W. Blackstone, *Commentaries* (1765), 2. Robert Goodin cites Frank Snare, "The Concept of Property," *American Philosophical Quarterly* 9 (1972): 200–206; and C. B. Macpherson, "Human Rights as Property Rights, *Dissent* 24 (1977): 72–77.

39. Robert Goodin puts the point as follows: "The right to destroy is usually not part and parcel of the central incidents of the right to property, as ordinarily understood." Robert Goodin, "Property Rights and Preservationist Duties," paper presented at the Conference Group on Political Economy, American Political Science Association Annual Conference, Chicago, September 1987, 3.

40. John Locke, *Second Treatise of Government*, chap. 5, sec. 46.

41. For discussion, see William Rodgers, "Bringing People Back: Toward a Comprehensive Theory of Taking in Natural Resources Law," *Ecol-*

ogy *Law Quarterly* 10 (1982): 205, 248–51. Rogers cites about twenty relevant cases at 249 nn. 214–16.

42. Locke, *Second Treatise*, chap. 5, sec. 27.

43. 56 Wis. 2d 18, 201 N.W.2d 768.

44. Ibid., 17.

45. For discussion of the "Lockean Proviso," see Robert Nozick, *Anarchy, State, and Utopia* (New York: Basic Books, 1974), 174–82.

46. Ellen Frankel Paul, "The Just Takings Issue," *Environmental Ethics* 3 (1981): 309, 320.

Bart Gruzalski

Chapter 7

Assessing Acts of Pollution

When we assess an act of pollution on moral grounds, we tend to think we can do so on the basis of its harmful consequences. When we need to determine the degree of accountability of those who contributed to pollution, it seems pertinent to discover what harmful consequences their individual actions actually caused.

In this chapter I clarify and defend each of these beliefs for those difficult situations where, because an individual action is only one among many, its consequences may seem insignificant or even irrelevant to the subsequent harm. Although my two main examples of harms involve harms to human and nonhuman animals, nothing in what follows is intended to limit our assessment of harm in this way. In addition to harming animals, our actions may also harm plants, ecosystems, and even the planet itself.

Assessing the Morality of an Action in Terms of Its Own Consequences

Although almost all of us are concerned about pollution, we frequently tend to think that none of our individual actions makes any significant contribution to pollution-related harms. This thought is not implausible. The large-scale effects about which we are concerned typically occur only after a threshold of activity has been crossed and, usually, more than enough actions are performed to cross the threshold. As a result, your or my individual action seems immaterial, especially in retrospect, to the occurrence of these threshold harms.

The following imaginary example will allow us to highlight the difficulties in threshold cases. Consider the *Mercury Poisoning Case*:

> Suppose four chemical plants discharged waste water into a river during the same period of time and at roughly the same location, that the effluent from each plant contained roughly as much methyl mercury chloride as the effluent from each other plant, and that together the joint discharge of methyl mercury caused the level of mercury in the fish downstream to be .6 ppm, or .2 ppm above the "safety" level. Suppose further that the only relevant harm comes from eating these contaminated fish downstream and that were the methyl mercury in the fish below the .4 ppm level, there would be no harm. Finally, suppose that an endangered fish-eating species, for whom the valley was the sole remaining natural habitat, was killed off because the mercury level in the fish was no longer below .4 ppm.[1]

In this example, each chemical company can show that if it had acted *alone*, the resulting chemical concentrations would have caused no harm downstream. Moreover, there would have been mercury poisoning downstream, including the kill of the endangered species, *whatever* any one company had done. In this way it becomes somewhat plausible to think that the amount of waste any particular chemical plant discharged into the river was immaterial to the harmful result. The "logic" of the *Mercury Poisoning Case* parallels the "logic" in many ordinary cases where we think that the consequences of our own individual acts make no difference because the harmful results will occur whatever we do. For example, I may think that my dumping my automobile oil into the local landfill or your throwing your garbage overboard into the ocean will be immaterial to the ecological harms that occur when many people act in similar ways.

Such pollution cases are especially problematic for an act consequentialist because the performance of any particular act of pollution seems to make no difference to the result, and so we seem unable to condemn an individual act of pollution in terms of its own consequences. The best-known act-consequentialist theory, and the one around which I structure my discussion, is act utilitarianism. According to act utilitarianism, whether an act is right, wrong, or obligatory is a function of its actual or foreseeable consequences. The *Mercury Poisoning Case* poses a potential counterexample to this theory of moral obligation.

The Act Utilitarian Solution

A problematic feature of the *Mercury Poisoning Case* is that there is a threshold that must be crossed before any damage occurs, and it is unclear whether any particular act is necessary or sufficient to cross that threshold. Derek Parfit recently illustrated the threshold problem with a series of imaginative examples, including the following:

> *The Harmless Torturers.* In the Bad Old Days, each torturer inflicted severe pain on one victim. Things have now changed. Each of the thousand torturers presses a button, thereby turning the switch once on each of the thousand instruments. The victims suffer the same severe pain. But none of the torturers makes any victim's pain perceptibly worse.[2]

In his discussion of this example, Parfit claims that we cannot assess the wrongness of an act of torture on the basis of its own consequences.[3] But the following observation suggests a "solution" for how to assess each act of button pushing in terms of its own consequences: Each act occurring below or at some pain threshold may have that threshold effect as a consequence if that threshold effect would not have occurred had the agent done something else instead.[4]

One difficulty with this "solution" is that it does not answer the following complaint in the *Mercury Poisoning Case*: We know, at least in retrospect, that any particular company's discharging waste was unnecessary to cross the "safety" threshold. In the *Harmless Torturers*, an analogous problem occurs: Even though the crossing of a pain threshold may be the result of a particular button pusher pushing a button, it may also *not* be a result of that act, and so there is no good reason for condemning any particular act of button pushing on the grounds that it *in fact* had the crossing of a pain threshold as a consequence.

This problem does not undermine the intuition that we are able to assess an individual act morally in terms of that action's consequences. The so-called problem rests primarily on thinking of act utilitarianism as a moral view on which we are to assess actions in terms of their *actual* consequences rather than as a function of their *foreseeable* consequences. This fundamental misunderstanding of act utilitarianism— thinking of it as an actual-consequence—leads to a host of unnecessary anomalies. On the actual-consequence view, actions will not infrequently be morally wrong because of actual results that were unforeseeable on the evidence available at the time of action. For example, a person driving on a busy two-lane road nears the top of a hill on a blind curve. We know that a driver in such a situation, unable to know that passing will not result in a catastrophic head-on collision, should not pass. If the driver does pass, and as a result avoids being killed by an unseen boulder rolling down the side of the mountain, that does not make the action morally permissible. Yet, on the actual-consequence view, because passing on a blind curve would in fact have had the best consequences, that act is right, and it is morally wrong to have done otherwise.[5] To attempt to account for this deeply counterintuitive result, the actual-consequence theorist distinguishes between the assessment of an action as right or wrong and the assessment of an agent as praiseworthy or blameworthy. But this distinction leads to the result that in many cases people ought to do what is morally blameworthy or should be praised for failing to do what they ought. These tensions between the artificial language generated by actual-consequence theorists and our ordinary usage violate our moral sensibilities and strain our moral concepts. These anomalies do not typically arise in another way of viewing act utilitarianism that seems closer to what John Stuart Mill had in mind when he wrote of the tendencies of actions, namely, as a foreseeable-consequence account according to which an action is assessed in terms of those consequences foreseeable at the time of action. From a foreseeable-consequence view, a person will generally be praiseworthy for doing what is obligatory and blameworthy for doing what is wrong.

When we examine the foreseeable-consequence view, we note that each action usually has several mutually exclusive forseeable consequences that are of different values (in our automotive example, passing safely or causing a terrible accident are two foreseeable consequences of passing). We take these foreseeable possibilities into account by assigning a number to each to represent its desirability. We then multiply the desirability of each foreseeable consequence by its probability, and the sum of the products of the likelihood and desirability of each of the foreseeable consequences is the expected desirability of the action. On the formulation of act utilitarianism we employ for the remainder of this chapter, it is our obligation to perform one of the available actions whose expected desirabilities are no less than the expected desirabilities of any alternative:

Foreseeable-consequence act utilitarian principle: An act is right if and only if the expected desirability of that act is no less than the expected desirability of any available alternative.

This principle allows us to account for our moral intuitions in the case of the *Harmless Torturers* as well as in the *Mercury Poisoning Case*.

Consider again Parfit's example. If there is a foreseeable possibility that this (or some later) pain threshold might not be crossed unless a particular act of button pushing is performed, then the crossing of that pain threshold is among the foreseeable consequences of that button pushing, and we must take this foreseeable effect into account in determining the expected desirability of that action. Since in any realistic version of the example there will be some probability that an act of button pushing will have the crossing of some pain threshold among its consequences, and assuming that the other foreseeable consequences of this act and its alternatives are relatively value neutral, an act of button pushing would be wrong on the foreseeable-consequence act utilitarian principle because of its negative net expected desirability. Since, *ex hypothesi*, the expected desirability of each action is the same, we are able to condemn each act of button pressing as morally wrong with a straightforward application of the foreseeable-consequences principle.

We can also apply this reasoning directly to the *Mercury Poisoning Case*. In our example of chemical plants discharging wastes into the river there are numerous thresholds that can be crossed by each individual act of pollution, although we have identified only one specific threshold in the example, that is, the mercury in the fish downstream being .4 ppm. Crossing this threshold kills off the members of the endangered species downstream and causes various degrees of mercury poisoning for any other fish-eating animals. In a real version of the *Mercury Poisoning Case*, it will probably not be clear, before the fact, that the actions of each chemical plant will not cause this .4 ppm threshold to be crossed, and so each act of discharging mercury-laden wastes into the river will have, among its foreseeable consequences, the tremendous harm caused by the crossing of this threshold. In addition, in this and other pollution examples—including examples involving the pollution of aquifers as well as the Greenhouse Effect—the greater the degree of pollution, the greater the amount of harm caused. Hence, each act of pollution will have, among its foreseeable consequences, the causing of these additional harms. In our example, any additional acts of pollution performed after the .4 ppm threshold has been crossed will also foreseeably cause additional harm, and so be wrong.[6]

This reasoning is generalizable over a range of apparently less dramatic but commonplace situations. For example, dumping oil into the local landfill has, among its foreseeable consequences, increasing the contamination of groundwater and so likely causing harm or increased harm. Assuming that the other foreseeable consequences of this act and its alternatives are value neutral, then the act of oil dumping would be wrong on the foreseeable-consequence act utilitarian principle because of a negative net expected desirability that is primarily a function of the value of foreseeable harms due to increased water contamination. Likewise, throwing garbage into the ocean increases the likelihood of individual sea animals being harmed and increases the possibility of thresholds being crossed that would produce much greater harms.

The Problem of Imperceptible Effects and Another Probabilistic Approach

The above account also solves the problem currently referred to as the problem of imperceptible effects. Parfit describes the problem in the following way:

> If some act has effects on other people that are imperceptible, this act cannot be morally wrong *because* it has these effects.

> An act cannot be wrong because of its effects on other people, if none of these people could ever notice any difference.[7]

The theoretically troubling cases of imperceptible effects involve threshold effects. Because the threshold-related consequences of each contributory act appear to be imperceptible, we seem unable to assess any of these actions in terms of the perceptible-threshold effect that occurs after all of them are performed. In the case of the *Harmless Torturers*, which Parfit uses to illustrate the problem of imperceptible effects, the expected desirability of one torturer's act of turning a switch is a function of the probability that this act will cause perceptible harm to one or more victims because it might cause the crossing of a pain threshold. From the foreseeable-consequence perspective, we can therefore provide an account of why turning the switch is wrong.[8]

Kristin Shrader-Frechette offers an alternative approach, the *measurable-risk approach*, which attempts to dissolve the problem of imperceptible effects by noting that when we assess an action's consequences at sufficiently fine-tuned microphysical levels in terms of their probabilistic risk, it is questionable whether there are any imperceptible effects.[9]

In contrast to the foreseeable-consequence utilitarian's acceptance of a problem of imperceptible effects, the measurable-risk theorist questions whether there is a problem of imperceptible effects. According to the measurable-risk approach, in these cases we "are able to talk about increased and decreased *risk*, or . . . probability of harm" that is perceptible because detectable "at the molecular level through sophisticated instrumentation":

> A great many problems associated with allegedly imperceptible differences can be understood in terms of finer microphysical discriminations, for example, among cell abnormalities having a propensity to develop into cancer. The point is that, if one looks at allegedly imperceptible harms with fine enough medical and scientific know-how and instrumentation, then it is questionable whether there are any genuine effects of nonmental acts which are imperceptible.[10]

From the measurable-risk account, there are perceptible *qua* measurable harms even if no one experiences them on the non-microphysical level.

The foreseeable-consequence and measurable-risk approaches may seem similar because each introduces and emphasizes a probabilistic feature in the assessment of individual actions.[11] Although these two approaches share important similarities, they are significantly different, as the following examples illustrate:

> *The Simple Digoxin Case:* Sally is the caretaker for her uncle, who has a heart condition. At dawn, Sally gives her uncle a maximum (for him) dose of digoxin, thus causing cellular changes that affect myocardial contraction. He will receive no other drugs that day, and without the digoxin would have died late that night.

It might seem that the measurable-risk theorist would assess as positive the digoxin-related cellular changes. But consider the following:

> *The Digitalis Intoxication Case:* As in the *Simple Digoxin Case*, Sally gives her uncle a maximum (for him) dose of digoxin at dawn. But unlike in the *Simple Case*, she knows that her dose of digoxin was medically contraindicated because this is the one day each week when the visiting nurse will give her uncle a drug that, in combination with the morning dose of digoxin, will cause him to die from digitalis intoxication.

These cases pose a problem for the measurable-risk approach when we examine the measurable effects of Sally's action at the cellular level. In the first case, Sally's actions seems to cause a measurable benefit. In the second case, because of the nurse's foreseeable action, Sally's action seems to cause a lethal risk. The key issue is whether this risk is measurable at the cellular level. If this lethal risk is measurable at the cellular level, then, since what Sally causes at the cellular level is the same in both cases, it is also a lethal risk in the *Simple Digoxin Case*, which is counterintuitive. If this risk is not measurable at the cellular level, then on the measurable-risk approach the consequences of Sally's action in the *Digitalis Intoxication Case* do not constitute a lethal risk, which is counterintuitive for a measurable-risk assessment of Sally's action.

What differentiates Sally's act in the *Simple Digoxin Case* from her act in the *Digitalis Intoxication Case* is a factor not measurable at the microphysical level: the foreseeable behavior of others. The foreseeable-consequence theorist, unlike the measurable-risk theorist, is able to take the foreseeable behavior of others into account in assessing actions, since the expected desirability of an action is a function of, among other things, the foreseeable behavior of others. In the *Simple Digoxin Case*, Sally's action would be right from the foreseeable-consequence perspective. In the *Digitalis Intoxication Case*, the cumulative dose is foreseeable, and Sally's act would therefore be wrong on the foreseeable-consequence principle.

The interplay between these two cases illustrates a systematic problem with the measurable-risk approach and the superiority of foreseeable-consequence act utilitarianism. In many cases, we cannot tell whether a measurable effect is a risk without first assessing what might result given the foreseeable behavior of others or other foreseeable events. Yet if we introduce these foreseeable factors into the measurable-risk account, it would no longer be an alternative to foreseeable-consequence perspective but would become fully imbedded within it. In more general terms, we cannot tell whether the effects of some molecular change are positive, negative, or evaluatively neutral until we know the relationship between those changes and the resulting perceptible effects of pain, disease, disability, and death.

It might be thought that we should combine the foreseeable-consequence approach with an "independent" measurable-risk approach that excluded these foreseeable factors. We should resist this thought. Foreseeable-consequence act utilitarianism *simpliciter* is superior to the hybrid of a foreseeable-consequence approach and an "independent" measurable-risk approach because the complexities of the hybrid are unnecessary.[12] Not only are the sophisticated apparatuses that we use to discover and trace molecular changes caused by pollution—the "sophisticated instrumentation" to which Kristin Shrader-Frechette refers—among the arsenal of what we bring to a proper application of foreseeable-consequence act utilitarianism, but the relevant effects of death, pain, cancer, and so forth—the basis of the measur-

able-risk theorist's negative assessment of specific cellular changes—
are fully taken into consideration when we apply the foreseeable-consequence principle in cases involving imperceptible effects.

After-the-Fact Assessments of
Causal Accountability

After damage has been done, there are many reasons for investigating
what actions actually caused all or part of the damage. We may want
to have the damage corrected, we may want to have it compensated,
or we may even want to punish in order to discourage others from
acting in the same way. Concerns about responsibility and accountability raise a number of questions: How much did the agent know?
What was the agent's intention? Was he or she acting under duress?
Will holding this agent accountable discourage others from acting in
similar ways? How much damage can we causally link or attribute on
causal grounds to this agent's action? Although each of these five
questions is relevant to the issue of responsibility, it is only the last
question that I investigate here. It is important, however, to keep in
mind that this question of *causal attribution is only part of what is
involved in a more general assessment of responsibility and that it is
only this limited question that I am exploring in what follows.* As
H. L. A. Hart and A. M. Honore remind us:

> There is nothing to compel any legal system to accept a causal
> connexion with harm as either necessary or sufficient for lia-
> bility, and, where it seems just to do so, it may introduce spe-
> cial principles of "policy" or scope rules to enlarge or cut short
> liability independently of causal connexion.[13]

In what follows I do not focus on general questions of responsibility
or accountability but *only* on the question of the causal connection
between individual acts and subsequent harms, especially threshold-
related harms.

The foreseeable approach is not useful for this task. When people
have acted in ways that would be wrong on the foreseeable-consequence principle and no harm results, we are simply not inclined to
hold them accountable for a harm that never occurred.[14] In contrast,

when a harm has been caused, we want more than the rough estimate of the likelihood and value of the consequences associated with a particular action. We want to know what actually happened and to what extent an individual act can be considered causally accountable for what happened. This is not provided for us by the foreseeable-consequence act utilitarian principle.[15]

It might be useful to begin with a suggestion by David Lyons that, if correct, would supply us with an answer for these after-the-fact assessments. In cases involving the causal overdeterminism of threshold results, Lyons argues that we must employ a principle of "complete ascribability," that is, if n acts have jointly produced an effect E, then the effect can be completely ascribable to each of the n acts taken individually. The most rigorous statement of this principle offers for acts that are exactly similar with respect to all their effects.[16] For such acts, the effect is *completely ascribable* as follows:

> *Complete ascribability:* If n equally efficacious acts jointly have T as a consequence, then each act has a consequence T/n.

Using complete ascribability in our opening example, we would attribute one-fourth the harm to the endangered species to the actions of each chemical polluter. Lyons offers several illustrations of complete ascribability. Consider: If k equally efficacious votes have some election result V, then each can be ascribed $1/k$th the election result V. Or, if eight people push a car up a hill and each push equally hard, each act has a consequence one-eighth of the car's reaching the top of the hill. Lyons's defense of complete ascribability does not rest on examples but on the claim that if complete ascribability were not true, then "some effects would be mysteriously appearing or disappearing. And of course effects do not disappear (in this sense), nor can they just appear; they are not, for example, ascribable here to anything other than the n acts."[17]

Unfortunately, this principle is demonstrably false. For example, suppose four persons simultaneously drop one-third a lethal dose of strychnine into a fifth person's orange juice. No one act was necessary or sufficient to cause the fifth person's death, and so this death cannot properly be thought of as the consequence of any of the acts considered individually. Under complete ascribability, each act has, as a consequence, one-fourth the death. Yet this is, strictly speaking, absurd. It makes no sense to talk of one-fourth of a death; nor even does it make sense to divide an election result (e.g., the placing of a candidate into office) into parts, or to divide into parts an automobile's reaching the top of a hill. In short, although Lyons has identified a general causal notion of contributory causation that is intuitively compelling, we must conclude that the details of his first suggestion are defective.

Although Lyons's principle does not hold up under scrutiny, it nonetheless is an intuitively plausible beginning. What Lyons overlooked, and what allows us to devise a suitable account of causal accountability, is that between these overdetermined threshold effects and the individual acts that contribute to them there are intermediate causes and effects.

Consider again the *Mercury Poisoning Case*. The person who wants to ascribe some consequential value to each act of discharging mercury into the river must find some way of doing so that rests on sound causal and evaluative principles. One plausible strategy is to identify a factor that is part of the cause of the death of the endangered species *and* a consequence of each act of polluting. Since such a factor is part of the cause of a harmful situation, that factor would plausibly be undesirable. Since each act has, as a consequence, this undesirable factor, then each act has at least one undesirable consequence.

In our example, the river's having more than enough mercury in it to raise the ppm in the downstream fish to .4 ppm, or above this level, is the cause of the loss of the endangered species. If the cause of an effect "inherits" the value of that effect, then the river's containing sufficient mercury to cause this high ppm level in its fish is very undesirable. In our case, this mercury has been discharged into the river by the chemical companies. We can analyze this whole—the amount discharged by the chemical companies—into four equal parts.[18] Since the whole is very undesirable, it seems reasonable that one-fourth of the whole is undesirable. Since each act has, as a consequence, one-fourth of the whole, each act of polluting has this undesirable consequence. Following this line of reasoning, we are able to ascribe back to the contributing actions the *value* of an effect that none of the actions is either necessary or sufficient to produce.

The Value of Causes and the Value of Parts

Our proposal involves two claims about how events acquire extrinsic value. The first concerns the *value* an event may derive by being a *cause* (hereafter shown as "VC"), whereas the second concerns what *value* an event may derive from being a *part* (hereafter, "VP"):

VC: If X is the cause of Y, and if X has value G, then X, *as cause of Y*, has the extrinsic value G.

VP: If X is one of n indistinguishable similar parts of Y, and the value of Y is G, then X, *as part of Y*, has the extrinsic value G/n.

We next examine each of these in turn.[19]

The Value of Causes (VC). VC corresponds to the way we typically evaluate events insofar as they are causes. For instance, in calling a thing "good," we frequently mean that it is a means to an end that is good. "Good" in this sense presupposes both a causal relation between something valued as good and that good's cause. If Fred's being killed is undesirable, then, other things being equal, it is undesirable that he be decapitated. If it is desirable that the crops have water, then, other things being equal, it is desirable that the clouds be seeded. The undesirability of DDT in the food chain is sufficient reason, other things being equal, for evaluating the use of DDT on grains as undesirable. In these examples, the phrase "other things being equal," often referred to as the *ceteris paribus* condition, expresses the appreciation of several complexities, two of which are significant for us.

When we say that Fred's being decapitated is as undesirable as his being killed, *other things being equal*, the *ceteris paribus* condition alerts us to those background conditions given which, if a person is decapitated, that person has been killed. This use of the *ceteris paribus* phrase is a way of identifying the condition of being decapitated as the cause of being killed by implicitly referring to the appropriate background conditions—for example, that recapitation is not yet a viable medical procedure or that, if it were, Fred is not sufficiently near a medical facility that performs this operation. Such background conditions are always implicit whenever we identify some event as the cause of another.[20] In other cases, the *ceteris paribus* condition alerts us to ways that some factor may be valuable other than as the cause of a specific result. Consider the statement that using DDT on grains is as undesirable, other things being equal, as having DDT in the food chain. Here the *ceteris paribus* condition requires us to discount, temporarily, other aspects of DDT that may outweigh the undesirability of having it in the food chain or may even make the presence of DDT in the food chain only one of DDT's lesser evils. When these other aspects of DDT are included, the evaluation of its use may change.

Although these clarifications enhance the plausibility of VC, the following may appear to be a decisive counterexample. A politician is shot, the bullet puncturing his lung. He dies. We can imagine various plausible situations in which the politician's life would have been saved. Were he shot near a hospital, were a doctor at the scene, had a helicopter been available to fly him to a hospital, had his blood type not been so unusual—any of these not implausible factors, had they obtained, would have prevented the politician's death. Since the absence of *all* these conditions is abnormal, we are inclined to say that some of the undesirability that we might otherwise attribute to the act of shooting must be attributed to these other factors, namely, the abnormal grouping of background conditions. But this attribution of value is plausible only so long as the background conditions remain vague and implicit. Once these conditions are made explicit, such examples conform to VC. Given that there is no hospital nearby, no doctor on the scene, and that the politician has a rare blood type—in short, given conditions that make it plain that a bullet puncturing a lung will cause death—it is no less undesirable from the point of view of achieving death that the politician be shot through the lung rather than be decapitated.

The Value of Parts (VP). We may begin examining VP's plausibility by considering the following example: Suppose a landowner wants four stumps removed from his property. He negotiates with a contractor who will remove each stump for $100 each only if all four are to be removed. The landowner agrees to pay $400, but claims that each stump is not worth $100 to remove even if the other three are also removed. We are puzzled, since the landowner seems to be both affirming and denying that the job is worth $400. In saying that the job is worth $400 but that the sum of the value of the equal parts is not worth $400, we take the landowner to be contradicting himself precisely because we presuppose VP.

It may be objected that this example does not support VP because in this case, as in many others, we need focus only on the value of a whole, and there is no necessity to attend to the value of parts *as parts*. Because such a further distribution of value is pointless, to claim that our ordinary intuitions support VP is gratuitous. This point may be illustrated by modifying our original example. Suppose the landowner agrees to pay $40 for one stump only if all four are removed, $80 for another only if all four are removed, $120 for the third only if all four are removed, and $160 for the fourth only if all four are removed. Is there any reason to opt for an equal valuation rather than this new unequal valuation? If the contractor were to say that he would do the job only given the landowner's agreement that each stump be worth $100 only if all four are removed, *his* requirement would seem silly. What is at issue is the value of the whole job. Since there is not reason or need to distribute the value of this whole among its parts, any particular distribution of value is arbitrary, and VP is not confirmed in the original example.[21]

This objection permits the making of an important point. Suppose a similar stump-removal example, except that there is no individual contractor and that the functions of contractor are equally shared by four men who have comparable skills for the job. Each man is to remove one stump, and it will take the same amount of time, energy, and so on to remove each stump. The whole job, valued at $400, is the removal of all four stumps. In this further modified example there is a reason (i.e., payment) to evaluate the parts (each part is removing one stump when all four are removed) *as* parts. It is reasonable to evaluate each part, which is one-quarter of the whole, as one-quarter the value of the whole. It would be unreasonable to evaluate the parts of the job such that one was worth $40, one $80, one $120, and one $160. The example is idealized, but the point is that, in a case clearly within the range of VP, VP is confirmed. Note, however, that this rationale for VP requires that there be a *need* to distribute the value of the whole among the parts and that the need to do so, at least in our example, is to pay for work already completed. Since VP conforms to our intuitions in cases of such need for distribution, I conclude that VP is the correct analysis of how such parts are valued as parts and is a legitimate principle of evaluation, at least when we are assessing an individual contributing to what has been completed or agreeing on compensation for what will be completed.

Although VP seems plausible, the plausibility may be questioned on the grounds that VP is remarkably similar to the familiar but false principle G. E. Moore stated as follows: "Where a whole consists of two factors, A and B, the amount by which its intrinsic value exceeds that of one of these factors must always be equal to that of the other factor."[22] This principle, the *value* of *wholes* ("VW"), may characterized as:

> VW: If Y and Z are parts of X, and the intrinsic value of X is G, then the intrinsic value of Y and the intrinsic value of Z must equal G.

Since our concern is the legitimacy of VP, and since VW is false, it is important to determine whether VP and VW are sufficiently different to account for the plausibility of VP given that VW is false.[23]

Although the parts within the domain of VP need not be similar and indistinguishable, the parts within the domain of VW need not be similar. For example, the goodness of a person and this person's happiness constitute, for Moore and for William David Ross, a whole that is within the domain of VW, and it is such wholes that provide counterexamples to VW. According to Ross, the combination of a person's happiness and goodness provides "at least one case which illustrates the doctrine" that VW is false.[24] This case includes nine persons who are good and one person who is evil, and the characteristic of one person being very happy. Ross's point is that it makes a difference in the value of the whole whether one of the good persons is very happy or whether it is the evil person. In this counterexample to VW, the parts are clearly distinguishable and not similar in the way in which each hundredth of a $600 fund is similar to each other hundredth. Not only is VW different from VP in this respect, but because of this difference the few examples used to show that VW is false do not fall within the domain of VP and, for that reason, do not impinge on the legitimacy of VP.

Taken together, VC and VP are plausible evaluative principles that permit us to solve our original problems: the ascription of value to actions that contributed to a causally overdetermined valuable effect. This is the sort of case Lyons discussed when focusing on his own indefensible principles of contributory causation:

> If it takes six men to push a car up a hill and, not knowing this, eight lend a hand and do the job, what are we to say? If all actually pushed, and pushed equally hard, and delivered equal forces, are we to say that only some of them actually contributed to the effects because fewer *could* have done the job?[25]

In Lyons's example, there is a reason for assessing the contributory value of each action to the valuable whole, namely, to give credit to each actual contributor. In other cases, the reason may be payment or the collection of damages. When there is a reason for assessing the value of an act because of its contribution to a valuable whole, VC and VP are principles of evaluation we are justified in using.

The VC/VP analysis is legitimate and useful for a range of after-the-fact consequential assessments where there is a need to assess the contribution of an individual action. After the damage has been done, after the good has been achieved, at that point the VC/VP analysis is a plausible account of how to distribute reward, blame, payment, or compensation. In the *Mercury Poisoning Case*, the VC/VP analysis yields the useful result that each of the chemical companies caused one-fourth of a very negative whole, and hence, if compensation is appropriate, a consequential assessment would require one-fourth of the total compensation from each. The VC/VP analysis is also legitimate and useful in Lyons's example of eight people pushing a car up a hill. An after-the-fact analysis yields the result that each act of pushing was equally causally accountable for the result.

The VC/VP analysis is even more useful than may be apparent from these illustrations because VP is even more flexible in making after-the-fact assessments than we have so far indicated. Suppose, as a modification of the *Mercury Poisoning Case*, that one of the chemical plants discharged 40 percent of the mercury into the river, and each of the remaining three plants discharged 20 percent of the total. In this new case, although the actual contributions of the chemical plants are not equal, the whole of the mercury waste may be divided into five (equal) parts (of 20 percent) each, with one company having produced two of these parts, and each of the other three companies each having produced one part of this negative whole. Insofar as responsibility or compensation is based solely on a consequential assessment, then the one company is accountable for 40 percent of the damages, whereas each of the other three companies is accountable for 20 percent of the damages.

Conclusion

The VC/VP analysis of contributory causation, which plays no role in answering the question of what, on act utilitarian grounds, a person should do, has an important use in after-the-fact ascriptions of value, as in the *Mercury Poisoning Case*, where it provides a causal analysis for determining the accountability of each individual polluter.[26] In contrast, when we want to determine what a person should do in cases involving threshold effects or "imperceptible effects," we straightforwardly apply the foreseeable-consequence act utilitarian principle. In short, there is no problem of contributory causation or of imperceptible effects for the act utilitarian, either before or after the fact.

Appendix: The Promise and Defeat of Utilitarian Generalization

It would be remiss to omit from a discussion of the consequentialist solution to these problems a brief examination of a once-popular utilitarian approach. The problem of causally associating a specific individual action with important threshold results was explicitly noted by R. F. Harrod over fifty years ago:

> *There are certain acts which when performed on* n *similar occasions have consequences more than* n *times as great as those resulting from one performance.* And it is in this class of cases that obligations arise. It is in this class of cases that generalizing the act yields a different balance of advantage from the sum of the balances of advantage issuing from each individual act.[27]

Harrod's recommendation was that we abandon act utilitarianism and instead employ a Kantian form of utilitarianism according to which actions are right or wrong depending on the consequences *that would obtain were everyone to perform actions of the same kind*, a view more recently referred to as *utilitarian generalization*.[28] Although utilitarian generalization seems intuitively compelling, it faces two difficulties so severe that it is not even an advantage over an *actual-consequence* version of act utilitarianism.

Each difficulty stems from how we answer this question: How are we to specify those who are able to perform an action of the same kind? Consider our example of several companies discharging minute amounts of mercury into the river. When the Widget Company discharges wastes, is it discharging *when three other companies are discharging wastes into the river*, or is it discharging wastes into the river *simpliciter*? Which description we use to describe Widget's action for the application of utilitarian generalization makes all the difference to the outcome of our application. Whereas the first description takes the behavior of others to be relevant to the description of what the Widget Company is doing, the second description does *not* take the behavior of others to be relevant.

David Lyons has argued that the behavior of others is relevant in describing actions for an application of utilitarian generalization.[29] But when we take the behavior of others into account in describing our actions, the results of applying utilitarian generalization and an *actual-consequence* act utilitarianism are equivalent, often because we are applying utilitarian generalization to classes of actions that include only one member. For example, when we assess the Widget Company's action on actual-consequence act utilitarianism, we seem to find that it produces no additional harm to the endangered species and so, we will assume, its consequences are no worse than the consequences of any alternative. When we assess the Widget Company's action on utilitarian generalization, we ask what would happen if everyone did what Widget Company did, that is, discharge wastes into the river when three other companies were already doing so. As Lyons argued, we come up with the same answer. The reason is that if everyone does what Widget Company can do (i.e., discharge wastes into the river when three other chemical companies are already doing so), there is no harm to the endangered species, since the pollutants dumped by the other three companies will kill off the endangered species anyway.

The alternative, for which Marcus Singer has argued, is that we do not take the behavior of others into account in applying the generalization test.[30] That leaves us able to articulate the kind of generalization in which we are interested, since we can now ask what would happen if everyone were to act in the same way, regardless of how others were or were not acting in this way. When we understand the generalization test in this way, we can use it to assess each company's actions regardless of how many other companies are or are not acting in this way. But excluding the behavior of others in this way leads to our second difficulty with utilitarian generalization. What if the damage is so severe that one more participant adding to it causes little or nothing more that is bad, but if one individual does not participate in the harmful group behavior, that nonparticipation will create significantly more harm? The following industrial-environmental dilemma illustrates this possibility.

Imagine a company that is substantially more careful with wastes than is required by law and stands head and shoulders over its competition in all things affecting the environment. Suppose this company, with so many environmental safeguards in place that it has become a model for how an industry can change in the direction of environmental safety, realizes that it could stop externalizing the cost of removing a toxic waste in its smokestacks by adding expensive scrubbers that are not legally required. Should it do so? The generalization test would say it should, since the results of everyone doing that would be better, and the results of everyone not doing that are bad. Yet if our environmentally aware company puts the expensive scrubbers in place, it will put itself out of business, and the only consequence will be that the company most enlightened about the environment will no longer exist.[31]

This difficulty seems to show that utilitarian generalization is inadequate to account for our moral obligations. When we combine the difficulties borne by each horn of the dilemma on the behavior of others, we seem forced to abandon the generalization test and utilitarian generalization as adequate alternatives to actual-consequence act utilitarianism in these cases: Either the results of applying the test are the same as the results of applying actual-consequence act utilitarianism or the results of applying the test lead to a new group of counterexamples. Fortunately, as we have seen, the problem confronting act utilitarianism is illusory because the foreseeable-consequence approach is perfectly adequate to solve these problems.

Notes

Acknowledgments: I am grateful to Lawrence Becker, Dale Jamieson, Raymond Frey, Alan Gewirth, Stephen Nathanson, Moreland Perkins, Holbrook Robinson, Donald Scherer, W. E. Schlaretzki, Kristin Shrader-Frechette, and Henry West for commenting on earlier versions of this paper; to Allan Gibbard for discussions about the concept of consequences; to Brian Barry and Derek Parfit for discussions about contributory issues, and, finally, to Jackie DuPont for encouraging me to abandon an abysmal title.

1. Since this chapter is not a case study but an examination of the consequential approach to these and similar problems, I have posited, for the sake of discussion, typical but controversial assumptions that I would challenge if I were discussing a case study of mercury pollution. The most questionable assumption in the example is that, government "safety" levels aside, levels of mercury poisoning in fish below .4 ppm do not cause damage. Note also that throughout the chapter I am exploring the adequacy of consequential and causal analyses for cases that do not involve synergistic effects.

2. Derek Parfit, *Reasons and Persons* (Oxford: Clarendon Press, 1984), 80. Parfit claims his example of the *Harmless Torturers* "derives entirely from the stimulus of this [Glover's] brilliant example" (p. 511). Glover's example involves 100 unarmed tribesmen, each eating a lunch of 100 baked beans, and 100 bandits, each of whom steals one bean from each tribesman. See Jonathan Glover, "It Makes No Difference Whether or Not I Do It," *Proceedings of the Aristotelian Society* 49 (1975): 174–75.

3. For this reason, Parfit embraced a multiact form of consequentialism akin to utilitarian generalization. For a discussion of the inadequacy of Parfit's specific proposal, see Bart Gruzalski, "Parfit's Impact on Utilitarianism," *Ethics* 98 (1986). For a brief discussion of utilitarian generalization, see the appendix to this chapter.

4. This follows from a straightforward application of the orthodox "avoidance conception" of consequences according to which an event is a consequence of an action if that event would not occur were the agent to perform an alternative to the action in question. On this analysis of "consequence," an event is among the consequences of an action only if there is some alternative the agent could perform that would not be followed by the event in question. For discussions of this notion of consequences, see Lars Bergstrom, *The Alternatives and Consequences of Actions* (Stockholm: Amqvist & Wiksell, 1966), esp. 127–32; Allan Gibbard, "Doing No More Harm Than Good," *Philosophical Studies* 25 (1973): 158–73, esp. 160–62; J. Howard Sobel, "Utilitarianisms: Simple and General," *Inquiry* 13 (1970): 394–449; and Richard Brandt, *A Theory of the Good and the Right* (Oxford: Clarendon Press, 1979), 271–72.

5. This example is from Bart Gruzalski, "Foreseeable Consequence Utilitarianism," *Australasian Journal of Philosophy* 59 (June 1981): 167, and is close to one used to make the same point in Brian Ellis, "Retrospective and Prospective Utilitarianism," *Nous* 15 (1981): 325–40, at 327

6. An arithmetic calculation of the expected desirability would require calculating not only the probabilities involved but also the value of the "costs" of polluting against the "benefits." My working assumption is that destroying the members of an endangered species in its last natural habitat and causing such harms as Minamata disease outweigh any plausible benefits.

7. Parfit, *Reasons and Persons*, 75.

8. See "Parfit's Impact on Utilitarianism," 782, where I first proposed this solution to Parfit's problem.

9. Kristin Shrader-Frechette, "Parfit and Mistakes in Moral Mathematics," *Ethics* 98 (October 1987): 50–60.

10. Ibid., 60.

11. Shrader-Frechette writes: "Gruzalski . . . makes a *similar* point. He notes that Parfit has not been able to solve the problem of contributory causation because he uses an actual-consequence version of act utilitarianism, rather than a foreseeable-consequences (*risk*) version." Ibid., 56 n. 18; italics added.

12. One technical complexity is that the hybrid suggested in the text would lead to a double weighting of consequences unless this were ruled out by an ad hoc device. For example, if an action caused lethal microphysical changes, on this hybrid view that action would have both the negative consequence of a lethal microphysical change *and* a death as a consequence, thus double counting the value of the death.

13. H. L. A. Hart and A. M. Honore, *Causation in the Law* (Oxford: Clarendon Press, 1959), 124.

14. We may want to hold them accountable for doing wrong by risking such harm, but that is a separate assessment.

15. Should this lack of inexactitude seem to be a weakness of the foreseeable-consequence approach, it is worth recalling Aristotle when he wrote: "Our discussion will be adequate if it has as much clearness as the subject-matter admits of, for precision is not to be sought for alike in all discussions. . . . Now fine and just actions, which political science investigates, admit of much variety and fluctuation of opinion. . . . We must be content, then, in speaking of such subjects and with such premises to indicate the truth roughly and in outline . . . for it is the mark of an educated man to look for precision in each class of things just so far as the nature of the subject admits" (1094b12–26).

16. Lyons refers to such acts as "causally homogeneous." See David Lyons, *Forms and Limits of Utilitarianism* (Oxford: Clarendon Press, 1965), 76.

17. Ibid., 76–77.

18. Recall that we assumed each plant was discharging an equal amount of methyl chloride into the river. For extending this approach to unequal contributions to a harm, see the last paragraph of this part.

19. These principles are to be understood in such a way that the possibility of double counting has been ruled out. Consider two acts, A and B. Let A be the act of pressing a button that causes a lever to move. The movement of the lever causes an M&M candy to fall into the hands of Mickey, who is thereby pleased. Act B is the act of giving Mickey an M&M candy directly. It has, as a consequence, Mickey's being pleased. The effect of A is a lever moving which causes an M&M falling into the hands of Mickey which, in turn, is the cause of Mickey's being pleased. Hence, if Mickey's being pleased is assigned some numerical value, say $+5$, then, on VC, the candy falling into Mickey's hands would also have a value of $+5$, and, also on VC, the lever's moving would have a value of $+5$. It would seem to follow that the total value of the consequences of act A would be $+15$, since the consequences of act A include the lever's moving, the M&M falling into Mickey's hands, and Mickey's being pleased. On the other hand, the total value of the consequences of act B would only be $+5$. Yet it is ridiculous to accept the conclusion that the value of the consequences of pressing a button that has, as its eventual consequence, Mickey's receiving an M&M candy and so being pleased is greater than the value of the consequences of Mickey's being given,

straight out, an M&M candy. To avoid this result, double counting is prohibited: Both VC and VP must be understood not to be applicable when a factor (some X) deriving extrinsic value from another factor (some Y) are *both* among the consequences of an act that is being consequentially assessed.

20. See Raymond Martin, "Singular Causal Explanations," *Theory and Decision* 2 (1972): 221–37.

21. I am indebted to W. E. Schlaretzki for this objection.

22. G. E. Moore, *Ethics* (New York: Holt and Company, 1912), 126.

23. A difference not relevant to this concern is that VW characterizes a relationship between intrinsic valuables, whereas VP identifies only the extrinsic value of the parts of wholes.

24. William David Ross, *The Right and the Good* (Oxford: Clarendon Press, 1930), 72.

25. Lyons, *Forms and Limits*, 89.

26. There is a strong theoretical reason for thinking that the VC/VP analysis is irrelevant as a guide to action and corresponding assessments of moral obligation. Recall the objection to VP that the assessment of equally sized parts as having equal value was as arbitrary as assessing these equally sized parts as having unequal value. The crucial step in answering this objection was that there was a need or necessity for the parts of the whole to be assessed individually. Given that the foreseeable-consequence account satisfactorily accounts for our obligations in such cases, there is no need within the foreseeable-consequence framework to employ the VC/VP analysis, and hence that objection to VP cannot be answered within a probabilistic framework. It follows that VP is not a legitimate principle of value assessment in probabilistic contexts.

27. R. F. Harrod, "Utilitarianism Revised," *Mind* 45 (1936): 148; italics in original.

28. Harrod writes: "He who wishes people so to act that the ends of sentient beings should be best served, must wish them to act in accordance with the Kantian and not the crude utilitarian principle. He will find it necessary to refine the crude utilitarian principle by applying the process of generalization in all relevant cases, that is in all cases where the consequences of n similar acts exceed n times the consequences of any one. . . . The test is always—Would this action if done by all in similar relevant circumstances lead to the breakdown of some established method of society for securing its ends?" (pp. 148–49). He continues: "Now when the process is applied there will be loss of advantage in particular instances; but there is a gain if it is applied in a large number of instances" (p. 151).

29. Lyons, *Forms and Limits*, 91–115.

30. Marcus Singer, *Generalization in Ethics* (New York: Knopf, 1961).

31. This argument is developed at length in Bart Gruzalski, "The Defeat of Utilitarian Generalization," *Ethics* 93 (1982). See also Glover, "It Makes No Difference," 177.

Alan Gewirth

Chapter 8

Two Types of Cost–Benefit Analysis

The general idea of cost–benefit analysis (CBA) seems eminently rational. CBA is both a method of analysis and a set of precepts based on that method. According to CBA in general, in deciding to engage in any action, one should estimate the costs of performing the action and the benefits expected to result from it, and one should not do the action unless its expected or actual benefits are greater than its costs. In this broad sense, CBA is a version of the traditional pleasure–pain calculus upheld by utilitarians, which in turn goes back to that "art of measuring" pleasures and pains that Socrates declared to be "the salvation of life."[1]

Cost–Benefit Analysis and Human Action

Even apart from the controversial equation of benefits with pleasures and costs with pains, CBA in the general form just presented is intrinsically connected with the nature of human action. For all action aims at purposes that seem to the agent to be of some good or value; as Aristotle said, "Every art and every inquiry, and likewise every action and choice, seems to aim at some good."[2] This purposive good, which of course varies enormously in its specific content from one action to another, is the envisaged benefit of the action; thus, benefit of some sort or other is intrinsically connected with action as its intended purpose.

Cost is also a part of every action, in at least two interrelated respects. First, whatever action is undertaken requires, at least at the the time of the action, that one forgo other actions, and hence other purposes with their intended benefits, that might then be available to the agent. As Lionel Robbins put it in a perhaps overly dramatic way, "Everywhere we turn, if we choose one thing we must relinquish others which, in different circumstances, we would wish not to have relinquished. . . . Economics brings into full view that conflict of choice which is one of the permanent aspects of human existence. Your economist is a true tragedian."[3] These omitted choices count as what economists call *opportunity costs* of the action one undertakes. Second, action toward fulfillment of purposes often requires work and effort. Although some actions may be intrinsically pleasant or otherwise valued for their own sakes, many or most are not; functioning as means to desired ends, they involve costs that necessarily accompany the action.

In pointing out these connections of costs and benefits with action, I am not to be understood as implying that all agents actually follow CBA in their actions, nor am I endorsing the "economic approach to human behavior" according to which all agents always act according to stable preferences whose fulfillment they maximize on the basis of market constraints.[4] The fact that upholders of this approach must constantly guard against the accusation of tautology suggests some of its limitations; others are indicated below.

I have so far discussed actions, and thus costs and benefits, including their implicit criteria, only from the standpoint of the individual agent. But the criteria of "costs" and "benefits," as well as the actions and projects that involve them, may also be more general and social. An especially important aspect of CBA that proceeds from a social standpoint is that here it is not a matter of the individual agent's calculating his or her own costs and benefits from within his or her own value criteria, but that some social agency, especially (but not only) the state, calculates costs and benefits for a whole society by criteria that are themselves more social.

Now these concepts of "costs and benefits for a whole society" and "social criteria" are initially very vague. We can begin to clarify them by connecting them with the previous standpoint of the individual agent. The whole tradition of moral philosophy can be understood largely as focusing on three central questions about this connection between the individual and the social.[5] First, there is the *authoritative* question: Why should one be moral, where being moral consists in the individual agent's giving favorable consideration to the interests of many or all other persons even when this conflicts with his or her own interests? Or, to put it another way, why should the individual agent follow a social consideration, whereby he or she takes positive account of costs and benefits to other persons, when he or she engages in his or her own purposive actions? Second, there is the *substantive* question: *Which interests* of other persons should receive such favorable consideration from the individual agent and thereby count as benefits to be weighed against costs? Third, there is the *distributive* question: To the interests of *which other persons* should the individual agent give such favorable consideration: of all persons or only of some, and if of all, then of all equally, and if of some, then of which persons as against which others, and on what basis? The substantive and distributive questions ask in two different but related ways for the criteria of estimating the benefits and the costs that enter into CBA, and hence also for the precepts that are set forth on the basis of those criteria.

Economic and Moral Cost–Benefit Analyses

These three central questions of moral philosophy have received many different answers throughout the history of the subject. I now want to focus on two different types of CBA that are distinguished by their different answers especially to the second and third questions, in that they provide different substantive and distributive criteria for estimating costs and benefits and for giving the resultant precepts. I call these types the *economic* and the *moral*. It may seem question begging to confine "moral" to one type as against another when each type can be construed as providing answers to the central questions of moral philosophy. My initial reason for this is that even though the type I call "economic" takes account of costs and benefits to persons other than or in addition to the individual agent, its criteria for this accounting are primarily *monetary* and thus economic in a directly recognizable sense. The criteria used by the type I call "moral," in contrast, are the *moral rights* of persons, especially their human rights. To estimate costs and benefits in terms of money may give results that are very different from those that emerge when moral rights are made fundamental. The differences partly coincide with the divergences that have traditionally divided utilitarian and deontological criteria of moral rightness; but because the economic type of CBA focuses on monetary criteria of costs and benefits, it leads to further differences both from traditional utilitarianism and from the moral type based on human rights.

This distinction between monetary and rights criteria may be challenged on the ground that monetary considerations are themselves also considerations about rights. For money is a form of property rights, and these may be moral as well as legal. This obligation can be answered in at least four different ways. First, the distinction I have drawn is between property rights and *other* kinds of moral rights, defined as having objects other than money: life, health, safety, education, and many others. Second, the distinction between monetary and rights considerations still holds, in the important respect that one (but not the only) central problem area of CBA in general concerns the ways in which the moral rights of some persons are affected by the monetary expenditures or nonexpenditures of other persons. Third, many of the objects of moral rights cannot be measured or bought for money, so the property rights involved in money are of lesser extension than moral rights generally. Fourth, moral rights in some of their most important aspects serve to criticize and evaluate property rights, including the ways or respects in which all property rights, including those involved in money, deserve to be regarded as moral rights, and in what morally justified ways money ought to be used.

A further challenge to the distinction between the economic and the moral CBAs is the contention that the economic CBA takes account of the very values—especially human life, health, and safety—that are the focus of the moral CBA. Indeed, the objection may be pressed further; it may be held that it is a category mistake to oppose monetary values to moral rights because money can be used to measure how strongly one moral right is preferred to another or to other values. Hence, the monetary criterion has an extension that includes but also goes beyond moral rights.

There is some truth in this contention. It is not my aim here to ignore or downgrade the many valuable contributions that the economic CBA can make and has made to the achievement of rational decisions on matters of social policy ranging from energy and environment to medical care and education. Nevertheless, in distinguishing between the economic and the moral CBAs as I do here, I aim to bring out sharply those aspects of the economic CBA that are most questionable and most in need of supplementation because they tend to reduce questions of life, health, and safety exclusively to monetary considerations. The point is that there are other, normatively prior ways of assessing basic human values—ways that view these values as objects of rights and hence as setting normatively necessary duties to protect the values, quite apart from monetary considerations. It is for this reason that I here differentiate between measurement exclusively in terms of money and measurement or assessment by reference to those most vital human interests that are the objects of moral, especially human, rights. I subsequently take up a further objection to the dichotomy between the economic and the moral CBAs (see the section "Substantive Criteria of the Moral Cost–Benefit Analysis").

The Economic Cost–Benefit Analysis

Since the economic CBA has already been the subject of a vast literature, and since my main concern here is to bring out its contrasts with the moral CBA and the reasons why the latter is needed, I shall be very brief concerning the economic CBA. First, we must note the distinction between it and cost-effectiveness analysis.[6] In cost-effectiveness analysis, envisaged benefits are held constant as ends to be maintained or achieved, and the analysis is concerned solely with the most efficient means for realizing the end, where "most efficient" signifies minimum cost. An example is "the choice between hemodialysis (i.e., treatment by artificial kidneys) and transplantation as means of prolonging the lives of people with chronic renal disease."[7] Here it is not the envisaged end or benefit—prolonging life—but only the alternative means that are subjected to monetary measurement and calculation.

In the economic CBA, in contrast, both benefits and costs are estimated in money terms. Whether the envisaged benefit should be promoted at all by the project in question is to be decided by comparing its monetary value with the monetary costs of achieving it. The decision is to be affirmative only if the benefit's monetary value exceeds its cost. As usually analyzed, such a decision requires that the project achieve a "Pareto improvement."[8] According to this, one allocation of resources is an improvement over another if it involves at least one person's being made better off while no person is made worse off. The criterion of being made better off consists simply in the preferences of the person concerned, so that if some person prefers allocation X to allocation Y, then that person is made better off by X than by Y. And if no person prefers Y to X, then the change from X to Y is a Pareto improvement. The criterion of such preference, in turn, is the person's willingness to pay (or to be paid) in money for accepting X as against Y. Thus whether a project involving some envisaged benefit is to be undertaken, according to the economic CBA, is to be determined by whether the persons affected by the project are willing to pay, or to be paid, for that benefit despite its other costs. In a further version, the determining criterion is extended so that it consists simply in the *possibility* of being paid to compensate for losses.

On this view, then, even when some project threatens the lives of various persons, such as industrial workers in risky occupations, the economic CBA's decision whether to pursue it is to be determined by the minimum sum of money those persons are willing to accept to compensate for the risk of losing their lives. Thus, for example, the risk of cancer may be imposed on some person in some job if he or she is willing to accept that risk on payment of a certain sum of money.[9] Since that person prefers working at some carcinogenically risky job, and hence earning money, to not working at all, or prefers a carcinogenically riskier job at more pay to a less risky job at less pay, while in each case no one else is made worse off, it follows that the former situation is in each case a Pareto improvement over the latter. Thus the economic CBA sanctions that even the benefit of preserving human life is to be measured in monetary terms through the willingness of persons to pay, or to be paid, for that preservation.

Substantive Criteria of the Economic Cost–Benefit Analysis

This brief characterization already indicates what are the substantive and distributive criteria of the economic CBA and what problems they raise. On the *substantive* side the criterion is money, specifically, willingness to pay. This is a *homogeneous* or *unidimensional* criterion because it assumes that all the benefits and costs of projected policies can be measured by a single common monetary standard. But this assumption seems very doubtful, for reasons similar to those that perplex the utilitarian attempt to assess all goods in terms of "pleasure," "happiness," or "utility." The willingness to pay may be an adequate criterion for a single person contemplating a choice between buying two different kinds of ice cream. But can the criterion encompass the more complex values that enter into such social policies as the choice between greater employment and carcinogenic dangers, or between the building of income-producing football stadiums or airfields and the displacement of lifelong residents?

More generally, if we recur to the connection indicated above between CBA and human action, there is the question whether all values, goods, or benefits can or should be estimated in money terms. How about personal love or the civil liberties and other democratic values?[10] In opposition to such questions, a noted economist has protested that "treatises on the subject [of economic CBA] make clear that certain ethical or political principles may dominate the advantages and disadvantages capturable by cost–benefit analysis."[11] There remains, however, the question what are these "dominating" ethical and political principles, especially when such values as life, health, and safety are themselves included in the calculations that are subject to the economic CBA.

Of special concern is the fact that the economic CBA treats human life, health, and safety not as basic goods whose protection must be given primary consideration but as "costs" that are to be weighed against the "benefits" of various productive arrangements and commodities. In this commodification of human life and health the economic CBA mistakenly assumes that some great risk of death can be compensated for by a certain amount of money. Even more important, perhaps, the medical application of the economic CBA raises sinister possibilities that have been held to assimilate it to the downgrading of the right to life that was characteristic of Nazi Germany. "There, racism overrode personal autonomy; here, it might be an economic rationale—the attitude that we won't spend so much per year to keep somebody alive."[12]

To this objection about the potential evil of monetarizing human life it is frequently replied that this same "evil" is found in such innocent and indeed beneficial contexts as life insurance. In buying life insurance, one implicitly places a certain monetary value on one's life. It is a mistake, however, to generalize from such contexts to medical, workplace, and other situations where the value of human life and health is held to be measured by money. For example, the willingness to work for more pay, such as in carcinogenically risky occupations, is interpreted as accepting a certain "cost" in return for the social "benefit" of making such products as asbestos and vinyl chloride. But there is an important difference between this kind of situation and the buying of life insurance—a difference that derives from the role of human freedom in the sense of the ability to control one's choices and outcomes in incurring costs and achieving benefits. In buying life insurance, one recognizes that death is inevitable for everyone sooner or later, and one does not thereby voluntarily incur the serious risk of death. But to undertake the risk of cancer by one's work is not itself inevitable, so the compensation involves putting a market price on one's life in the context of a controllable, avoidable choice. The economic CBA's Pareto criterion thus involves that one's life is to be given a monetary value not simply as a matter of an unavoidable outcome but in the context of a freely chosen line of action whereby one voluntarily subjects oneself to the risk of death in return for various economic benefits. In this respect, human life is treated as one marketable, voluntarily dispensable commodity among others.

Distributive Criteria of the Economic Cost–Benefit Analysis

Closely related to these substantive issues are problems about the *distributive* criterion of the economic CBA. The difficulties here are similar to those that confront traditional utilitarianism with its purely aggregative criterion of maximizing utility overall. As Mishan puts it, "In cost–benefit analysis we are concerned with the economy as a whole, with the welfare of a defined society, and not any smaller part of it."[13] But from this it follows that when the economic CBA recommends some project or policy because it yields monetary benefits in excess of its costs, no account is taken of how these benefits are distributed: "The quantitative outcome of a cost–benefit calculation itself carries no distributional weight; it shows that the total of gains exceeds the total of losses, no more."[14] Despite the Pareto criterion's requirement that no one is to be made "worse off" by some projected change, because a "compensating variation" can be provided for those who lose by the change, the fact that this compensation may be only "potential" entails that some persons or groups may be very adversely affected, including even those who are already worse off:

> A project that is adjudged feasible by reference to a cost–benefit analysis is, therefore, quite consistent with an economic arrangement that makes the rich richer and the poor poorer. It is also consistent with manifest inequity, for an enterprise that is an attractive proposition by the lights of a cost–benefit calculation may be one that offers opportunities for greater profits and pleasure to one group, in the pursuit of which substantial damages and suffering may be endured by other groups.[15]

In opposition to this unequalizing and inequitable distributive possibility of the economic CBA, it may be contended that its concern for maximizing benefits over costs assimilates it to the traditional utilitarian concern for maximizing utility, with a resultant tendency toward equal distribution. Traditional utilitarians, beginning at least with Hume, have argued that because of the diminishing marginal utility of money, a simple monetary unit, such as a dollar, adds more utility to a poor person than to a rich one, and so, in order to maximize utility, money or wealth should be redistributed until equality is reached. The utilitarians at once add, however, that in order to provide incentives for working to produce more utility, this equalizing trend should be severely limited, so drastic inequalities are still justified.[16] A further point is that the "inefficiency costs" of effectuating monetary transfers from the rich to the poor may be so great that they drastically decrease the total amount of resulting utility.[17]

A more specific distributive difficulty of the economic CBA derives from its application of the Pareto criterion to workers in risky occupations. Since the poorer a person is, the greater is the marginal utility for him or her of a given sum of money, whereas the opposite is true the richer a person is, the poor are willing to accept much greater risks—such as those that stem from working with carcinogenic chemicals—for much less money. This casts doubt on the Paretian "preference" model where workers "voluntarily" accept compensation for risks and thereby show that they consider themselves to be "better off" than they would be without the risks and the compensation. Many workers are in effect confronted with a forced choice, since the alternative to their having the risky job with its slightly added compensation is their not having any job at all.

When it is replied that in such cases the carcinogenic risk is imposed on workers with their consent, the further question remains of how *informed* is this consent. This is another aspect of the role of freedom, to which I referred above. Is each of the persons who chooses among alternatives able to know the degree of risk of the possibly carcinogenic alternatives for which compensation is required? Industrial workers in factories making asbestos, kepone, vinyl chloride, and other lethal substances were surely not aware of the risks during the years that elapsed between their initial exposure and the time when some of them came down with cancer. For them, consequently, the Pareto criterion would not apply insofar as it assumes that persons who express their preferences by their acceptance of compensation for risks are aware of the magnitude of the risks. And even when, as is increasingly the case in recent years, research is pursued into carcinogens and the results are made public, there remains the question whether complicated statistical calculations can be understood by the workers who are most vulnerable to their possibly varying implications.

Can There Be a Rights-Centered Cost–Benefit Analysis?

In view of these moral shortcomings of the economic CBA's substantive and distributive criteria, it is important to examine whether there can be another type of CBA that avoids these difficulties. For this purpose, I turn now to the moral CBA, whose criteria of costs and benefits are not money payable or receivable but the moral rights of persons.

Most appeals to morality in connection with CBA have invoked moral criticisms such as the ones presented above against the economic CBA. There have also been some discussions of moral CBAs as alternatives to the economic CBA; but these discussions, while suggestive, have been mainly programmatic and taxonomic rather than attempts to provide actual contents for a rationally justified moral CBA.[18] And they have been concerned almost exclusively with distributive criteria rather than substantive ones. In this section I try to go beyond these valuable prior attempts by focusing on a determinate kind of moral criterion—human rights—and by building on some of my previous work concerned with the rational justification and contents of a moral rights principle.

At the outset, the idea of a moral CBA centered on rights may seem anomalous for at least two reasons. First, to use moral rights as the criteria of costs and benefits raises the difficult prior question what are the criteria of moral rights. The paying and receiving of money is a quite "objective" standard, in that money dealings are relatively easy to verify and measure even if the "willingness" aspect may raise problems. Similarly, the existence of *legal* rights is relatively easy to confirm by reference to the statute books of municipal law. But it is objected that there are no similar intersubjectively recognized *moral* rights, and so to use them as criteria of costs and benefits may serve to reinforce doubts and conflicts rather than resolve them.

This objection is too pessimistic. It ignores the wide acceptance of the idea of human rights; even if such of their contents as social and economic rights are controversial, the development of the modern welfare state has done much to resolve the controversies. The objection also ignores the philosophical elucidations that the idea of human rights has received, which give rationally grounded arguments for the existence and contents of moral rights. It will be helpful for understanding what follows if I give a brief summary of one such elucidation, which I have worked out in considerable detail elsewhere.[19]

The main idea is directly related to the point made above about the intrinsic connection of CBA with human action. For human rights are also intrinsically connected with human action because their purpose is to protect equally the general abilities of agency on the part of all persons. The rights serve this function because their objects, what they are rights to, are the generic features and necessary conditions for goods of action and successful action in general, and because the rights involve that all persons have equal dignity in that they have equal claims or entitlements to these goods as their personal due.

In their most general aspect, the necessary goods and generic features of action are freedom and well-being. Freedom is the *procedural* necessary condition of action; it consists in controlling one's behavior by one's unforced choice while having knowledge of relevant circumstances. Well-being, as here understood, is the *substantive* necessary condition of action and generally successful action; it consists in having the general abilities and conditions needed for achieving one's purposes. Such well-being falls into a hierarchy of three levels that are progressively less needed for action. Basic well-being consists in having the essential prerequisites of action, such as life, physical integrity, mental equilibrium. Nonsubtractive well-being consists in having the general abilities and conditions needed for maintaining undiminished one's general level of purpose fulfillment and one's capabilities for particular actions. Additive well-being consists in having the general abilities and conditions needed for increasing one's general level of purpose fulfillment and one's capabilities for particular actions. Examples of nonsubtractive well-being are not being lied to, stolen from, or threatened with violence. Examples of additive well-being are self-esteem, education, and opportunities for earning wealth and income. Of course, not all the rights to these kinds of well-being have governments as their respondents or protectors. But since the rights in question are claim rights, they entail correlative duties to assist or forebear with a view to supporting the right holders' having the objects of their rights. For this reason, the rights serve to protect the important action-related interests of persons.

The distinction of levels of well-being already shows how differences in degrees of importance of various human goods or interests can be ascertained objectively. Basic well-being is normatively prior to the other kinds of well-being because it is more needed both for action and for generally successful action; and this priority also holds for the respective rights. A similar priority obtains in general for nonsubtractive rights in relation to additive rights, although this priority may be reversed according to the criterion of degrees of needfulness for action. With regard to freedom, the matter is more complicated; but some kinds of freedom are subordinate to basic well-being, according to the criterion of degrees of needfulness for action. These levels of well-being and freedom function in a way analogous to the "lexicographical order" set forth by John Rawls.[20] But because of their derivation from the needs of agency, they have a justification that is more firmly and objectively grounded than the somewhat intuitionist basis that Rawls adduces for his ordering.

The general principle of human rights is that all persons have equal rights to freedom and to well-being in its three levels. I call it the *Principle of Generic Consistency* because the argument that justifies it combines the material consideration of the generic features or goods of action with the formal consideration of the avoidance of self-contradiction on the part of every agent. This argument provides an answer to the "authoritative question" mentioned earlier. I have presented this argument in considerable detail elsewhere,[21] but for reasons of space I omit recapitulation of it here. Instead, I focus in this chapter on the implications of the Principle of Generic Consistency for the substantive and distributive questions.

I turn to a second objection against the idea of a moral CBA. It might be contended that nothing analogous to the kind of calculation of monetary costs and benefits that enters into the economic CBA can be found in the sphere of moral rights because these are not subject to weighing and compromise. This, however, would be to regard all rights as absolute, such that none can be overridden in any circumstances. That this is mistaken can be seen from the fact that moral rights may conflict with one another. Now an essential criterion for resolving such conflicts is provided by the derivation of rights from the needs of action and successful action in general, and the resulting distinction between degrees of needfulness for action pointed out above. For since the purpose of the human rights is to protect or secure persons' abilities of agency, rights whose objects are more important because more needed for action take precedence over rights whose objects are less needed for action.

Substantive Criteria of the Moral Cost–Benefit Analysis

It is in terms of such rights and their objects that the moral CBA weighs costs and benefits. I first discuss the substantive side of this criterion and then the distributive side. The *substantive* side—which interests are to count in determining costs and benefits—can be initially illustrated by a familiar example from small-scale human relations. Suppose A can save innocent B's life only by telling a lie to C. (To avoid certain complications, let us assume that C is not the would-be killer and is entirely innocent in this regard.) Here there is a conflict between two different interests that are the objects of two different rights: the right of B not to be killed and the right of C not to be lied to. Each of these rights is grounded in the needs of agency. This is obvious in the case of the basic right not to be killed, but it is also true in the case of the nonsubtractive right not to be lied to. For if someone is lied to about some fact, then he or she is led to base present or future action on a false conception about that fact, and this tends to decrease his or her action's effectiveness or likelihood of success.

Because, in the situation envisaged here, C's right not to be lied to is in conflict with B's right to life, the benefit of fulfilling either right can be obtained only at the cost of infringing the other right. In this conflict of rights, the moral cost–benefit calculation does not, like the economic CBA, proceed by considering the monetary values of fulfilling or infringing the respective rights. Suppose, for example, A is quite poor while C is very rich and is willing to pay a large sum of money to A if A will divulge B's whereabouts. On one version of the economic

CBA, the cost to C of being lied to for the purpose of saving B's life would be outweighed by the benefit to A of truthfully telling C where B is.

But on the moral CBA, it is required that A lie to C in order to save B's life, because B's right to life overrides C's right not to be lied to. So we have here a case of CBA in which the primary objects of the analysis are moral rights and their corresponding interests, and the criterion for arriving at a justified decision is the degrees to which the objects of the conflicting rights are needed for action. A similar result emerges in such a case as where D, lost and starving in the wilderness, stumbles upon E's well-stocked cabin and breaks in for the purpose of avoiding starvation. Here the cost to E of having a property right infringed is outweighed by the benefit to D of avoiding starvation and thus preserving his or her right to life.

As these examples indicate, the costs and benefits that enter into the moral CBA, while not homogeneous and unidimensional like the economic CBA's monetary criterion, are not simply a random collection. Instead, they are *multidimensional* but also *hierarchically ordered* because of the varying degrees of their needfulness for action. From this it follows that a parallel account cannot, in general, be given for situations in which nonsubtractive rights conflict with one another or additive rights with one another unless some further relevant differences can be found in the respective rights. But such differences will often be found by considering the respective degrees of needfulness for action.[22]

The thesis just presented may be used, however, to mount another objection against the dichotomy of the economic and the moral CBA. It may be contended that what I have called the moral CBA is simply one variety of the economic CBA because of the very fact that it calculates the relative importance of rights in terms of the degrees of their needfulness for action. For this fact shows that the calculation in question is economic, in a general but basic sense. In a tradition that goes back at least to Hume, the economic is not restricted to money or to material goods; its definition is far more general: It deals with "economizing," the allocation of scarce resources having alternative uses.[23] Now, in what I have called the moral CBA, these resources are rights, and they are scarce at least in the sense that, in the situations envisaged above, they cannot all be fulfilled. Indeed, it has been argued that a calculative procedure like the one I have described amounts to a "utilitarianism of rights," because it regards the minimization of rights violations as a desirable end state to be achieved by violating lesser rights in order to prevent the violation of greater rights.[24] Hence, the moral CBA is just one version of the economic CBA, in the broader sense of "economic" just indicated.

There are at least three replies to this objection. First, the phrase "utilitarianism of rights" is seriously misleading here if it implies a constant readiness to interfere with rights for the sake of regularly achieving some sort of weighted minimization of rights violations. A "utilitarian" approach of this sort is different from considerations restricted to wide disparities in degrees of importance between the interests that are the objects of the respective rights, as in my above examples. Second, either the objection assumes, quite unsoundly, that all rights are absolute and thus never to be infringed or else it does not provide any alternative way of dealing with conflicts of rights. Third, in assimilating the moral CBA's calculation of the relative importance of rights to an "economizing" procedure, the objection overlooks the hierarchic ordering whereby some rights are so important that they are not to be made parts of a calculus at all, but instead must be held inviolate. I next discuss this point more fully.

The Moral Cost–Benefit Analysis and the Right to Life

The simple interpersonal schemes of the moral CBA that I have presented so far can be augmented in various ways, including extensions to problems of social policy. They bear directly, for example, on the issue discussed above of workers in carcinogenic occupations. The economic CBA requires that the benefits of preserving the workers' lives, health, and safety be weighed against the costs of providing such assurance, with the workers' willingness to accept added pay as a decisive criterion. This has all the shortcomings outlined above. The moral CBA, in contrast, requires that the benefits of workers' lives, health, and safety be maintained as basic rights that are not to be subjected to cost bargaining with a view to attaining an overall situation wherein monetary benefits as a whole are maximized regardless of their impacts on basic well-being. There may indeed be calculation of the most efficient way to preserve the rights in question amid the various benefits of industrial production; but the interests that are the objects of the rights must not be weighed against, and possibly endangered by or even sacrificed to, other potential benefits and costs. In this last kind of example, the moral CBA is very close to, if not identical with, the cost-effectiveness criterion I mentioned above, since what enters into the calculation is not the benefit-end itself but only the alternative means that figure as diverse costs of maintaining the end.

How far can the moral CBA carry us? I seem to be saying that because life and health are more needed for action than are other goods, the rights to life and health must always take precedence over the rights to these other goods. But it may be objected that if this is taken strictly, then no policy that even remotely threatens life should ever be undertaken for the sake of other values. Consider, for example, the making of automobiles. This gives employment to many workers and provides great convenience in transporting persons from one place to another. But it also creates risks of auto accidents resulting in death. Hence, by the moral CBA as so far interpreted, no automobiles should ever be built, since the cost in deaths outweighs the benefits of employment and convenience. But such a drastic conclusion is surely implausible.

An important reply to this objection focuses on the role of human freedom in the risk of death stemming from automobile accidents. This aspect was also mentioned above in connection with the contrast between buying life insurance and accepting pay for risky work as two ways of putting a monetary value on one's life. The crucial difference is the presence of freedom in the sense of control over one's behavior. The driver of a car has a certain, usually large, control over the degree of risk. He or she can markedly lower this risk by driving carefully and indeed defensively and by abstaining from liquor and drugs. Since it is the driver who mainly controls whether and to what extent his or her life will be endangered, he or she is still enabled to give primary weight to the right to life, despite the statistical possibility of mortal accidents. Thus the hierarchic priority of the right to life over the right to drive automobiles is not refuted by the lethal possibilities of the latter right.

This consideration can also be extended to the passengers who entrust their lives to the driver, since they are in a position to ascertain how much the driver can be trusted to protect their rights to life. To a lesser degree, and with special reference to various statistical considerations, a similar point applies to airplane passengers.

This point also permits a deeper understanding of the right to life. As was suggested above in the connection of both CBA and moral rights with human action, the "life" that is here in question is not mere vegetative existence; instead, it is a part of the whole context of agency, the general right to which is the source of all other moral rights. Agency includes freedom: the control of one's behavior by one's unforced choice while having knowledge of relevant circumstances. The right to life hence includes the right to control the circumstances that impinge on one's continuing to live. Such control is not arbitrary; viewed within the context of moral rights in general, it involves both wanting to live and being in a position to determine how this want will be best satisfied. For this reason, the driver's control over his or her driving serves to protect rather than to threaten the right to life.

The Moral Cost–Benefit Analysis and Medical Economics

The hierarchic primacy of the substantive values of human life, health, and safety as upheld by the moral CBA is also challenged by the whole vast area of medical economics. We may distinguish three different applications of CBA to the provision of health care. The first involves a direct use of the economic CBA. Here, the costs of providing health care are weighed against the economic benefits that result from it. For example, when antibiotic therapy was used against pneumonia, "work lost through sickness from this cause fell from 1,550,000 days in 1954 to 800,000 days in 1967, representing a saving in production of some £2.8 million per year."[25] In this context, medical care is viewed simply as an economically efficient device, on a par with labor-saving machinery and other technological procedures. By this criterion, however, in some circumstances medical care should be withheld; for example, "preventing premature deaths in young adults should bring short-term economic benefits, while prolonging life among those about to retire does the reverse."[26] Similarly, the polio immunization campaign in Britain in the late 1940s and early 1950s should not have been continued because "the costs of immunization exceeded what would have been the total economic cost of the disease."[27]

This application of the economic CBA raises an obvious question. Why should human life and health be evaluated solely or mainly as means to economic benefits, instead of being regarded as objects of rights that are supremely important goods or interests? A possible answer is the following: Only by measuring health-care benefits monetarily can one know whether the money to pay for their costs will be available. For if the benefits do not outweigh the costs economically, then one may not be able to cover those costs. This answer, however, makes the assumption that we have seen to be characteristic of the economic CBA: that all benefits and costs are homogeneous and unidimensional, to be assayed solely in monetary terms, so the only criterion for determining which policies yield "benefits" is their monetary excess over the monetary costs of those policies. This overlooks the distinct claim of human life and health to be regarded as essential human benefits, which deserve protection even if monetary losses in other areas result therefrom.[28]

This brings us to a second medical application of CBA. Here, the costs of providing certain kinds of health care are measured not against possibly resultant economic benefits but against the benefits for life and health that may result from alternative kinds of health care. In this application, a central consideration focuses on situations where "the distinct possibility exists that widespread use of some particular therapy would divert resources from other more effective health measures."[29] An example may be the kidney dialysis program as universally provided in the United States.

In this application, there is no departure from the moral CBA's hierarchic primacy of life and health. Taking this as a *general* end, the moral CBA engages in inquiries as to cost/effectiveness aimed at ascertaining how this end can be maximally achieved. But it is not to be sacrificed to other goods whose pursuit may bring greater monetary benefits.

A third health-care application of CBA weighs the costs of providing health care against other benefits that may be forgone because of those costs. Unlike the first application distinguished above, this one does not focus exclusively on the monetary benefits of health care; instead, it calls attention to the vast array of other human values and needs that may be jeopardized because of the overwhelming costs of medical care. "Resources are scarce. Funds spent for heart transplants could go for food programs for poor mothers or even into general economic development activities—not to mention education, environment, transportation, and defense."[30]

This application of CBA does not depart in principle from the hierarchic conception of the moral CBA, but it emphasizes that that conception must not be interpreted in an overly simple way. The primacy of life, health, and safety for human action must be viewed dynamically rather than statically. As such, it requires that attention be paid to causal factors ranging from the availability of food and shelter to the environmental circumstances that are among its necessary conditions. Thus the moral right to medical care must be supplemented by rights to various other goods that are needed not only for action in general but also for having general chances of success in achieving purposes for which one acts.

Nevertheless, the hierarchic ordering of moral rights calls attention to the relevant priorities; in particular, it emphasizes the degrees of importance of which public policies must take account. Three objections must be considered here. The first, stemming directly from the third health-care application of CBA distinguished above, is that the hierarchic ordering may jeopardize the fulfillment of other values. For example, when the right to unpolluted air, especially for such groups as asthmatics and the elderly, is upheld over lesser goods, such as "somewhat higher living standards for the rest of us," it is objected that "this defends the entitlement by assuming the costs involved are both trivial and diffused. Suppose, though, that the price to be paid is not 'somewhat higher living standards,' but the jobs of a number of workers?"[31]

This objection skirts the hierarchic issue by opposing one area of high rights-based need to another. Why should it be "a number of workers" who, by losing their jobs, have to pay the price of avoiding air pollution? Can there not be other, nonpolluting jobs for them? Here it is an indispensable, rights-securing function of government, at least as a last resort, to prevent there being such forced choices between polluting or carcinogenic jobs and no jobs at all.

A second, related objection concerns the contrast between the economic CBA with its criterion of workers' willingness to accept pay for risky jobs and the moral CBA's emphasis on the right to a safe work environment, with its concomitant requirement that government regulate the degrees of risk. The objection is that such governmental protection of rights is an elitist interference with workers' freedom. "Uniform standards do not enlarge worker choices; they deprive workers of the opportunity to select the job most appropriate to their own risk preferences. The actual 'rights' issue is whether those in upper income groups have a right to impose their job risk preferences on the poor."[32]

This objection, with its appeal to "risk preference," ignores the severe, objective disvalue for workers of life-threatening conditions of work, as well as the possibility of maintaining safety standards with costs of lesser degree to other persons, as against the high health-related costs of nonregulation. So here too the hierarchic ordering of rights in the moral CBA can be upheld by protecting workers from forced choices of lethal risks.

A third objection focuses on a perhaps deeper issue of freedom, in such a familiar example as where a needed blood transfusion is rejected because of religious beliefs. Here it would seem that the hierarchic priority of the right to life can be maintained only at the cost of violating the religious person's right to freedom, in the form of the nonviolation of his or her most cherished convictions. This issue, which I have discussed in some detail elsewhere,[33] returns us to the basis of human rights in the necessary goods of agency. Because of this basis, "where it is conclusively established that some person is unable or unwilling to accept or consent to what is needed for his having these goods, there is no point in forcing him to have them."[34] Such an extreme case, however, should not be extended to those kinds of forced choice where lethal risks can be avoided only at the cost of loss of livelihood.

Distributive Criteria of the Moral Cost–Benefit Analysis

Thus far I have been discussing the moral CBA from the substantive side: the goods or interests that enter into the calculations as objects of moral rights. Let us now turn to the *distributive* side: the persons or groups whose interests or rights are to be protected or promoted. The substantive and distributive sides are of course related, for if one maintains that certain interests, such as health, are among the benefits of which CBA must take account, then this also helps to determine which persons must have their interests promoted, namely, those who have or embody those interests. Similarly, if one holds the substantive position that interests X—such as health—take precedence over interests Y—such as money—in the calculation of costs and benefits, then if there is a conflict between X and Y, the distributive conclusion will follow that the persons who have a right to X must be given preference over the persons who have a right to Y.

Nevertheless, it is also important to consider the distributive side separately because its full criteria have essential aspects that are not exhausted by the substantive side. For example, even if it is agreed that the right to life must take precedence over the right to property, there still remain such questions as these: What is to be done when two persons' or groups' rights to life are in conflict, such as when limited resources require that choices be made between different lethal diseases as objects of funded research and hence between extending the lives of different groups of persons?[35] And in what proportion are various rights to be distributed among persons? The answer to this latter question may range from equality to various degrees of inequality.

The reason for this possible distributive range is that to determine the relative or comparative distribution of certain goods among persons requires the consideration not only of the goods themselves but also of a distinct criterion for distributing those goods. There is a considerable difference, for example, between such distributive criteria as contribution and need. Thus, according to Aristotle, distribution is to be determined by contribution, in that the persons who receive greater honors and political authority in a society must be those who contribute more to the ends for which the society exists, and who therefore have greater merit according to those ends. In an aristocratic society, dedicated to the inculcation and practice of the moral and intellectual virtues, the persons who embody and foster these virtues must have the highest political authority, while in oligarchic and democratic societies, dedicated respectively to wealth and freedom, political authority goes to the wealthy and to persons of free birth, respectively.[36] A closely similar criterion is upheld by utilitarians who argue that "value to society" should determine who gets various kinds of medical care, although here the criterion of contribution primarily figures not retrospectively, in terms of past contribution, but prospectively, in terms of how the rewarding of contributions serves to maximize utility.

Now, as we saw above, the economic CBA, with its focus on aggregative benefits for a whole society, has no independent concern for how those benefits are distributed among different persons or groups within the society. The reason for this is that "distributional effects" are "changes that occur in well-being of one group of individuals at the expense of another group"; they are "transfers from one set of purchasers and sellers to another, rather than increases in productive activity," and so they are not "real benefits."[37]

In contrast to this position, distributive considerations are of fundamental importance in the moral CBA because of its concern for equal rights to the necessary conditions of action and generally successful action. Its primary distributive criterion is not the meritocratic one of contribution but rather need. Here, the proportion in which relevant substantive goods are to be distributed is determined by persons' relative needs for those goods. For since, according to the Principle of Generic Consistency, moral rights are derived from the needs of agency, which are fundamentally equal for all actual or prospective agents, it follows that all persons have equal rights to freedom and well-being. But it also follows that if some persons are less capable of fulfilling these rights for themselves by their own efforts, they must receive greater assistance toward such fulfillment.

There is a contrast here with the economic CBA's willingness-to-pay criterion, according to which, amid its primary concern for aggregative benefits, the interests of the richer may take precedence over the interests of the poorer, even when the interests are substantially of the same kind. For according to the moral CBA, greater efforts must be made to protect the comparable interests of poorer persons precisely because they are economically less capable of defending their morally equal rights. Thus, in determining the value of some social policy, such as governmental provision for paying health-care costs, the benefits to poorer persons must be weighted higher than those to richer persons, and the costs arising from medical assistance to poorer persons must be given lower weights than the costs for richer persons. If this involves transfers made "at the expense of" wealthier groups, it is nonetheless not a violation of the latter's own rights, because of the moral CBA's hierarchic priority of basic rights over rights whose objects are less important for action. But at the same time, the moral CBA upholds a policy of helping poorer persons to acquire the productive skills that enable them to be less dependent for basic goods on transfers from other persons.

Conclusion

The economic CBA has the important merit that it provides a quantifiable measure for evaluating projected social investments and other policies. But it also has the important demerit that its monetary measure may blur and distort the nonmonetary values involved in such policies, as well as the requirements of equity in the distribution of costs and benefits. The moral CBA focuses on the most important of these values, those that are the objects of moral rights. It calls direct attention to the ways in which these objects are affected by projected policies, evaluating both the costs and the benefits of the policies in terms of their consequences for moral rights, including their distribution according to need. Although the moral CBA does not have the quantifiable precision available to the economic CBA, it can make full use of the latter's monetary calculations, but always as subordinate or ancillary to its own concern for equal rights. It not only avoids the economic CBA's often misleading and potentially disastrous reduction of important human interests to monetary considerations but it also provides ways of measuring the relative importance of rights in terms of the degrees of their needfulness for human action.

These considerations show that the economic and the moral CBAs are not two normatively parallel alternatives, but that the moral CBA is the normatively superior method and doctrine. This is so not only because it makes moral rights central but also, ultimately, because, as was indicated above, no agent can reject the moral principle on which the moral CBA is based, on pain of self-contradiction.[38] For to reject this principle, the Principle of Generic Consistency, would mean rejecting the necessary conditions that make agency possible. In this way, the argument for the Principle of Generic Consistency provides a decisive answer to the "authoritative question" presented near the beginning of this chapter.

The economic and the moral CBAs eventuate in different kinds of societies. When the economic CBA is given predominant or exclusive emphasis in the formulation of social policies, its monetary criterion of "willingness to pay" serves to annul or obscure the intrinsic importance of nonmonetary values, and it tends to favor the rich over the poor and to downgrade efforts at redistribution not only of wealth but also of resources for acquiring wealth. When the moral CBA is made predominant, in contrast, the most important interests of persons are given independent recognition as rights that require primary protection and support, and monetary considerations, including the economic CBA, are viewed only as efficient means of helping to provide such protection and support. The moral CBA thus eventuates in a community of rights whereby mutual aid and respect are upheld in a context of social solidarity.

Notes

1. Plato *Protagoras* 356D ff.

2. Aristotle *Nicomachean Ethics* 1.1.1094a1.

3. Lionel Robbins, *An Essay on the Nature and Significance of Economic Science*, 2nd ed. (London: Macmillan, 1952), 15, 30.

4. See Gary S. Becker, *The Economic Approach to Human Behavior* (Chicago: University of Chicago Press, 1976), chap. 1. For a more elaborate development of this idea, see Ludwig von Mises, *Human Action: A Treatise on Economics*, 3rd rev. ed. (Chicago: Regnery, 1966).

5. I have previously distinguished and discussed these questions in Alan Gewirth, *Reason and Morality* (Chicago: University of Chicago Press, 1978), 1–7.

6. See Henry M. Levin, *Cost-Effectiveness: A Primer* (Beverly Hills: Sage, 1983), 17–26; Robert Sugden and Alan Williams, *The Principles of Practical Cost–Benefit Analysis* (Oxford: Oxford University Press, 1978), 190–93.

7. Sugden and Williams, *Practical Cost–Benefit Analysis*, 191.

8. See E. J. Mishan, *Elements of Cost–Benefit Analysis*, 2nd ed. (London: Allen and Unwin, 1978), chap. 2; E. J. Mishan, "Evaluation of Life and Limb: A Theoretical Approach," *Journal of Political Economy* 79 (1971): 687–705; M. W. Jones-Lee, *The Value of Life: An Economic Analysis* (Chicago: University of Chicago Press, 1976), chaps. 1–3.

9. Here and in the following paragraphs I repeat a few sentences from my earlier article "Human Rights and the Prevention of Cancer," *American Philosophical Quarterly* 17 (1980): 117–25, reprinted in Alan Gewirth, *Human Rights: Essays on Justification and Applications* (Chicago: University of Chicago Press, 1982), 181–96, and, in part, in *Ethics and the Environment*, ed. Donald Scherer and Thomas Attig (Englewood Cliffs, N.J.: Prentice-Hall, 1983), 170–77.

10. See Steven Kelman, "Cost–Benefit Analysis: An Ethical Critique," *Regulation* 5, no. 1 (January–February 1981): 35 ff.

11. Robert M. Solow, "Defending Cost–Benefit Analysis," *Regulation* 5, no. 2 (March–April 1981): 41.

12. Laurence McCullough, "Biomedical Ethics and the Shadow of Nazism," *Hastings Center Report* 6, no. 4 (August 1976): 15.

13. E. J. Mishan, *Cost–Benefit Analysis*, 2nd ed. (New York: Praeger, 1976), x.

14. Mishan, *Elements of Cost–Benefit Analysis*, 15. Another writer puts this point even more bluntly: "No distributional weights need to be used; i.e. analysis based on efficiency alone is worth its face value with no need for a distributional proviso. In short, a dollar is a dollar." Yew Kwang Ng, *Welfare Economics* (New York: Wiley, 1980), 244.

15. Mishan, *Elements of Cost–Benefit Analysis*, 13. See also Mishan, *Cost–Benefit Analysis*, 392 ff.

16. See David Hume, *Enquiry Concerning the Principles of Morals*, ed. Selby-Bigge, sec. 3, pt. 2, pp. 193 ff.; Jeremy Bentham, *Theory of Legislation*, ed. C. K. Ogden (London: Routledge and Kegan Paul, 1928), 104; Henry Sidgwick, *Principles of Political Economy* (London: Macmillan, 1901), 519 ff.; Henry Sidgwick, *Elements of Politics* (London: Macmillan, 1919), 160 ff. For a more recent statement of the same position, see Richard B. Brandt, *A Theory of the Good and the Right* (Oxford: Clarendon Press, 1979), 310 ff. It is significant that the same recourse to the need for incentives

is used by the antiutilitarian John Rawls to set a limitation on economic equality. Although the word "incentives" is not found in the index to *A Theory of Justice* (Cambridge: Harvard University Press, 1971), the word is frequently invoked for this purpose: see pp. 78, 149, 151, 164, 279.

17. See Arnold C. Harberger, "Basic Needs vs. Distributional Weights in Social Cost–Benefit Analysis," *Economic Development and Cultural Change* 32 (April 1984): 455–74, at 457 ff.

18. See Allen V. Kneese, Shaul Ben-David, and William D. Schulze, "The Ethical Foundations of Benefit-Cost Analysis," in *Energy and the Future*, ed. Douglas MacLean and Peter G. Brown (Totowa, N.J.: Rowman and Littlefield, 1983), 59–74; and K. S. Shrader-Frechette, *Science Policy, Ethics, and Economic Methodology* (Dordrecht, Holland: Reidel, 1984), chap. 8: "Ethically Weighted Risk-Cost-Benefit Analysis" (pp. 261–85). Shrader-Frechette's discussion is especially valuable both for its clear justification of the need for ethical weights and for its careful development of the various ways in which "transitive, lexicographically ordered rules" can be used "to represent the priority weightings of different ethical claims within a given ethical system" (p. 269). In a different direction, see the discussion of the "participatory alternative" in James T. Campen, *Benefit, Cost, and Beyond: The Political Economy of Benefit-Cost Analysis* (Cambridge: Ballinger, 1986), chap. 10.

19. See Gewirth, *Reason and Morality*, 52 ff.; Gewirth, *Human Rights*, 3 ff.

20. Rawls, *A Theory of Justice*, 43.

21. Gewirth, *Reason and Morality*, chaps. 1–3. For briefer versions of the argument, see Gewirth, *Human Rights*, 41–67; "The Epistemology of Human Rights," *Social Philosophy and Policy* 1, no. 2 (Spring 1984): 1–24; "The Rationality of Reasonableness," *Synthese* 57 (1983): 225–47.

22. For a fuller discussion of how conflicts of rights are to be resolved, see Gewirth, *Reason and Morality*, 338–54.

23. See Robbins, *Economic Science*, 16.

24. See Robert Nozick, *Anarchy, State, and Utopia* (New York: Basic Books, 1974), 28 ff.

25. G. Teeling-Smith, "A Cost-Benefit Approach to Medical Care," in *The Economics of Medical Care*, ed. M. M. Hauser (London: Allen and Unwin, 1972), 150.

26. Ibid., 148.

27. Ibid., 152.

28. It is perhaps significant that this point is made by exponents of the economic CBA more often as applied to education than in the application to

health care. See, e.g., C. B. Padmanabhan, *Economics of Educational Planning in India* (New Delhi: Arya Book Depot, 1971), 90: "Decision making in educational planning cannot be guided by economic considerations alone because education is not merely a means for attaining certain ends or objectives but also an end or good in itself. Therefore, economic analysis should be used along with other kinds of analysis." See also Hans H. Thias and Martin Carnoy, *Cost–Benefit Analysis in Education: A Case Study of Kenya* (Baltimore: Johns Hopkins University Press, 1972), 3: "Cost–benefit analysis can perhaps measure the direct economic return to education investment, but education is justifiable for many other reasons." The authors reply to this objection by citing "Kenya's official policy" that "at Kenya's stage of development, education is much more an economic than a social service" (p. 7). By analogy, health care would likewise be justified primarily as an aid to "development." The underlying premise here may be the distinction between degrees of needfulness with regard to action.

29. Marc J. Roberts, "Economics and the Allocation of Resources to Improve Health," in *The Price of Health*, ed. George J. Agich and Charles E. Begley (Dordrecht, Holland: Reidel, 1986), 16.

30. Ibid., 19.

31. James V. DeLong, "Defending Cost–Benefit Analysis," *Regulation* 5, no. 2 (March–April 1981): 39.

32. W. Kip Viscusi, *Risk by Choice: Regulating Health and Safety in the Workplace* (Cambridge: Harvard University Press, 1983), 80.

33. Gewirth, *Reason and Morality*, 262–66. My position on this issue has been misunderstood by Marcus G. Singer; see his "Gewirth's Ethical Monism," in *Gewirth's Ethical Rationalism*, ed. Edward Regis, Jr. (Chicago: University of Chicago Press, 1984), 29 ff. I have replied to Singer in "Replies to My Critics," ibid., 252–53.

34. Gewirth, *Reason and Morality*, 263.

35. See the essays collected in Steven E. Rhoads, ed., *Valuing Life: Public Policy Dilemmas* (Boulder, Colo.: Westview Press, 1981).

36. Aristotle *Nicomachean Ethics* V.3.1131a 24 ff.; *Politics* 111.9. 1280a8 ff.

37. Arthur P. Hurter, Jr., George S. Tolley, and Robert G. Fabian, "Benefit–Cost Analysis and the Common Sense of Environmental Policy," in *Cost–Benefit Analysis and Environmental Regulations: Politics, Ethics, and Methods*, ed. Daniel Swartzman, Richard A. Liroff, and Kevin G. Croke (Washington, D.C.: Conservation Foundation, 1982), 95.

38. See note 21.

About the Contributors

Alan Gewirth is Professor Emeritus of Philosophy at the University of Chicago. His distinguished career has been marked by several honors including the presidency of the American Philosophical Association. *Reason and Morality*, his 1978 book, perhaps most clearly defines the concern for human liberty and human rights that underlies the argumentation he has developed concerning environmental pollution.

Bart Gruzalski is Professor of Philosophy at Northeastern University. His professional reputation focuses on his work on utilitarianism, and he is widely published in leading journals on the subject. His contribution to the volume advances his general defense of act utilitarianism by arguing how it responds to threshold problems.

Dale Jamieson is Professor of Philosophy and Director of the Center for Values and Social Policy. He is an applied philosopher whose work spans questions in the philosophy of science and ethics. He is known for his work on methodology in the sciences and its impact on public policy. His paper applies and extends this work to the study of the Greenhouse Effect.

James W. Nickel is Professor of Moral Philosophy at the University of Colorado. His work, which extends into many applied areas of ethics, prominently includes his arguments concerning the problems that political boundaries create for moral evaluation and policy formulation. Daniel Magraw, his coauthor, is Professor of Law at the University of Colorado. He is a specialist in international law and is currently writing a text in the field. He is widely published in international law and, particularly, in the implications of international law for environmental concerns.

Ernest Partridge is a Visiting Associate Professor of Philosophy at California State University, Fullerton. His philosophical interests include applied and theoretical ethics, policy analysis, environmental ethics, and within the latter field, the duty to posterity. Professor Partridge has taught at the Santa Barbara, Riverside, and Irvine campuses of the University of California and has studied the ethics of earthquake prediction under a grant from the National Science Foundation. He is the editor of the anthology *Responsibilities to Future Generations.*

Mark Sagoff is Senior Research Associate and Director of the Institute for Philosophy and Public Policy at the University of Maryland. He is widely published in philosophy and law review journals, being best known for his insights into our ambivalent attitudes toward the environment that betray our more principled concerns.

Donald Scherer is Professor of Philosophy at Bowling Green State University. A pioneer of applied philosophy and environmental ethics, he is on the advisory boards of the *International Journal of Applied Philosophy* and *Environmental Ethics.* Chief environmental ethics consultant to the Ohio Humanities Council for environmental ethics for the proposals they have invited on the theme of Upstream-Downstream Issues in Environmental Ethics, Scherer is the author of "A Disentropic Ethic: The Ethics of Extraterrestrial Space Exploration," the lead article in the Winter 1988 *Monist.*

Kristin Shrader-Frechette is Graduate Research Professor of Philosophy at the University of South Florida. She is renowned for her work on problems in the methodology of the sciences and the impact of those problems on public policy. The author of *Risk Analysis and Scientific Method: Methodological and Ethical Problems with Evaluating Societal Hazards,* she is widely published in environmental ethics. Professor Shrader-Frechette is editor-in-chief of Oxford's book series on environmental ethics and science policy.

Index

CARDIFF
UWCC LIBRARY